Trade and the Environment

Princeton Series in International Economics

Series Editors
Gene Grossman and Pierre-Olivier Gourinchas

Sponsored by the International Economics Section of the Princeton University Department of Economics, the Princeton Series in International Economics includes commissioned works by leading scholars in international trade, international macroeconomics, and international finance. The volumes in the series are intended to span the important policy and research topics in international economics and to help define and direct scholarship in the field. This work is published in collaboration with The International Economics Section of the Department of Economics, Princeton University.

Trade and the Environment: Theory and Evidence
by Brian R. Copeland and M. Scott Taylor

Trade and the Environment
Theory and Evidence

Brian R. Copeland and
M. Scott Taylor

Sponsored by the
International Economics Section
Department of Economics
Princeton University

Princeton University Press
Princeton and Oxford

Published by
Princeton University Press, 41 William Street,
Princeton, New Jersey 08540

In the United Kingdom:
Princeton University Press, 3 Market Place,
Woodstock, Oxfordshire OX20 1SY

Library of Congress Cataloging-in-Publication Data
Copeland, Brian Richard.
Trade and the environment : theory and evidence / Brian R. Copeland
and M. Scott Taylor.
p. cm. — (Princeton series in international economics)
Includes bibliographical references and index.
ISBN 0-691-11355-6 (alk. paper)
1. International trade—Environmental aspects. 2. Free trade—Environmental aspects.
3. Environmental policy—Economic aspects. 4. Economic development—Environmental
aspects. I. Taylor, M. Scott (Michael Scott), 1960– II. Title. III. Series.
HF1379 .C657 2003
363.73'2—dc21   2002042461

British Library Cataloging-in-Publication Data is available

Sponsored by the International Economics Section of the
Princeton University Department of Economics

This book has been composed in Palatino

Printed on acid-free paper. ∞

www.pupress.princeton.edu

Printed in the United States of America

10 9 8 7 6 5 4 3 2 1

Contents

Preface

We started this project with the hope of providing an answer to the question, "Is free trade good for the environment?" We soon realized that a complete answer would require a consideration of both local and global pollution, the impact of international trade on natural resource use, and also contain empirical work estimating the impact of trade and testing competing hypotheses. In short, this was not a book-length project that we could complete, but a question requiring an entire research agenda fueled by the contributions of many. In fact over the last thirty years, many *have* contributed to answering this question, and these earlier researchers provided the intellectual foundation for much of the analysis in this book. But while the existing literature contained many useful insights, it was fragmented: authors adopted very different assumptions regarding abatement, market structure, the efficacy of policy, and the tradability of both goods and factors; and the integration of theory with empirical work was rare. This made it difficult to identify key hypotheses, to focus future research on unanswered questions, and to convince both our students and our colleagues of the benefits of future research in this area.

Most progress in our discipline occurs when research efforts coalesce around a theoretical framework, develop its many implications, and examine these predictions empirically. Accordingly, we decided that a shorter and more focused effort would be of value in providing researchers with a simple and unified framework for analysis. We hope that by demonstrating how to identify and isolate the environmental impacts of trade, growth, and pollution policy, we will stir the interest of graduate students and prospective future entrants to the literature; by adopting a simple framework, we hope to lead readers to speculate about the robustness of our results and provide them with the tools for extension and qualification; and by presenting empirical evidence, we hope we have provided a provocative but partial answer to this literature's main question, while demonstrating the usefulness of combining theory with empirical work.

We have written a research monograph and not a textbook. It contains both known results and new research contributions. Chapters from the book have been taught to both advanced undergraduates and graduate students at the University of Wisconsin and the University of British Columbia. It would be suitable as a primary text in a special topics course, or as a supplementary textbook in either graduate international or environmental economics courses. Some of the material will be difficult for all but the most advanced undergraduates, but we have had great success in communicating the main ideas of the book to undergraduates by heavy use of the book's diagrams. We have tried very hard to make the book user friendly and enlarge its potential audience. Courses in agricultural economics, in public policy schools, and in specialized environmental programs may find the book useful.

Many people have helped us during this project. We are especially grateful to our colleague, Werner Antweiler, who collaborated with us on the empirical work that forms the basis of chapter 7. Gene Grossman provided excellent and detailed comments on every chapter. His input increased the book's clarity and focus. Both Sjak Smulders and Cees Withagen provided very helpful detailed comments on the book, based on their experience using the manuscript in a course at Tilburg. Arik Levinson, Larry Karp, Carol McAusland, and Chia-hui Lu also read the entire manuscript and made a number of helpful suggestions, as did several anonymous reviewers. Our students provided wonderful feedback that affected the book in very significant ways. We have also benefited from the input of seminar and conference participants at the National Bureau of Economic Research and at too many universities to mention. Research funding was provided by the Social Sciences and Humanities Research Council of Canada (Copeland) and the National Science Foundation (Taylor).

The biggest debt we owe is to our families for their patience and support during the book's very long gestation and somewhat painful labor.

1

The Trade and Environment Debate

1.1 Globalization and the Trade versus Environment Debate

"It was the best of times, it was the worst of times." This line, written by Charles Dickens over 100 years ago, captures the present-day divide between supporters and critics of globalization. During the 1990s, North America and much of Europe enjoyed its longest peacetime expansion, unemployment rates hit historic lows, and real income growth in much of the developing world soared. To many these are the fruits of globalization. But this same decade saw little progress in addressing climate change, a decline in fish and tropical forest stocks, and by some measures, rising inequality in the world distribution of income. To many others, these are its costs.

Debates over "globalization" have been going on for some time. But nowhere has the divide between the two views of globalization been more apparent than in recent discussions concerning trade liberalization and the environment.

For the last ten years environmentalists and the trade policy community have squared off over the environmental consequences of liberalized trade.[1] This debate was fueled by negotiations over the North American Free Trade Agreement and the Uruguay round of General Agreement on Tariffs and Trade (GATT) negotiations, both of which occurred at a time when concerns over global warming, species extinction, and industrial pollution were rising. The debate intensified with the creation of the World Trade Organization (WTO) and proposals for future rounds of trade negotiations.

Trade negotiators saw the WTO as a step forward because of its improved dispute settlement procedures and because it closed loopholes

---

1. For a good discussion of the policy issues involved, see Esty 1994.

in previous trade agreements. Environmentalists, however, were disturbed by the intrusion of trade agreements into what many thought were purely domestic matters. Perhaps not surprisingly, then, an attempt to initiate a new round of multilateral trade negotiations in Seattle became a flashpoint for growing unrest with globalization and efforts at further trade liberalization.

The purpose of this book is to study the interaction between international trade and the environment using both economic theory and empirical analysis. Our objective is to move the discussion forward by developing useful theory and devising methods to help in the empirical estimation of key magnitudes. We hope to enlist readers in further discussion and evaluation of trade's environmental effects, and this book is designed to equip them with the tools for doing so. In the end, differences of opinion will of course remain because the effects of international trade on the environment are still not fully understood. But we hope to give researchers and policymakers a common language and framework within which to discuss, debate, and continue their investigations.

1.2 Two Questions and a Preview of Our Answers

Throughout the book, we focus on two key channels through which trade can affect the environment. The first is via its effects on the level, or *scale*, of economic activity. If trade spurs economic activity, then the pure income-generating effects of trade may be harmful to the environment. The second channel is via a *composition* effect—a change in the mix of economic activity in countries, caused by trade. Many environmentalists are concerned that trade may lead to a shifting of polluting industry from rich to poor countries, and this global composition effect may also raise world pollution.

As we will see, both of these channels are more complex than these simple arguments suggest, and this leads to the two key questions that unify the book:

1. *How does the increase in economic activity induced by international trade affect the environment?*

Many in the "deep green" environmental movement believe unfettered access to world markets is necessarily harmful to the environment. While arguments differ in the details, the primary objection is that international trade leads to a greater scale of economic activity—be it transportation services, more production of goods and services, or more consumption—and that economic activity per se harms the environment. In this view, if international trade stimulates economic activity and if this activity is inherently environmentally damaging, then so too is international trade.

This concern forces us to think about the link between economic activity and environmental quality more generally and not just with regard to international trade. It leads us to define a measure of the scale of economic activity and to then link this measure to changes in the economy brought about by trade liberalization. But since any change in the scale of economic activity also affects incomes, we must also take into account the impact of income gains on environmental regulation.

If higher real incomes generate a greater ability and willingness to implement and enforce environmental regulations, then the logical chain linking trade liberalization to environmental destruction is broken. A trade liberalization that raises the scale of economic activity will then also lower the dirtiness of production techniques, and its full environmental impact can only be resolved through careful empirical investigation.

We address this first question by using our theoretical framework to separate the impact of economic growth on the environment from that caused by trade liberalization.[2] We show that the relative strength of *scale* versus *technique* effects depends on how government policy is formed and how quickly it changes in response to new conditions. We also set out the theoretical conditions under which either the scale or the technique effect is stronger. But since theory alone cannot determine the answers to our questions, we also present empirical work undertaken using a large cross-country data set on measured sulfur dioxide concentrations in over 100 major cities in the world.

By isolating the pure scale and technique effects of trade,[3] we estimate that a trade liberalization that raises the scale of economic activity by 1% raises pollution concentrations by 0.25 to 0.5% via the scale effect, but the accompanying increase in incomes per capita drives concentrations down by 1.25–1.5% via a technique effect. These estimates imply a strong policy response to trade-inspired income gains. As we show, they also imply that economic growth created by neutral techno-

---

2. Economic growth is modeled as once-and-for-all changes in either technologies or endowments. For a discussion of the relationship between growth and the environment in a dynamic setting see Smulders 2000.

3. Trade also generates composition effects, which we will discuss shortly.

logical progress will both raise real incomes and improve environmental quality, but economic growth fueled by capital accumulation alone will worsen the environment.

Our estimates and analysis are important in establishing that we need to identify the source of income gains before we predict its environmental consequences. For example, neutral technological progress favors no industry, and we find that it improves environmental quality through its role in raising incomes and tightening techniques of production. And while capital accumulation raises both incomes and scale, it favors the production of dirty, capital-intensive processes. Hence capital accumulation creates an additional effect leading to a worsened environment. Trade liberalization can be environmentally friendly since it brings income gains and will lead some countries to specialize in relatively clean industries. But not all countries can specialize in the production of clean goods, and hence it is important to determine which countries are likely to specialize and export relatively dirty products. This brings us to our second question.

2. How does environmental policy affect a nation's trade pattern?

This second question arises from concerns that dirty industries will leave tightly regulated countries and migrate to countries with lax regulations. As a result, international trade could alter the composition of output across countries, leading poor countries with relatively weak environmental regulation to specialize in the production of dirty goods while rich and tightly regulated countries specialize in clean goods. Even if trade liberalization had no effect on the scale of economic activity or on the dirtiness of the techniques of production, it could create pollution havens in the developing world by altering the *composition* of their output toward dirty goods.

Dirty industry migration is a serious concern because it would imply that poor less developed countries are bearing the pollution burdens of rich developed country consumption. Despite the claims of some economists that this may well be efficient, it would be unpalatable to many. Dirty industry migration may also raise concerns about competitiveness and cause regulatory chill in the developed countries which could slow down ongoing efforts to raise environmental protection. At worst it could usher in a worldwide race to the bottom in environmental protection as nations relax standards to forestall dirty industry migration.

These are valid concerns that need to be seriously addressed. To examine dirty industry migration and the creation of pollution havens we investigate how differences across countries in both environmental regulations and other country characteristics interact to determine a country's trade pattern. We also have to isolate changes in the composition of output created by trade liberalization from those created by more mundane sources such as taste changes or ongoing growth in a nation's productive capacity. To do so we employ our theoretical framework to isolate the composition effect of trade liberalization on pollution.

Isolating changes in the composition of output created by trade is critical to examining whether lax-regulation countries are destined to become pollution havens. While this may appear obvious to some, it too is an empirical question. While developed and less developed countries differ widely in the stringency of their environmental regulations, they also differ widely in average education levels, in available infrastructure, and in capital equipment per person. If these other differences are significant determinants of production costs, then it is no longer clear that lax regulations alone create a cost advantage in dirty good production.

In fact, our empirical work indicates that greater access to international markets creates only relatively small changes in pollution via the composition effect, and that conventional determinants of production costs are more important in determining "international competitiveness" than are differences in meeting the costs of environmental regulation. We find little evidence for dirty industry migration, or the pollution haven hypothesis. Our empirical results suggest just the opposite: that relatively rich developed countries have a comparative advantage in dirty goods. As a result, freer international trade shifts dirty good production from lax-regulation countries to more stringent-regulation countries. If this is correct, then the global composition effect of trade lowers world pollution. Combining our estimates of scale, composition, and technique effects created by a trade liberalization yields a surprising conclusion: freer trade appears to be good for the environment—at least for the average country in our sample and for the pollutant we consider.

While this result will be of interest to policymakers because of the importance of sulfur dioxide pollution and its close connection to other equally noxious pollutants, the most important contribution of this book is the theoretical framework it presents, the methods it espouses, and its discussion of competing hypothesis linking international trade to environmental outcomes.

1.3 Our Method of Analysis

We do not present an exhaustive account or review of all that is known about international trade and the environment, but instead develop a simplified but cohesive framework to investigate the relationship. We show that our framework is useful for understanding the links between economic growth and the environment, useful in disentangling the many different motives for trade in environmentally damaging goods, and useful as a springboard for empirical work that estimates the environmental consequences of liberalized trade. The strength of the book lies in the consistent application of our theoretical approach to various questions and our integration of this approach with empirical work.

Some readers may prefer different methods to discuss different issues, or wish for a presentation less encumbered by formal theory. We chose to be constrained by our theoretical framework because much of the current debate is not constrained by either theory or empirical work, and this has produced an astonishingly high ratio of rhetoric to results. Strong ideologies are at play here. There are those for whom free trade is a goal in and of itself and who speak of it in reverential tones; and there are also those who scorn any exercise to evaluate trade's environmental impact because they view its costs as clearly self-evident. This is an area of public policy debate sorely in need of guidance from further theory and empirical work. Accordingly, our goal is to introduce the reader to a new set of issues and build understanding. To do so we use theory to identify the main forces at work, motivate our empirical approach, and constrain the conclusions that we can draw.

While the appeal of doing "international environmental economics" has surely been present before, various difficulties face those who attempt it. The key difficulty is in introducing public goods into a general equilibrium model rich enough to explore the implications of trade, yet tractable enough to examine policy and to serve as the basis for empirical work.

We have attempted to strike a constructive balance between model complexity and tractability. Our analysis is marked by three characteristics: we adopt general equilibrium models; we assume environmental policy can be altered in light of changed economic conditions; and we adopt relatively simple economic models where the economy is aggregated into only two sectors. Throughout we examine only local pollution, although our methods can be extended to consider transboundary or global pollution.[4]

General Equilibrium

General equilibrium methods are necessary because they allow us to consider the full implications of international trade on the environment. For example, a partial equilibrium model of a clean industry might predict that the clean industry expands as a result of trade liberalization. Since the clean industry does not pollute, the partial equilibrium model does not predict any effects on the environment. But a general equilibrium analysis recognizes that as the clean industry expands, it must draw resources from other parts of the economy. If these other parts of the economy pollute, then the expansion of a clean industry can lead to a fall in the country's pollution.

In addition, a general equilibrium analysis allows us to grapple with income effects, which have played a central role in the debate over the effects of trade and growth on the environment. If trade stimulates a dirty industry, it will tend to increase pollution. But if trade also raises real incomes via general equilibrium effects, then it will increase the demand for environmental quality, and this can have a dampening effect on the increase in pollution via an endogenous policy response.

Some of the tools we employ are commonly used in competitive general equilibrium trade theory, but will be unfamiliar to many readers.[5] In an attempt to engage those unfamiliar with general equilibrium methods, we develop special cases of our models in some chapters to

---

4. A serious consideration of transboundary or global pollution would require a much longer book. Interested researchers can amend our analysis along the lines of Copeland and Taylor 1995, 2000.

5. Although chapter 2 sets out a more or less self-contained exposition of the principal tools we use, some readers may want to consult the book-length treatments of trade theory by Woodland (1982) and Dixit and Norman (1980) for background and a far more general treatment.

provide explicit solutions and derivations of main results. The examples we provide have the twin purpose of clarifying and simplifying the more general analysis we present elsewhere, and on occasion demonstrating surprising counterexamples.

Endogenous Policy

Endogenous policy is necessary if we are to capture the response of pollution policy to rising incomes and changing prices brought about by free trade. Much of the literature has focused on the role of differences in environmental policy between rich and poor countries in influencing the trade pattern and in determining the effects of trade on the environment. But if policy differences are caused in part by income differences, and if trade affects incomes, then we cannot evaluate the long-run effects of trade liberalization without taking into account the effects of changes in income and relative prices on environmental policy.

To facilitate a simple analysis of endogenous policy, we assume that the government maximizes an objective function that reflects the weighed sum of preferences of agents in the economy. In many cases, we assume all agents are identical; however, we will also consider a simple political economy model where the government places different weights on "Brown" consumers who benefit from dirty good production than it places on "Green" consumers who benefit mainly from clean good production.

While endogenous and fully responsive policy is a useful benchmark, it may not always reflect real-world conditions. Environmental economics was born out of the recognition of market failure and imperfect policy. Accordingly, wherever possible we present our analysis first under the assumption that policy is rigid and imperfect, and then present the case of optimal and flexible policy. This is useful not only because it may represent a reasonable representation of short- versus long-run outcomes, but also because the rigid policy analysis is often a pedagogically useful precursor to the analysis of optimal policy.

Simple Models

Finally, throughout the book, we limit the complexity of our models. Previous work in this area has sometimes been hampered by a well-intentioned effort to use very general models. This can often lead to complicated analysis in which many of the results are ambiguous. Our goal in the book is to introduce the reader to a new set of issues and build understanding. Relatively simple economic models can do just that—they shed light on different questions, they provide insight, and they guide—but not completely determine—the direction of empirical work. There are surely more general formulations that will overturn some of our results and introduce other complications, and we encourage readers to pursue these advances. But given the severe limitations researchers face in obtaining environmental data, adding further theoretical nuances will be for naught if we lack data necessary to explore their strength or validity. At present, getting the simple logic right seems a worthy goal. We leave it to readers and future researchers to elaborate on our findings.

1.4 Plan of the Book

We begin by developing our two-sector general equilibrium pollution and trade model in chapter 2. One special case of the model is a simplified version of the pollution haven model in Copeland and Taylor (1994). Another special case gives us the canonical Heckscher-Ohlin model that links relative factor abundance to international trading patterns. Chapter 2 is a difficult one, as it develops in detail the model's theoretical structure, starting with a consideration of pollution as a joint product of output and ending with a discussion of optimal pollution policy using the constructs of pollution demand and supply. Readers may wish to skip certain sections of this chapter, safe in the knowledge they may return to clarify a derivation or definition that they find puzzling in a later chapter.

After laying out the theoretical foundation in chapter 2 we proceed in chapter 3 to investigate the *environmental Kuznets curve*. We start with an examination of growth because the environmental consequences of trade and growth share some common features and any credible analysis of the effects of trade on the environment has to disentangle changes in pollution caused by trade from those caused by growth.

This chapter demonstrates that our simple pollution demand and supply framework can be employed to discuss the most commonly cited explanations for the environmental Kuznets curve. But this chapter is more than review and exercise. We present new theoretical results detailing the conditions under which strong policy responses alone can generate an EKC, new results linking increasing returns to abatement (at the industry level) to the EKC, and new results regarding the link between the sources of economic growth and environmental quality.

Following our discussion of growth, we proceed to trade liberalization in chapter 4. We identify the scale, composition, and technique effects created when a country liberalizes its trade and find that the positive and normative effects of trade liberalization depend critically on whether a country is a dirty good importer or exporter. We consider both a reduction in transport costs and a fall in tariffs as the motivations for further trade and introduce a simple political economy model as well.

In chapters 5 and 6 we turn to a discussion of the pattern of trade. We start in chapter 5 by demonstrating that differences across countries in pollution policy alone can lead to the *pollution haven hypothesis*. But since policy differences should arise endogenously from more basic assumptions about country characteristics, we then link differences in the stringency of pollution regulation to cross-country differences in institutions, in income levels, and in the fragility of environments. In each case, we demonstrate how differences in country characteristics lead to differences in the stringency of regulation and hence trade. Although in each case free trade results in the lax-regulation countries exporting dirty products, we show that this trade need not be either welfare reducing or environmentally damaging.

In chapter 6 we broaden the potential motives for trade to demonstrate that differences across countries in other characteristics can also influence relative production costs. We focus on differences across countries in their capital stocks and labor forces because these differences are at the basis of the *factor endowments hypothesis*. We examine how differences in income levels and factor endowments interact to determine the pattern of trade. This chapter contains several new results. We demonstrate that rich but capital-abundant countries may export dirty goods, while poor and capital-scarce countries export clean goods. We show that when differences in other country characteristics lead to cost advantages that overwhelm the pollution haven motives for trade, many of the dire consequences of international trade disappear. We demonstrate that world pollution can fall with trade, that imperfectly regulated and poor developing countries must both gain from trade and see an improvement in their environment, and that pollution may fall in both rich and poor countries with trade liberalization. All of these results are in direct opposition to predictions of the pollution haven hypothesis.

In chapter 7 we present empirical work estimating the strength of scale, composition, and technique effects. We employ many of the results developed in earlier chapters to develop a simple reduced form estimating equation linking pollution concentrations to country characteristics, and measures of both openness to trade and comparative advantage. This equation is then estimated on a large panel data set containing measures of sulfur dioxide pollution concentrations drawn from cities in 44 developed and developing countries over the 1971 to 1996 period.

Chapter 8 presents a short conclusion and suggestions for future research. Some of these suggestions are topics that we had hoped to include but did not because of limited time or space. Others are suggestions for further empirical or theoretical work addressing unanswered questions regarding linkages between trade and the environment.

2   Pollution in a Small Open Economy

This chapter develops the simple general equilibrium model we employ in the all subsequent chapters and provides a foundation for our analysis of trade and environmental policy. This is a "tools" chapter, and some readers may prefer to skim it and move on to the "issue" chapters that follow. But since many of the key assumptions we use throughout the book are laid out here, it is worthwhile spending some time on this chapter before proceeding.

Because the book straddles two fields—environmental economics and international trade—we develop basic concepts from each field. At times it may seem that we are being pedantic, but our objective is to ensure that readers from either field can follow and extend our analysis.

The model we develop is deliberately simple.[1] We assume two industries (one dirty and one clean) and two primary factors of production. In addition, because the pollution level in a free market may be unacceptably high, we include in our model a government that regulates pollution. Despite its simplicity, the model contains as one special case the standard Heckscher-Ohlin model of international trade, and as another, a version of our Pollution Haven model (Copeland and Taylor

---

1. The model builds on previous work in trade and the environment. The structure of our model is closest to that of McGuire (1982), who developed a two-sector model with two primary factors of production and treated pollution as an input as we do. Earlier work by Pethig (1976) used a two-sector model with one primary factor. Markusen (1976) used a two-sector model with two primary factors but did not allow for variable levels of emission intensity—in his model, pollution is directly proportional to output. More recent work has sometimes used more complicated models than we use here. Copeland (1994) uses a general equilibrium model that allows for many goods, many factors, and many different pollutants. Rauscher (1997, chap. 5) uses a two-sector model with one primary factor, but allows for pollution to harm producers as well as consumers, and he allows for consumption-generated pollution. Copeland and Taylor (1994) use

1994). Both factor endowments and pollution regulations play a role in determining a country's comparative advantage. This ensures the model has sufficient richness to address the issues at hand.

While much of environmental economics makes use of partial equilibrium analysis, we need a general equilibrium approach to examine the interaction of trading economies. By the end of the chapter we will have constructed a simple general equilibrium pollution demand and supply system determining equilibrium pollution as a function of world prices, endowments, technology, preferences, and government type. Environmental economists would refer to our constructs as general equilibrium marginal abatement cost and marginal damage schedules, and this is what they are. This system will then be used to examine the environmental consequences of growth in chapter 3, trade liberalization in chapter 4, and so on.

It is easy to lose the forest for the trees in a chapter with over 80 equations. And while the chapter contains many derivations and diagrams, it is organized around the development of just four key concepts. Before we launch into the specifics it may be useful to spell them out here.

First, in much of the book we treat pollution as if it were an input into the production of goods.[2] In fact, pollution is a joint (and undesirable) output. In section 2.1, we show how the two approaches are equivalent given some restrictions on the technology. We define a joint production technology where pollution and final goods are produced from primary inputs, and show how one can derive an equivalent technology where pollution (or access to environmental services) plays the role of an input into production. This allows us to use standard tools, such as isoquants and unit cost functions, in analyzing the economy.

Second, we need a model rich enough so that both factor endowments and pollution regulations play a role in determining a country's comparative advantage, but also tractable enough so that we can do comparative statics. For factor endowments to play a role in determining comparative advantage independently of pollution regulations, we

a model with one primary factor, but allow for a continuum of goods, all with different pollution intensities.

2. The treatment of pollution as an input has been standard in the general equilibrium literature on trade and environment. See, for example, Pethig 1976; McGuire 1982; Copeland 1994; Copeland and Taylor 1994; Rauscher 1997; and others. Siebert et al. (1980), Rauscher (1997, chap. 2), and Copeland and Taylor (1994) discuss the conditions under which this approach is equivalent to treating pollution as a joint output.

specify a model with two primary factors (capital and labor). This allows us to consider countries that differ in relative capital abundance. However, because pollution is also treated as an input, this gives us a model with three inputs. To keep the model tractable, we make two key assumptions: we assume the abatement activity employs factors in the same proportions as does production of the dirty good; and we assume a specific form for the abatement production function. With these two assumptions our three-factor model simplifies tremendously. For example, if we hold emissions per unit output in the dirty industry constant, our model inherits all the comparative static properties of the Heckscher-Ohlin model of international trade. Specifically, as we show in section 2.2, the Stolper-Samuelson theorem holds: an increase in the relative price of the dirty good raises the real return to capital and lowers the real return to labor. In addition, the Rybczinski theorem holds: an increase in the supply of capital raises the output of the capital-intensive dirty good and lowers the output of the labor-intensive clean good. This is an important feature of our model because, as we will show in later chapters, it allows us to separate the role played by factor endowments from those of pollution policy in determining trade patterns.

Third, the focus of the book is on how exogenous changes in the economy (such as trade liberalization) lead to changes in equilibrium levels of pollution. To facilitate this analysis, we develop two diagrams that illustrate how equilibrium pollution is determined. The first diagram exploits the production frontier. Given pollution policy, we show how to determine the level of goods production on the production frontier, and then project down onto a pollution frontier to determine emissions. This diagram is also useful in illustrating how changes in pollution caused by shocks to the economy can be decomposed into *scale*, *composition*, and *technique* effects. This decomposition is employed to examine the consequences of trade liberalization and growth in chapters 3 and 4; and in chapter 7, we estimate these effects empirically.

The second diagram uses a general equilibrium demand-and-supply approach to determine the equilibrium level of pollution. Once we treat pollution as an input, we can then ask how much firms would choose to emit for a given price of pollution emissions. This gives us the general-equilibrium derived demand for pollution. On the other hand, the supply of pollution reflects the willingness of the regulator to allow increased emissions and depends on the policy regime. If an aggregate pollution quota is in place, the supply curve is simply a vertical line, and its intersection with the demand curve determines the equilibrium price of emissions. If the regulator imposes a fixed pollution tax, the supply curve is horizontal and its intersection with the demand curve determines the equilibrium quantity of emissions. In much of the book, however, we need a model where pollution policy is endogenous, and since we have already argued that one can think of pollution as an input, it is natural to think of the willingness to allow pollution as similar to a problem of endogenous factor supply. We can therefore derive the pollution supply curve from optimizing behavior of the regulator. Its intersection with pollution demand determines both the equilibrium price and the quantity of emissions.

The final key concept developed in this chapter is the use of national income or GNP functions to represent the supply side of the economy. This is motivated by the central role that income plays in our analysis. One of the prominent issues in the debate on the effects of trade and the environment is the interaction between per capita income, pollution policy, and the pattern of trade. According to the pollution haven hypothesis, for example, high-income countries have relatively stringent pollution policy and this shifts dirty good production to poorer countries via international trade. We need a tool that allows us to analyze the role of income in determining the supply of pollution, but which also takes into account the endogeneity of income. To deal with these complications in a tractable manner, it is useful to employ national income or GNP functions. These are commonly used in the international trade literature, but their use in environmental economics is less common. A GNP function exploits the result that if the conditions for production efficiency hold, then profit-maximizing firms will in aggregate end up maximizing the value of national income at producer prices. We can therefore represent the value of national income at producer prices as a maximum value function. This is a very convenient tool to exploit when modeling the dependence of pollution policy on per capita income. In addition, because the GNP function is a maximum value function, it satisfies a number of useful properties that expedite our comparative statics analysis.

We complete the chapter in section 2.4 by determining the efficient level of pollution using our pollution supply and demand framework. Our pollution supply and demand can be interpreted as general equilibrium marginal damage and marginal abatement cost schedules, and so this section clearly links our approach to standard textbook treatments of pollution in environmental economics.

With these tools in hand, the reader will be well equipped to examine the relationship between pollution and growth in chapter 3, and between pollution and trade in subsequent chapters.

2.1 Technology

We start by considering a small open economy that faces fixed world prices.[3] At least two goods are needed for trade to occur, and for trade to be interesting, the two goods should differ in pollution intensity. Consequently, we assume the economy produces two goods, X and Y. Good X generates pollution during its production, and good Y does not.[4] We let good Y be the numeraire (so that $p_Y = 1$), and denote the domestic relative price of good X by p. Throughout the chapter world prices and domestic prices are identical, but at some points we distinguish between the two for clarity.

There are two primary factors, capital and labor (K and L), with market returns r and w. Both factors are inelastically supplied.[5] X is capital intensive and Y is labor intensive. This means that for any w and r, the capital/labor ratio in X is higher than in Y:

$$\frac{K_x}{L_x} > \frac{K_y}{L_y}. \tag{2.1}$$

We assume the capital-intensive sector is also the polluting sector. For industrial pollution, this is consistent with the evidence.[6]

To keep things simple, we assume that pollution from any given firm harms consumers but does not affect productivity in other firms.[7] In addition, we rule out pollution generated during consumption.

---

3. We consider endogenous world prices starting in chapter 5.
4. It is straightforward to generalize the model to allow both goods to pollute, but for most of our purposes, this would just add unneeded complexity. For an example of a model with more than one polluting good, see Copeland and Taylor 1994, where we consider a model with a continuum of goods, each with a different pollution intensity.
5. Recently, one branch of the environmental literature (the double dividend literature—see Fullerton and Metcalf 1998 for a review) has focused on models with endogenous labor supply in order to analyze the interaction between pollution taxes and distortionary labor taxes. As our focus is on trade, we follow the standard international trade literature and treat labor supply as exogenous.
6. See chapter 7.
7. See Baumol and Bradford 1972 and Copeland and Taylor 1999 for an analysis of some of the complexities that arise when there are cross-sectoral production externalities.

Both goods are produced with a constant returns to scale technology. The production function for good Y is

$$y = H(K_y, L_y). \tag{2.2}$$

We assume that H is increasing and strictly concave in inputs.

The X industry jointly produces two outputs—good X and emissions Z. However, abatement is possible, and so emission intensity is a choice variable. To capture the possibility of abatement very simply, suppose that a firm can allocate an endogenous fraction θ of its inputs to abatement activity. Increases in θ reduce pollution, but at the cost of diverting primary factors from X production. The joint production technology is given by

$$x = (1 - \theta) F(K_X, L_X), \tag{2.3}$$

$$z = \varphi(\theta) F(K_X, L_X), \tag{2.4}$$

where F is increasing, concave, and linearly homogeneous, $0 \leq \theta \leq 1$, $\varphi(0) = 1$, $\varphi(1) = 0$, and $d\varphi/d\theta < 0$. We discuss the interpretation of φ in detail below.

If $\theta = 0$, there is no abatement, and by choice of units, each unit of output generates one unit of pollution. We can think of $F(K_X, L_X)$ as potential output; this is the output of X that would be generated if there were no pollution abatement. That is, without abatement activity, we have

$$x = F(K_x, L_x), \tag{2.5}$$

$$z = x. \tag{2.6}$$

If firms choose $\theta > 0$, then some resources are allocated toward abatement. If a vector (K_x, L_x) of inputs is allocated to the X sector, then θK_x units of capital and θL_x units of labor are allocated to abatement.[8] Equivalently, we can think of the firm as producing a gross or *potential output* of $F(K_x, L_x)$, and using a fraction θ of this as an input for abatement. This leaves the firm with a *net output* $(1 - \theta) F(K_x, L_x)$, which is available for consumption and export.

It is convenient for expository purposes to put a little more structure on (2.4); hence we adopt the following functional form for abatement:

$$\varphi(\theta) = (1 - \theta)^{1/\alpha}, \tag{2.7}$$

---

8. We are assuming the abatement technology uses the same factor intensity as the production of the final good X. This is a simple way to capture the notion that abatement is

where $0 < \alpha < 1$. Using (2.3), (2.4), and (2.7), we can eliminate θ and invert the joint production technology to obtain

$$x = z^\alpha \left[F \left(K_x, L_x \right) \right]^{1-\alpha}, \tag{2.8}$$

which is valid for $z \leq F$, because $\theta \geq 0$. That is, although pollution is a joint output, we can equivalently treat it as an input.[9] This allows us to make use of familiar tools, such as isoquants and unit cost functions. One can think of pollution Z as the use of "environmental services," as the firm must dispose of its emissions in the environment. Alternatively, if we treat Z explicitly as pollution emissions, then we can think of the firm as requiring Z pollution permits in order to produce.

To help understand the technology in our model and its relation to others in the literature, it is useful to consider the abatement technology that lies behind (2.4). Many authors begin by specifying an abatement function, and then obtain pollution emissions as the difference between pollution potentially produced and the amount of abatement.[10] Our model can be interpreted in this way as well.

Abatement is like any other activity the firm undertakes in the X industry. The quantity abated depends on the amount of resources allocated to abatement, which we denote x^A, and the amount of pollution potentially produced, z^P. Define the abatement technology as $A(z^P, x^A)$, where A exhibits constant returns to scale. Pollution emissions are the difference between potential pollution and abatement:

$$z = z^P - A \left(z^P, x^A \right). \tag{2.9}$$

Because abatement is a constant returns activity, we can rewrite (2.9) as

$$z = z^P \left[1 - A \left(1, x^A / z^P \right) \right]. \tag{2.10}$$

---

costly, but avoids the complexity of modeling three activities (each with different factor intensities) in a general equilibrium model.

9. More generally, if we do not impose the added structure on the abatement technology, we have: $x = [1 - \varphi^{-1} (z/F)] F$, which is increasing and homogeneous of degree 1 in z and F. The specific functional form adopted in the text generalizes the model in Copeland and Taylor 1994 to allow for two primary factors. Separability ensures that the marginal rate of substitution between capital and labor is not affected by pollution taxes or quotas. This will allow us to use simple diagrams to illustrate much of our analysis, and later on to generate simple clean results on trade patterns. The unitary elasticity of substitution assumption implicit in (2.8) simplifies the algebra. Much of our work will generalize to the case where $x = \Phi [z, F (K_x, L_x)]$, with both F and Φ being linearly homogeneous. But we have opted for the simpler (albeit more restrictive) specification for clarity.

10. For an example of the explicit modeling of abatement in the trade and environment literature, see Barrett 1994 in a partial equilibrium context, and Siebert et al. 1980 for a general equilibrium approach.

Recall from (2.6) that potential pollution is equal to potential output (hence $z^P = F$) and that θ is the fraction of resources devoted to abatement (hence $\theta = x^A / F = x^A / z^P$). Hence we can write (2.10) as

$$z = [1 - A (1, \theta)] F (K_x, L_x) = \varphi (\theta) F (K_x, L_x), \tag{2.11}$$

where we have defined $\varphi (\theta) \equiv 1 - A (1, \theta)$. Thus our specification in (2.4) can alternatively be interpreted as being supported by an explicit abatement technology. This interpretation will be useful later on when we want to think about generalizing the model to allow for technological change or increasing returns to scale in abatement.

The particular form we adopted for φ in (2.7) corresponds to a particular abatement production function, A. Our choice in (2.7) has two benefits. First, it ensures we obtain the neat expression (2.8). This in turn requires the share of pollution taxes in the value of net output be constant. This aids in calculations as it did in Copeland and Taylor 1994. Second, it ensures the first unit of abatement has a bounded marginal product. This feature makes zero abatement optimal for firms when pollution taxes are low. This seems sensible, and in fact we show in the next chapter how this feature was exploited by Stokey (1998) in explaining the environmental Kuznets curve.

The relationship between net output, potential output, and the resources allocated to abatement can be illustrated using isoquants. In figure 2.1 we have drawn isoquants for two different levels of net output in the X sector. The higher isoquant (labeled X_1) corresponds to higher output. An isoquant illustrates the trade-off between "inputs" of potential output, denoted by F, and pollution emissions, denoted by Z, for a constant amount of net output. The constant returns to scale assumption implies all isoquants have the same shape: higher isoquants are radial blowups of lower isoquants.

At point A on the isoquant for X_1, no abatement is undertaken and pollution is proportional to output.[11] This corresponds to $\theta = 0$ in (2.3) and (2.4). Similarly, other points along the dashed ray through the origin correspond to the no-abatement points on other isoquants.

As we move down along an isoquant, pollution falls because firms allocate resources to abatement. To maintain a constant level of net output, the inputs into production as measured by F must increase as the pollution level falls.

---

11. Recall that we have chosen units to make the factor of proportionality equal to 1.

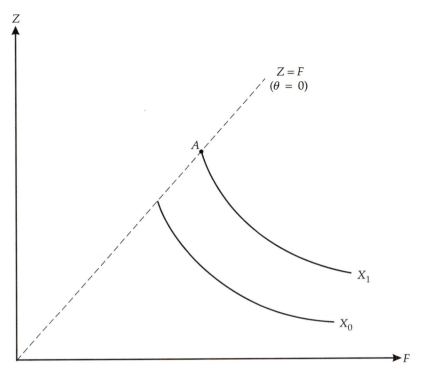

Fig. 2.1. Isoquants for the X Industry

Cost Minimization

In a competitive market, firms choose production techniques to minimize their cost of production. Because there is pollution, production costs depend on the regulatory regime. If there is no regulation, then there is no incentive to abate, and firms choose a point like A in figure 2.1. If there is regulation, the firm's problem is more complex: it must satisfy constraints imposed by the regulator as well as those coming from the market.

Our model can incorporate a variety of regulatory approaches. For example, in some jurisdictions, governments impose emission intensity restrictions. We could capture this regulation as a constraint that emissions per unit output not exceed some target. In other cases, governments charge an emission tax, which is a fee per unit of emissions released into the environment. And in other cases, firms must purchase emission permits if they want to pollute.

In much of the book, we assume that firms have to pay a fee for each unit of emissions they generate. The fee can either be an emissions tax, or it can be the market price for a pollution permit. We make this assumption in part because of its simplicity, but also because it ensures that the government's pollution target is implemented efficiently.[12]

Our focus is on the larger issue of how trade liberalization affects the environment, and we want to ensure that our results are not confused with side issues arising from the inefficient implementation of a pollution target. Notice we are not requiring the pollution target itself be efficient—we will spend considerable time on the implications of pollution policy that is too lax or too rigid.

Let us suppose then that firms face a price τ for each unit of emissions they generate. Given the price of emissions τ, and the prices of capital and labor (r and w), firms are now faced with a standard cost minimization problem. Moreover, because of the separability of our production function, we can break the firm's problem into two steps: first minimizing the cost of producing potential output F; and then finding the most efficient way to combine F with environmental services to produce net output X.

First, the firm can find the minimum cost of producing a unit of F (potential output). Because of constant returns to scale, a unit cost function for F exists, which we denote by c^F. That is, the firm has only to determine the most efficient techniques to produce one unit of F, because by constant returns to scale, multiple units are produced by simply scaling up production. The unit cost function for F can be found by solving the following problem:

$$c^F(w, r) = \min_{\{k, l\}} \{rk + wl : F(k, l) = 1\}. \tag{2.12}$$

The firm chooses the combination of capital and labor that allows it

---

12. A restriction on emissions per unit of output is not an efficient way to implement a pollution target—it can be shown to be equivalent to an emissions tax combined with an output subsidy. The output subsidy component of the policy leads to inefficiently high output. The problem is that if a firm is told to satisfy a restriction on emissions per unit of output, it can satisfy the regulation by either reducing emissions or by increasing output. In fact, in some cases, such a policy can lead to an increase in overall pollution. The policy can be rendered efficient if it is accompanied by an output tax, in which case it becomes equivalent to an emissions tax. In some strategic trade policy contexts, a government may actually want to subsidize output, and if production subsidies are illegal under trade rules, a devious choice of seemingly inefficient pollution instruments can actually be to a country's advantage. See Bruneau 2000. But these issues do not arise in a small open economy with perfectly competitive markets.

to produce a unit of potential output at lowest cost. The total cost of producing more that one unit of F is just $c^F(w, r)F$.

Next, the firm can determine how much abatement activity to undertake, by finding the unit cost function for net output, which we denote by c^x. Again, by constant returns to scale, it suffices to find the efficient production techniques for one unit. The firm weighs emissions charges against the cost of foregone potential output to determine the most cost-effective techniques of production. Formally, the firm solves the following cost minimization problem:

$$c^x(w, r, \tau) = \min_{\{z, F\}} \{\tau z + c^F(w, r) F : z^\alpha F^{1-\alpha} = 1\}. \tag{2.13}$$

The solution is illustrated in figure 2.2. The unit isoquant for net output of X is illustrated. The isocost line has slope $-c^F/\tau$, which is the relative cost of the two inputs (potential output and environmental services) used to produce net output X. The cost-minimizing choice of emissions and primary factor inputs (F_0, Z_0) is at point B.

To solve for the optimal level of emissions per unit of net output at a point like B, we can solve the problem (2.13), and rearrange the first-order conditions to obtain

$$\frac{z}{F} \frac{(1 - \alpha)}{\alpha} = \frac{c^F}{\tau}. \tag{2.14}$$

Because (2.8) is linearly homogenous, we must also have

$$px = c^F F + \tau z. \tag{2.15}$$

Therefore, using (2.15) and (2.14), we can solve for pollution emissions per unit of net output, which we denote by e:[13]

$$e \equiv \frac{z}{x} = \frac{\alpha p}{\tau} \leq 1. \tag{2.16}$$

The emission intensity falls as pollution taxes rise because emissions become more expensive. The emission intensity rises when the price of the polluting good rises because the resources used in abatement have become more valuable.

---

13. Those familiar with the properties of Cobb-Douglas production functions can obtain (2.16) more quickly by noting from (2.8) that at an interior solution, the share of emission charges in the total cost of production of X must be α; that is, $\tau z/px = \alpha$. Rearranging yields (2.16).

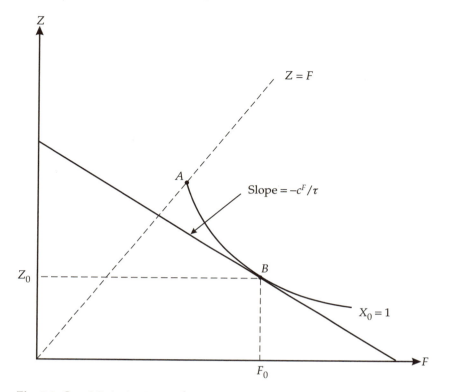

Fig. 2.2. Cost Minimization in the X Industry

The interior optimum depicted in figure 2.2 is not assured, though.[14] As the emission tax falls, the isocost line in figure 2.2 gets steeper; and for a sufficiently low emission tax, the firm will find that it is not cost-effective to abate at all and will choose point A in the diagram. To determine the conditions under which this occurs, define τ^* as the pollution tax that leaves a firm indifferent to abating or not. When there is no abatement at all, $z = x = F$ and $e = 1$. Evaluating (2.16) at this point yields

$$\tau^* = \alpha p. \tag{2.17}$$

For any pollution tax above τ^*, the firm actively abates, (2.16) is rele-

14. It would be assured if we adopted a formulation where the marginal product of abatement approached infinity with zero abatement as we did in Antweiler, Copeland, and Taylor 2001. We have deliberately chosen a formulation here where no abatement occurs for sufficiently low pollution taxes. This formulation facilitates our discussion of the environmental Kuznets curve and threshold effects in chapter 3.

vant, and emissions per unit of output, e, are less than 1. For any pollution tax below τ^*, the firm chooses not to abate and emissions per unit of output are equal to 1: pollution is simply proportional to output.

Once we have found the emissions intensity, the economy's overall quantity of pollution emissions is simply

$$z = ex. \tag{2.18}$$

Our main interest is in the level of pollution, and so the next step is to show how the economy's aggregate output of X is determined.

Net and Potential Production Possibilities

The simplest way to illustrate the determination of output in a general equilibrium model is with the aid of the production frontier. However, because pollution is endogenous, the production frontier in our model is three dimensional; that is, if we think of pollution and X as joint outputs, we have three goods: X, Y, and Z. Alternatively, if we interpret pollution as an input, then the feasible production of X and Y varies with the level of Z, and so there is no unique relation between X and Y.

However, by distinguishing between potential and net output, and exploiting some of the structure of our technology, we can illustrate the market equilibrium in a two-dimensional diagram, as depicted in figure 2.3.

First we can draw the production frontier for potential output. This indicates the maximum amount of potential output F in the X industry that can be produced for any level of Y, given factor endowments and technologies. That is, the potential output frontier illustrates the production possibilities for the economy if no abatement is undertaken. In figure 2.3, this is the outermost curve, labeled *Potential Frontier*.

In addition, we can draw a conditional (net) frontier, relating the maximum level of net output of X that can be produced for a given output of Y and for a given emission intensity e. In figure 2.3, we have drawn one such net frontier (for a particular level of e)—this is the innermost curve, labeled *Net Frontier*. All net frontiers lie inside the potential frontier because some resources are used for abatement unless the economy is specialized in Y.

For a given emission intensity e, we can derive the corresponding net frontier from the potential frontier as follows. Substituting (2.18) into (2.8) and rearranging yields

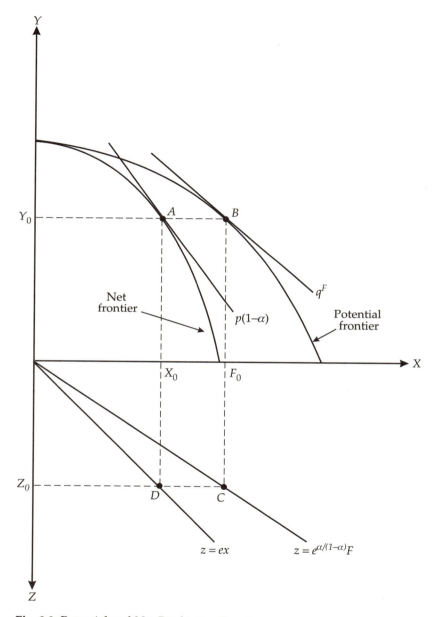

Fig. 2.3. Potential and Net Production Frontiers

$$x = e^{a/(1-a)} F(K_x, L_x).$$ (2.19)

If we recall that $e \leq 1$, (2.19) implies that net output is a fixed fraction of potential output. We can alternatively obtain a simple relation between net and potential output by referring to (2.3):

$$x = (1 - \theta) F(K_x, L_x).$$ (2.20)

Recall that θ is the fraction of resources allocated to abatement. Again, this shows that net output is a fixed fraction of potential output for a given emission intensity. Using (2.20), it is easy to derive the net frontier graphically from the potential frontier: given any Y, net output X is obtained by shifting in the potential output F by a fraction $1 - \theta$.

It is useful to combine (2.19) and (2.20) to obtain a relation between e and θ for future reference.

$$e = (1 - \theta)^{(1-a)/a}$$ (2.21)

Since θ is the fraction of value-added used in abatement, (2.21) neatly links pollution abatement costs to emissions per unit of output. Lower emissions per unit output come at the expense of higher pollution abatement costs.

Finally, we can invert (2.21) and use (2.16) to obtain an expression for θ in terms of prices:

$$\theta = 1 - \left(\frac{ap}{\tau}\right)^{a/(1-a)}$$ (2.22)

The share of resources allocated to abatement increases as the pollution tax τ increases, but fall as the price of X rises (since this reflects an increase in the opportunity cost of abatement).

2.2 Equilibrium along the Net and Potential Production Frontiers

We can now exploit our production frontiers to illustrate the equilibrium levels of output and pollution for a given market goods price p and pollution emission charge τ. We focus here on the case where τ is large enough so that firms allocate some resources to abatement.[15]

Output and pollution determination can be fully illustrated with the aid of either the net or the potential frontier alone. However, we will

---

15. If τ is so low that firms do not abate, then the net and gross frontiers coincide. Firms in X then receive $p - \tau$ per unit of X produced.

discuss both approaches (and demonstrate their equivalence) because each has its uses depending on the types of questions we ask.

We first illustrate the equilibrium using the net frontier. Firms in both sectors maximize profits. Profits π^x for a firm producing X are given by revenue, less payments to all labor and capital employed, and pollution charges:

$$\pi^x = pX(K_x, L_x) - wL_x - rK_x - \tau z, \tag{2.23}$$

where from (2.20) net output $X(K_x, L_x)$ is given by

$$X(K_x, L_x) = (1 - \theta) F(K_x, L_x). \tag{2.24}$$

Using (2.18), we can eliminate z from (2.23):

$$\pi^x = (p - \tau e) X(K_x, L_x) - wL_x - rK_x. \tag{2.25}$$

As long as the pollution tax is high enough so that abatement occurs, we can exploit the results of the firm's cost minimization problem by using (2.16) to eliminate e from (2.25). This yields

$$\pi^x = p(1 - \alpha) X(K_x, L_x) - wL_x - rK_x. \tag{2.26}$$

Firms in the Y sector do not pollute, so profits in Y are simply

$$\pi^Y = H(K_y, L_y) - rK_y - wL_y. \tag{2.27}$$

Each firm chooses inputs to maximize profits. This yields

$$\begin{aligned} H_K &= p(1 - \alpha) X_K = r \\ H_L &= p(1 - \alpha) X_L = w. \end{aligned} \tag{2.28}$$

Rearranging yields

$$\frac{H_K}{X_K} = \frac{H_L}{X_L} = p(1 - \alpha). \tag{2.29}$$

Finally, note that the slope of the net production frontier is given by[16]

---

16. To see this, solve for the maximum level of Y for a given level of X, subject to X and Y being on the net frontier:

$$Y(X) = \max\{H(K_y, L_y) : X = X(K_x, L_x), K_x + K_y = K, L_x + L_y = L\}.$$

Let λ denote the Lagrange multiplier for the constraint on X. Then the first-order conditions imply

$$\lambda = -\frac{H_K}{X_K} = \frac{H_L}{X_L}.$$

Using the envelope theorem, the slope of the net frontier is $dY/dX = \lambda$, which implies (2.30).

$$\frac{dY}{dX}\bigg|_{net} = -\frac{H_K}{X_K} = -\frac{H_L}{X_L}.\tag{2.30}$$

Combining (2.29) and (2.30) yields

$$\frac{dY}{dX}\bigg|_{net} = -p\,(1-\alpha).\tag{2.31}$$

That is, in aggregate, firms' behavior leads to a production point along the net frontier where the absolute value of the slope of the net frontier is equal to the producer price $q \equiv p\,(1-\alpha)$. This is point A in figure 2.3. Pollution can then be determined in the bottom half of the diagram, by recalling that $z = ex$. This yields point D in the diagram, which corresponds to a pollution level of z_0.

Alternatively, we can depict the equilibrium along the potential frontier. Using (2.20), we can rewrite (2.26) as

$$\pi^x = q^F F\,(K_x,\,L_x) - wL_x - rK_x,\tag{2.32}$$

where q^F is the producer price a firm obtains for producing one unit of potential output F:

$$q^F = p\,(1-\alpha)\,(1-\theta).\tag{2.33}$$

This producer price is less than p because only a fraction $1-\theta$ of output is available for sale outside the firm (the rest is used for abatement), and of that only a fraction $(1-\alpha)$ remains after pollution taxes are paid.

Hence, referring to (2.32), we can think of the firm's profit maximization problem entirely in terms of a decision about how much gross output to produce, providing that we use the correct producer price q^F.

Firms in the Y sector face the same problem as before, with profits there given by (2.27). Combining the profit maximization conditions for firms in both sectors yields

$$\frac{H_K}{F_K} = \frac{H_L}{F_L} = q^F.\tag{2.34}$$

But the slope of the potential frontier is given by

$$\frac{dY}{dX}\bigg|_{potential} = -\frac{H_K}{F_K} = -\frac{H_L}{F_L}.\tag{2.35}$$

and hence we have

$$\left.\frac{dY}{dX}\right|_{potential} = -q^F. \tag{2.36}$$

This is illustrated by point B in figure 2.3. Profit maximization by firms leads to a point on the potential frontier where the absolute value of the slope of the frontier is equal to the relative producer price for potential output q^F.

We can also illustrate equilibrium pollution by combining (2.18) and (2.19) to obtain

$$z = e^{1/(1-\alpha)} F.$$

For a given emission intensity, pollution is directly proportional to potential output, and this relation is plotted in the bottom half of figure 2.3. Consequently, once F is determined by q^F at point B, we can drop down to point C to determine pollution. This is the same level of pollution z_0 that we obtained when using the net frontier.

Finally, we can illustrate the equivalence of the potential and net output approaches to solving the model. Using (2.24), we can rewrite (2.30) as

$$\left.\frac{dY}{dX}\right|_{net} = -\frac{H_K}{(1-\theta)F_K} = -\frac{H_L}{(1-\theta)F_L}, \tag{2.37}$$

and hence we have

$$\left.\frac{dY}{dX}\right|_{net} = (1-\theta)\left.\frac{dY}{dX}\right|_{potential}. \tag{2.38}$$

Multiplying both sides of (2.31) by $(1-\theta)$, and using (2.33) and (2.38) yields (2.36). Hence the two approaches are equivalent and we can analyze the equilibrium by focusing either on point A or point B.

Uses of the Two Frontiers

The two frontiers can be used to clarify the distinction between production of final goods and production for abatement. In figure 2.3, point A represents the production point on the net frontier. This is the quantity of X actually available for consumption or trade. The distance BA represents that portion of gross X production used in the abatement process; and hence the ratio of BA to gross production B represents the share of value-added in the dirty industry allocated to abatement, that is, θ.

In addition, note that potential output (represented by the outer frontier) is determined by technology and endowments alone and is independent of the level of pollution. This is a useful reminder that an economy cannot pollute itself to prosperity. It can at best abate nothing and produce the maximum level of outputs consistent with its endowments and technology. This seems like a simple point, but often when authors adopt a formulation where pollution is an input it appears that generating more pollution generates more income. In fact, all a society can do is decide how to divide its potential output across two aggregate goods—pollution prevention and real consumption.

Improvements in the technology for producing goods shift out the potential and net frontiers uniformly, but improvement in the abatement technology alone shifts the net frontier outwards, leaving the potential frontier unaffected. For example, an improvement in abatement technology shifts the net frontier toward the potential frontier. The potential frontier is unaffected, but q^F must rise because with a constant product price and fixed tax, θ falls. The economy moves toward the dirty good industry.

And finally note that if emissions per unit of output are held fixed, then changes in potential and net output mimic one another. For example, if factor endowments change, then both potential output and net output change, but the ratio of the two remains the same.

Equilibrium Using Algebra

We can also use algebra to determine the production side equilibrium. We will specify the equilibrium conditions in terms of gross output; this corresponds to point B in figure 2.3. Net output can then easily be obtained by using (2.19) or (2.20).

Given that firms are profit maximizing, there are two sorts of equilibrium conditions for a competitive small open economy: free entry conditions and full employment conditions.[17] With free entry, if both sectors are active, we must have zero profits in each sector. This implies that unit cost must equal the producer price.

We previously derived the unit cost function for F in (2.12). Similarly, the unit cost function for Y is

---

17. The reader who wants more details on analyzing simple general equilibrium trade models is referred to Dixit and Norman 1980 and Woodland 1982.

$$c^Y(w, r) = \min_{\{k, l\}} \{rk + wl : H(k, l) = 1\}. \tag{2.39}$$

The producer price of Y is 1, and the producer price for gross output in sector X is q^F, which was defined in (2.33). Although q^F is endogenous and depends on θ, recall from (2.22) that given the exogenous world price p and the policy variable τ, θ is determined by cost minimization.

The free entry conditions are therefore

$$c^F(w, r) = q^F, \tag{2.40}$$

$$c^Y(w, r) = 1. \tag{2.41}$$

In each sector, the producer price must equal the unit cost when there is positive production. These two conditions jointly determined factor prices (w, r).

The full employment conditions simply require that the demand for each of the primary factors equals supply. The factor demands can be determined from the cost functions with the aid of Shephard's lemma.[18] For example, in sector Y, the amount of labor required to produce one unit of Y (which we denote a_{LY}) is obtained by taking the derivative of the unit cost function with respect to the wage:

$$a_{LY}(w, r) = \frac{\partial c^Y(w, r)}{\partial w}.$$

Total labor demand in sector Y is therefore $a_{LY}Y$, which is the total output of Y multiplied by the unit labor requirement. Other factor demands are determined analogously, and recalling that factor supplies are exogenous, we may therefore write the full employment conditions as

$$a_{LF}(w, r) F + a_{LY}(w, r) Y = L, \tag{2.42}$$
$$a_{KF}(w, r) F + a_{KY}(w, r) Y = K,$$

where $a_{Li} \equiv \partial c^i/\partial w$, and $a_{Ki} \equiv \partial c^i/\partial r$. The first condition requires that the demand for labor to produce F, plus the demand for labor to produce Y, must equal the supply of labor. The second equation is the analogous condition for the capital market.

---

18. See Dixit and Norman 1980 and Woodland 1982 for derivation of Shephard's lemma and its application to the analysis of simple general equilibrium trade models.

It is important to recognize that our system of endogenous variables resembles the standard two-sector Heckscher-Ohlin model.[19] Specifically, the system of equations (2.40)–(2.41) can be solved for equilibrium factor prices (w, r) as a function of q^F alone. With factor prices then determined, (2.42) solves for outputs (Y, F) as functions of K and L. Net output of X can then be determined by (2.19), and total pollution can be obtained from either (2.18) or (2.36).

Therefore, our system has the property that for a given emission price τ, we can solve for all remaining endogenous variables. The emission price is of course a policy choice, and we will discuss its determination later.

Comparative Statics

The system (2.40)–(2.42) looks very much like the standard two-sector competitive trade model—and indeed it is. The only difference is that the producer price q^F differs from the market price to take into account pollution taxes and abatement. This is very useful, because it means that for given pollution taxes (or given emission intensities), the model inherits the standard properties of the Heckscher-Ohlin model of international trade.

First, the Stolper-Samuelson theorem holds: an increase in the producer price of a good increases the real return to the factor used intensively in the production of that good, and lowers the real return to the other factor. To see this, note that as long as the economy is diversified in production, factor prices are determined by (2.40)–(2.41). This is illustrated in figure 2.4. The zero-profit conditions for F and Y have been illustrated (there are two zero-profit curves for F illustrated in the diagram, corresponding to two different levels of q^F). The zero-profit curves are level curves of the cost function, and so are downward sloping (along a curve of constant cost, an increase in w requires a fall in r to keep costs constant); and they are convex because cost functions are concave in input prices. Moreover, the absolute value of the slope of the zero-profit condition is the capital/labor ratio. To see this, consider the zero-profit curve for Y in the figure. Along the curve, we have

---

19. See Jones 1965 or any standard international trade textbook such as Bhagwati, Panagariya, and Srinivasan 1998.

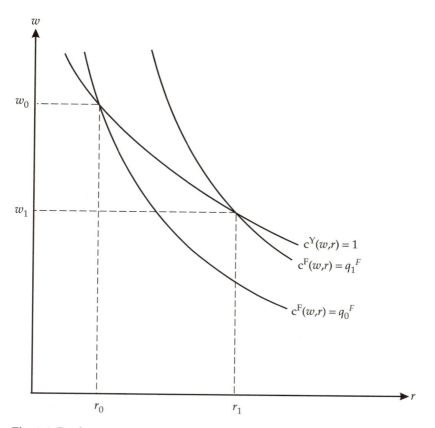

Fig. 2.4. Producer Prices and Factor Prices

$$\left.\frac{dw}{dr}\right|_{\bar{c}^y} = -\frac{\partial c^Y / \partial r}{\partial c^Y / \partial w} = -\frac{a_{KY}}{a_{LY}},$$

where the final result follows from using Shephard's lemma again. Because we have assumed that X is capital intensive relative to Y (recall
(2.1)), the zero-profit curve for F is steeper than that for Y. The initial
equilibrium factor prices are (w_0, r_0).

Now suppose that q^F rises from q^F_0 to q^F_1. This would happen either
if p rises or if the government lowers the pollution tax. Then the zero-
profit curve for F shifts out, and we can see that an increase in the
producer price of F causes r to rise and w to fall. That is, a reduction
in the pollution tax will raise the return to the factor that the polluting
sector uses intensively (capital) and reduce the return to the factor used
intensively in the rest of the economy (labor). This reflects the general

equilibrium adjustment to pollution regulation. A higher pollution tax causes the polluting sector to contract, and this reduces the relative demand for the factor used intensively by that sector.

Next, the Rybczinski theorem holds for a given emission intensity. An increase in the endowment of capital increases the output of the capital-intensive good (X or F) and reduces the output of the labor-intensive good (Y). To see this, first note that as long as the economy is diversified, changes in factor endowments have no effect on factor prices, because for a diversified economy, factor prices are completely determined by (2.40)–(2.41), and are not affected by factor endowment changes. Consequently, the effect of endowment changes can be obtained from (2.42), treating factor prices as constant. Adjustment to endowment changes takes place entirely via changes in output, not via changes in factor prices.

For constant factor prices, the equations in (2.42) are linear, as illustrated in figure 2.5. Because Y is labor intensive, the full employment condition for labor (the curve labeled L) is flatter than that for capital (two such curves are illustrated—labeled K_0 and K_1) . The initial outputs are (F_0, Y_0). Suppose the endowment of capital rises. Then the full employment condition for capital shifts out from K_0 to K_1. This increases the output of F (and hence also X), and reduces the output of Y. The intuition for this is that as the capital-intensive sector expands, it requires labor to be used in conjunction with the new capital. But this labor must be drawn from sector Y, so Y contracts (which in turn frees up even more capital to reinforce the expansion of the X sector).

The Rybczinski theorem will be important in helping us understand the incidence of pollution across the world. It implies, for example, that holding the emission intensity and goods prices constant, a capital inflow will stimulate the polluting industry and lead to a contraction of the clean industry.

Before moving on to analyze the comparative statics of the equilibrium, it is worth noting that we could reformulate the equilibrium conditions in terms of net output. If we divide both sides of (2.40) by $(1 - \theta)$, we obtain

$$\frac{c^F(w, r)}{(1 - \theta)} = p(1 - \alpha), \tag{2.43}$$

$$c^Y(w, r) = 1. \tag{2.44}$$

The left-hand side of (2.43) is the unit cost of producing X. To see this, note that each unit of X requires $1/(1 - \theta)$ units of potential output F

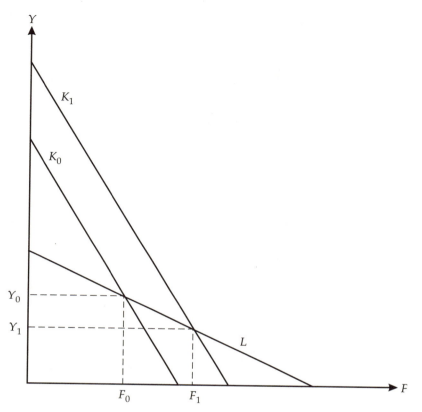

Fig. 2.5. The Effect of Endowment Changes on Outputs

because a fraction θ of the inputs are allocated to abatement. Hence the unit cost of net output X is $c^F / (1 - \theta)$. The right-hand side of (2.43) is the producer price of net output, taking into account pollution tax payments. Therefore (2.43) is simply the zero-profit condition for X producers.

Similarly, the full employment conditions can be written in terms of the net output of X:

$$L = a_{LX}(w, r) X + a_{LY}(w, r) Y, \tag{2.45}$$
$$K = a_{KX}(w, r) X + a_{KY}(w, r) Y,$$

which is equivalent to (2.42) once we note that

$$a_{LX}(w, r) = a_{LF}(w, r) / (1 - \theta), \tag{2.46}$$
$$a_{KX}(w, r) = a_{KF}(w, r) / (1 - \theta).$$

This follows for the same reason noted above. Each unit of net output requires $1/(1 - \theta)$ units of potential output. Hence we can obtain the unit input requirements for X by scaling up those for F by a factor of $1/(1 - \theta)$.

Because the system (2.43)–(2.46) is a transformation of the system (2.40)–(2.42), the two are equivalent, and either one may be used to analyze the equilibrium.

Finally, if we solve for outputs, we obtain

$$x = x\,(p,\, \tau,\, K,\, L), \tag{2.47}$$
$$y = y\,(p,\, \tau,\, K,\, L).$$

That is, outputs are determined by good prices, factor endowments, and pollution policy. To see this, first refer to (2.45) and (2.46), and note that x and y are functions of $(w,\, r,\, K,\, L,\, \theta)$. However, from (2.43)–(2.44), w and r are both determined by p alone; and from (2.22), θ is determined by p and τ. Hence we obtain (2.47).

An important property of the functions (2.47) is that both x and y are homogenous of degree 1 in $(K,\, L)$. That is, scaling up the factor endowments of the economy while holding pollution policy fixed will scale up outputs (and pollution). This follows from constant returns to scale. To prove this, let the new endowment vector be $(\lambda K_0,\, \lambda L_0)$, where $\lambda > 0$. Note from (2.43)–(2.44) and (2.22) that changes in K and L have no effect on w and r (provided both goods continue to be produced). Consequently, if x_0 and y_0 solve the full employment conditions (2.45), when endowments are $(K_0,\, L_0)$, then λx_0 and λy_0 must solve (2.45) when endowments are $(\lambda K_0,\, \lambda L_0)$.

Consumers

We assume there are N identical consumers in the economy. Each consumer cares about both consumption and environmental quality. Pollution is assumed to be harmful to consumers, and it is treated as a pure public bad (all consumers experience the same level of pollution). For simplicity, we assume that preferences over consumption goods are homothetic and that the utility function is strongly separable with respect to consumption goods and environmental quality. The utility function of a typical consumer is given by

$$U\,(x,\, y,\, z) = u\,(x,\, y)\, -\, h\,(z), \tag{2.48}$$

where $u\,(x,\, y)$ is increasing, homothetic, and concave, and h is increasing and convex.

Homotheticity is a standard assumption in the international trade literature, and it helps in two ways. First, it ensures that we can write the indirect utility function as simply an increasing function of real income: nominal income divided by a price index.[20] Thus it allows us to simplify our decision problem through a form of aggregation. The other benefit of assuming homotheticity is that it ensures that the relative demand for goods is unaffected by income levels. This is very helpful because it allows us to explain trade patterns as functions of regulation differences and relative costs alone.[21] The strong separability assumption means that the marginal rate of substitution between X and Y is not affected by the level of environmental quality, and it also limits the extent to which goods prices can affect the demand for environmental quality.

Each consumer maximizes utility, treating pollution, prices, and per capita income as given. This yields an indirect utility function of the following form:

$$V(p, I, z) = v(I / \beta(p)) - h(z), \tag{2.49}$$

where I denotes per capita income, β is a price index, and v is the indirect utility function dual to $u(x, y)$. The function v is increasing and concave because of the structure we imposed on u. Note that it is our homotheticity assumption that has allowed us to write indirect utility as a function of real income, defined as

$$R = \frac{I}{\beta(p)}. \tag{2.50}$$

National Income and Revenue Functions

National and per capita income will play a key role in our analysis of the effects of growth and trade on the environment. As we saw above,

---

20. To see this, note that a homothetic function is an increasing transform of a linearly homogenous function; that is, $u = g(f(x, y))$ where f is homogenous of degree 1 and g is increasing. If f is homogenous of degree 1, then demands are $x = b_x(p) I$, and $y = b_y(p) I$, and using linear homogeneity, we can write $u = g[f(b_x(p), b_y(p)) I]$. Define $\beta(p) = f^{-1}(.)$, and then we have $u = g[I/\beta(p)]$, where $\beta(p)$ is the price index specific to the function f. Utility is an increasing function of real income $I/\beta(p)$.

21. Without homotheticity over goods consumption, the relative demand for goods would vary with income: rich and poor countries would have different spending patterns, and trade would depend on the interaction between factor endowments, regulation, and income-induced differences in national spending patterns. This would compli-

consumer utility depends on income; and this means that a consumer's demand for both consumption goods and environmental quality will depend on income. This, in turn, means that efficient environmental policy depends on consumer income.

Because we have a general equilibrium model, income is endogenous. Income is the value of payments to all factors, including any pollution charges; or equivalently, it is the value of net goods production. Income will therefore depend on what the economy produces, as well as on goods prices and environmental policy. That is, the determination of income requires that we solve the entire general equilibrium of the economy.

Fortunately, there is a simpler way to obtain an expression for the economy's income that avoids having to resolve the entire model every time we want to undertake a comparative static exercise. As has become standard in the international trade literature, we can exploit the fact that profit-maximizing firms maximize the value of national income in a perfectly competitive economy.[22] The implied maximum value function (which we will call a national income or GNP function)[23] will have a number of very nice properties that help us in our analysis. An added benefit of this approach is that we can define a national income function for a very general economy, and so in some cases it will allow us to easily generalize our results beyond the confines of the simple technology we have assumed for our economy.

The result that profit-maximizing firms maximize the value of national income is a standard result in microeconomic theory, and can be most easily illustrated in our context for the case where the total amount of pollution in the economy is held fixed at z and firms have to buy permits in a competitive market if they want to pollute. (We will return to the case of endogenous pollution later in this section). Given a convex production technology, the endowments of K and L, and the fixed supply of pollution permits z, there will exist a concave production possibilities frontier as illustrated in figure 2.6. This represents the outer bound of the feasible production set given the aggregate allowable amount of pollution. Denote national income by G. Then $G = p^x x + p^y y$, which is the value of output at world prices. Al-

---

cate our model and distract from our main goals, but the interested reader should be able to extend the analysis to allow for this added motive for trade.

22. Here we exploit our assumption that pollution does not cause production externalities (that is, that pollution from one sector does not harm productivity in other sectors).

23. It is also sometimes called a revenue function.

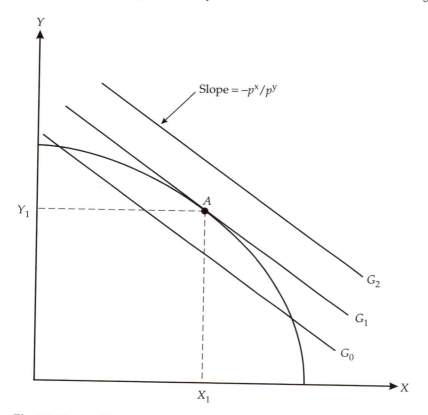

Fig. 2.6. National Income Function and the Production Frontier

though we usually treat Y as the numeraire, it is useful to refer explicitly to its price in what follows, so we have denoted goods prices as p^x and p^y.

In figure 2.6, we have drawn three iso-national-income lines, denoted by G_0, G_1, and G_2. The maximum feasible level of national income is G_1, and the outputs that support this are x_1 and y_1, denoted by point A. This is the point at which the absolute value of the slope of the production frontier is equal to the relative price ratio, p^x/p^y.[24] Profit-max-

---

24. We do not have to worry explicitly about the role of the price of pollution permits τ here as we did in figure 2.3 because we are treating the supply of pollution as fixed here and τ as an endogenous factor payment (recall that in figure 2.3, pollution was endogenous and the pollution price τ was fixed exogenously). Consequently, pollution plays the same role of capital and labor. Firms maximize profits subject to good prices and factor prices, and the factor prices adjust to ensure that markets clear and that production takes place on the frontier.

imizing firms will also induce the economy to end up at this point. Consequently profit-maximizing firms maximize the feasible value of national income. Note that G_1 depends on p^x, p^y, K, L, and z, as well as the underlying technology.[25] As we vary any of these variables, the maximum (or equilibrium) level of national income varies as well.

Let us now turn to the formal definition of the national income function. Start by assuming a somewhat more general technology than we have used so far.[26] Let $T(K, L, z)$ be a two-dimensional convex production possibility set with constant returns to scale. That is, T is the set of all combinations of net outputs (X, Y) that can be produced given the primary factor endowments K and L, and for a given level of pollution z. The production technology we specified in (2.2)–(2.8) is an example of such a technology. Now define the national income function G as follows:

$$G(p^x, p^y, K, L, z) = \max_{\{x, y\}} \{p^x x + p^y y : (x, y) \in T(K, L, z)\}. \qquad (2.51)$$

The function G tells us the value of national income at world prices, for any level of pollution and factor endowments, given the underlying technology. One can show that the first-order conditions for the solution to the maximum problem in (2.51) are exactly the same as the equilibrium conditions for our competitive economy.[27]

We have treated aggregate pollution as exogenous in (2.51), but will show how to make it endogenous below. Also note that although we suppress the price of Y throughout most of our analysis because we are treating it as the numeraire, we have included p^y in the equation above for clarity. In most of our applications, we will set $p^x = p$, and $p^y = 1$, and with slight abuse of notation will refer to the national income function as $G(p, K, L, z)$, where the role of the price of Y is suppressed.

---

25. See Woodland 1982 and Dixit and Norman 1980 for a detailed analysis of the national income function (sometimes called the revenue function). Copeland (1994) applies the national income function to economies with pollution.

26. We introduce a more general technology here because the specific technology assumptions used earlier in the chapter are not needed to derive the national income function. Our strategy in what follows will be to discuss some general results using the national income function, and then exploit the structure of our technology to discuss more specific results.

27. Woodland (1982) does this explicitly. The interested reader should demonstrate that the first-order conditions for (2.51) are equivalent to the equilibrium conditions already spelled out in terms of either gross or net output. To do so, it proves useful to solve for the cost function in (2.13) explicitly and then isolate $c^f(w, r)$.

The national income function has a number of very useful properties, many of which follow from its being a maximum value function. These are discussed in detail in Woodland 1982, and here we simply point out those properties that are of particular relevance.

First, Hotelling's lemma holds; that is, outputs can be recovered by differentiating with respect to goods prices:

$$\frac{\partial G\,(p^{x},\,p^{y},\,K,\,L,\,z)}{\partial p^{x}} = x, \qquad \frac{\partial G\,(p^{x},\,p^{y},\,K,\,L,\,z)}{\partial p^{y}} = y. \qquad (2.52)$$

This follows from the envelope theorem.

Next, the returns to capital and labor can be found by differentiating with respect to the relevant factor endowment:

$$\frac{\partial G\,(p^{x},\,p^{y},\,K,\,L,\,z)}{\partial K} = r, \qquad \frac{\partial G\,(p^{x},\,p^{y},\,K,\,L,\,z)}{\partial L} = w. \qquad (2.53)$$

The intuition for this is straightforward. Suppose the economy acquires an extra unit of capital. The derivative $\partial G/\partial K$ tells us how much national income rises because of the extra unit of capital. But this must be the value of the marginal product of capital, which in a competitive market is equal to the market return to capital. Similarly, an extra worker earns the value of his or her marginal product, which is the wage.

General Equilibrium Marginal Abatement Cost

Perhaps the most useful property for our purposes is that the derivative of the national income function with respect to pollution emissions is equal to the price the firms have to pay for the right to pollute:

$$\frac{\partial G\,(p^{x},\,p^{y},\,K,\,L,\,z)}{\partial z} = \tau. \qquad (2.54)$$

The intuition is the same as above: if firms are allowed to release one more unit of emissions, national income will rise by the value of the marginal product of emissions, which in a competitive market is equal to the price paid by firms for the right to pollute. If we think of environmental services as an input, then the logic is exactly the same as that we exploited in discussing factor returns above.

The expression $\partial G/\partial z$ can be interpreted as a general equilibrium *marginal abatement cost*. If we think of reducing emissions z, then the fall in national income due to a drop in allowable emissions is just

$\partial G/\partial z$; that is, it measures the cost to the economy of adjusting to a lower emission target. Reduced emissions will be achieved by private firms in two ways: by investing more in abatement activity, and by producing less of the dirty good X and more of the clean good Y. With either a market for emission permits or a pollution tax, firms will choose the most efficient combination of these two strategies. The derivative $\partial G/\partial z$ measures the cost to the economy of reducing emissions when the emission reduction is achieved at lowest possible cost.

Another interpretation of the result in (2.54), then, is simply that the pollution charge paid by the firm will equal the marginal abatement cost. This is a familiar result from environmental economics, although there it is usually presented in a partial equilibrium framework.

More Properties

Because G is a maximum value function, it has an important curvature property: it is convex in prices. The economic interpretation of this is that output supplies slope upwards. That is,

$$\frac{\partial^2 G}{\partial p^{x^2}} = \frac{\partial x}{\partial p^x} \geq 0, \qquad \frac{\partial^2 G}{\partial p^{y^2}} = \frac{\partial y}{\partial p^y} \geq 0. \qquad (2.55)$$

And because of constant returns to scale, G is concave in endowments:

$$\frac{\partial^2 G}{\partial K^2} = \frac{\partial r}{\partial K} \leq 0, \qquad \frac{\partial^2 G}{\partial L^2} = \frac{\partial w}{\partial L} \leq 0, \qquad \frac{\partial^2 G}{\partial z^2} = \frac{\partial \tau}{\partial z} \leq 0. \qquad (2.56)$$

That is, inverse demands for all factors slope downwards. Holding all other endowments fixed, increasing the supply of, say, labor, will typically reduce (or more generally, will not increase) the value of its marginal product. Most relevant to us is the last result in (2.56): it says that the general equilibrium marginal abatement cost curve slopes down, as shown in figure 2.7.

And finally, G has a couple of homogeneity properties. First, it is homogenous of degree 1 in prices; that is,

$$G\left(\lambda p^x, \lambda p^y, K, L, z\right) = \lambda G\left(p^x, p^y, K, L, z\right) \text{ for } \lambda > 0. \qquad (2.57)$$

This just says that doubling all goods prices doubles national income but has no effect on production decisions. Second, G is homogeneous of degree 1 in endowments. Doubling all endowments, but leaving prices unchanged, just scales up the economy.

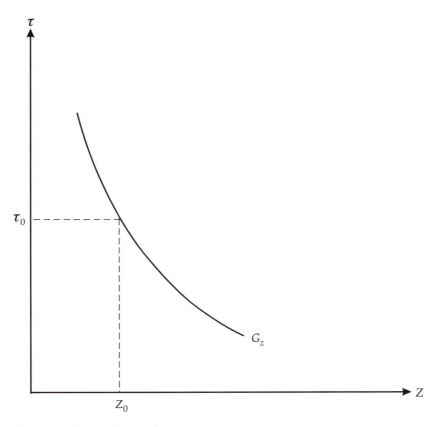

Fig. 2.7. Pollution Demand

$$G\left(p^{x}, p^{y}, \lambda K, \lambda L, \lambda z\right) = \lambda G\left(p^{x}, p^{y}, K, L, z\right) \text{ for } \lambda > 0.$$

This follows from constant returns to scale.

Endogenous Pollution with a National Income Function

It might appear that a potential limitation of (2.51) is that the emission level z is treated as exogenous when solving the optimization problem. This is fine if the government regulates pollution using an emission permit system. In that case the government specifies the overall supply of pollution permits, and the private sector through its competitive behavior ends up maximizing the value of national income, given the fixed available aggregate supply of emission permits. However, if there is no regulation, or if there is a fixed pollution tax in place, then we do not want to treat z as exogenous. It turns out there are two ways of defining a national income function with endogenous pollution; one involves using (2.51) but treating z as endogenous; and the other involves defining a different national income function. Because each approach has its uses, we will explain both.

First, we can exploit (2.54). If Z is exogenous, then (2.54) gives us the equilibrium market price of an emissions permit. But suppose instead that there is an exogenous pollution tax τ and that z is determined by the market response to the tax. Then if we treat τ as fixed, (2.54) determines z endogenously. Referring to figure 2.7, the policymaker can either choose a fixed z, in which case the market determines τ; or instead the policymaker can choose a fixed τ, and the market determines z. Using a combination of (2.51) and (2.54), we can therefore deal with either exogenous or endogenous aggregate emissions.

An alternative and perhaps more direct approach is to revert to the original interpretation of our technology as a joint production technology producing three outputs (X, Y, Z). Suppose that there is an exogenous pollution tax τ. Then standard competitive economic theory tells us that firms will collectively maximize the value of output given the prices of X, Y, and Z. This was illustrated by our discussion of figure 2.3. The only slight twist to keep in mind here is that the price of pollution is negative from the point of view of firms, because they must pay a tax on emissions. Therefore, we can define[28]

$$\tilde{G}\,(p^x,\,p^y,\,\tau,\,K,\,L) = \max_{\{x,\,y,\,z\}}\,\{p^x x + p^y y - \tau z : (x,\,y) \in T\,(K,\,L,\,z)\}. \quad (2.58)$$

This is the maximum value of net revenue generated by the private sector.

Recall that in our discussion of figure 2.3, we showed that given goods prices and the pollution tax, profit-maximizing firms would induce the economy to produce at point A. This is also the point that maximizes $\tilde{G}$. To see this, note that using (2.16), we have

$$p^x x + p^y y - \tau z = p^x\,(1 - \alpha)\,x + p^y y.$$

If we now think of maximizing national income at producer prices $p^x\,(1 - \alpha)$ and p^y given the optimal emission intensity (2.16), this corresponds to finding a point on the net production frontier that touches the highest line with slope equal to $-p^x(1 - \alpha)/p^y$. This is point A in figure 2.3. That is, the solution to (2.58) corresponds to point A.

28. This is the approach taken in Copeland 1994.

Before we can exploit (2.58), and to see the relation between G and $\tilde{G}$, we need to remember that national income also includes pollution tax revenue. Consequently, total national income is

$$G = \tilde{G}\,(p^x,\ p^y,\ \tau,\ K,\ L) + \tau z.$$

Notice that when we add pollution tax revenue to $\tilde{G}$, we are left with

$$G = p^x x + p^y y,$$

and so it should not surprise the reader that if we found the equilibrium pollution Z_0 that solved our problem (2.58), and confronted the economy with this fixed number of pollution permits Z_0, then (suppressing $p^y = 1$ as before) we would have

$$G\,(p,\ K,\ L,\ Z_0) = \tilde{G}\,(p,\ \tau,\ K,\ L) + \tau Z_0.$$

The function $\tilde{G}$ satisfies all the same properties as G that we outlined above, with the exception of (2.54) because it is a function of τ instead of Z. Instead, we have the following envelope property, which is an application of Hotelling's lemma:

$$\frac{\partial \tilde{G}\,(p,\ \tau,\ K,\ L)}{\partial \tau} = -Z\,(p,\ \tau,\ K,\ L). \qquad (2.59)$$

That is, we can obtain the derived demand for pollution by differentiating the national income function $\tilde{G}$ with respect to the pollution tax. Moreover, because $\tilde{G}$ is convex in all prices (including τ), we have $\tilde{G}_{\tau\tau} \geq 0$, which implies

$$\frac{\partial Z}{\partial \tau} \leq 0.$$

The derived demand for the right to pollute is decreasing in the pollution tax.

Finally, (2.59) and (2.54) are related. The former describes the derived demand for pollution; the latter is the inverse demand. Both describe the same curve in figure 2.6.

2.3 Scale, Composition, and Technique Effects

Much of our analysis will involve studying how changes to the economy, such as factor accumulation or trade liberalization, affect the environment. Because the linkages between the economy and the environment are both subtle and complex, it is useful to decompose changes in pollution into three fundamental forces: scale, composition, and technique effects. Grossman and Krueger (1993) used this approach in their influential study of the potential effects of NAFTA on the environment, and we have found it useful to help clarify both theoretical and empirical analysis. It is particularly useful in comparing the effects of different types of shocks to the economy. For example, both trade liberalization and capital accumulation tend to raise the productivity of the economy (this will lead to a scale effect in each case), but they may stimulate very different types of economic activity (their composition effects will differ). Moreover, because they both raise income and because environmental quality is a normal good, both types of changes could lead the government to tighten environmental policy (which will lead to a technique effect). By breaking the effects of policy changes into scale, technique, and composition effects, we can clarify how different types of shocks have both common and divergent effects on the economy. Moreover, this approach will also help us to disentangle empirically the effects of different types of shocks on the economy.

Definitions

In this section, we will define the scale, technique, and composition effects and give some examples to illustrate how to employ them.

Trade and growth both stimulate economic activity, and therefore both increase the economy's scale. To be more precise, we need a measure of the scale of the economy; that is, we need an index of output. There many ways to create such a quantity index. We will use the value of net output at world prices as our measure of the economy's scale. Our measure of scale, S, is defined as

$$S = p^0 x + y, \tag{2.60}$$

where p^0 denotes the world relative price of X prior to any shocks that we analyze. If world prices change, we continue to construct S using the old (base-period) world prices. This is so that scale will not change simply because of a change in valuation. But of course if the *outputs* of x and y change in response to world price changes, then our measure of scale will change—we evaluate the new outputs at the old prices.

Given this definition of scale, we now use (2.60) to write pollution as $z = e\varphi_x S / p^0$, where $\varphi_x = p^0 x / S$ is the value share of net output of x in total output evaluated at world prices. To make this expression a little less cumbersome we can choose the units we measure good X in so that $p^0 = 1$,[29] and this gives us

$$z = ex = e\varphi_x S. \tag{2.61}$$

Hence pollution emissions depend on the emissions intensity of production, e, the importance of the dirty good industry in the economy, φ_x, and the scale of the economy, S.

Taking logs and totally differentiating yields our decomposition:

$$\hat{z} = \hat{S} + \hat{\varphi}_x + \hat{e}, \tag{2.62}$$

where $\hat{z} = dz/z$, and so on.

The first term is the *scale effect*. It measures the increase in pollution that would be generated if the economy were simply scaled up, holding constant the mix of goods produced and production techniques. As an example, if there were constant returns to scale and all of the endowments of the economy grew by 10%, and if there were no change in relative prices or emissions intensities, then we should expect to see a 10% increase in pollution.

The second term is the *composition effect* as captured by the change in the share of the dirty good in national output. If we hold the scale of the economy and emissions intensities constant, then an economy that devotes more of its resources to producing the polluting good will pollute more.

Finally, we have the *technique effect*, captured by the last term in (2.24). Holding all else constant, a reduction in the emissions intensity will reduce pollution.

Let us illustrate these concepts using some diagrams. We will work through several examples both to illustrate how the model works, and to show how different sources of economic growth affect pollution in different ways. Because it is cumbersome to illustrate shifts in both net and gross frontiers, we will focus on the net frontier throughout.

---

29. To fix ideas, suppose X is steel and measured in units of 2,000 lb. tons; Y (our numeraire) is cloth and measured in units of 1,000 square yards. Then before we choose units of X, p^0 could be a number like 2.5 measured in units of cloth per unit of steel. Now measure steel in 800 lb. units rather than 2,000 lb. units. By choosing units that we measure steel in appropriately, we now have p^0 equal to 1; that is, at given world prices 1,000 square yards of cloth is worth 800 lbs. of steel.

The Scale Effect: Balanced Growth

To isolate the scale effect it is useful to assume that the emissions intensity is held fixed. This would be the case, for example, if the government had a fixed pollution tax. Now suppose we scale up the economy
by increasing each of the endowments by an equal percentage. That is,
denote the new factor endowment vector by $(\lambda K, \lambda L)$ and consider the
effect of increasing λ. Differentiating (2.61) logarithmically with respect
to λ yields an expression for the change in pollution decomposed into
scale, composition, and technique effects,

$$\frac{\frac{dz}{d\lambda}}{z} = \frac{\frac{dx}{d\lambda} + \frac{dy}{d\lambda}}{S} + \frac{\frac{d(x/S)}{d\lambda}}{\varphi_x} + \frac{\frac{de}{d\lambda}}{e}, \tag{2.63}$$

where we have made use of (2.60) and our units change to obtain
$p^0 = 1$.

   Recall from our discussion of (2.47) that x and y are homogenous of
degree 1 in K and L. This implies that

$$\frac{\frac{dx}{d\lambda} + \frac{dy}{d\lambda}}{S} = \frac{x(p, \tau, K, L) + y(p, \tau, K, L)}{x(p, \tau, \lambda K, \lambda L) + y(p, \tau, \lambda K, \lambda L)} = \frac{1}{\lambda} > 0.$$

The scale effect is positive: not surprisingly, scaling up endowments
also scales up the scale of production. Moreover, this is a pure scale
effect, as both the composition and technique effects are zero. The linear homogeneity of x and y in endowments implies that x/S is independent of λ. Hence $d(x/S) = 0$, and so, referring to (2.63), the composition effect is zero. And because both p and τ are fixed by assumption,
$de/d\lambda = 0$, and so there is no technique effect (the third term in (2.63)
is zero). Consequently, scaling up endowments in the presence of exogenous pollution taxes yields a pure scale effect:

$$\frac{\frac{dz}{d\lambda}}{z} = \frac{1}{\lambda} > 0.$$

   We illustrate this in figure 2.8. Point A indicates the initial output
point (on the net frontier) with producers receiving $q = p(1 - \alpha)$ per
unit of net output. In the lower panel of the figure we graph a pollution

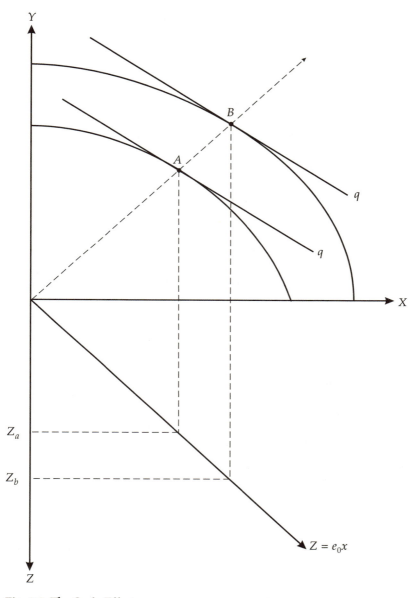

Fig. 2.8. The Scale Effect

emissions function $z = ex$ with a given fixed emission intensity of e_0. Given the initial production point, A, the initial level of pollution is Z_a. Suppose we scale up the economy by increasing each of the endowments by an equal percentage. Because of constant returns to scale, the new production frontier is just a radial expansion of the old one. The new production point is at point B, which must be on the same ray through the origin as A. Pollution has increased from $[Z_a$ to $Z_b]$, and this increase represents the pure scale effect.

There is no technique effect because we have held policy constant by assumption; and there is no composition effect because both the X and Y sectors expand equally. Therefore, we conclude that balanced growth in endowments in the presence of a fixed emission intensity will raise pollution via a pure scale effect.

The Composition Effect: Capital Accumulation

Next consider the composition effect. To illustrate an example of the composition effect, we again fix the emissions intensity, and now consider a change in only the endowment of capital. We will discuss the effects of this change first with the aid of figure 2.9, and then consider the algebra.

With capital accumulation, the outward shift of the production frontier is skewed toward the X-axis, because industry X is capital intensive. At a constant producer price $q = p(1 - \alpha)$, production in our economy moves from point A to point C. We know from the Rybczinski theorem that the economy produces more X and less Y at C than at A.

Both scale and composition effects are operative; and we now illustrate how to decompose the movement from A to C into these two effects. The line denoted P_0 measures the value of the initial output at our base-period world prices; this is the initial scale of the economy at point A. This line is steeper than the producer price line because of pollution policy.[30] For any movement along P_0, the scale of the economy is constant. We therefore decompose the total change in the economy into a movement from A to B, and from B to C.

The movement from A to B is a pure composition effect, because we have hypothetically held the scale of the economy constant and found the pure effect of increasing the share of X in the economy. This compo-

---

30. Note $p^0 = p > p (1 - \alpha)$.

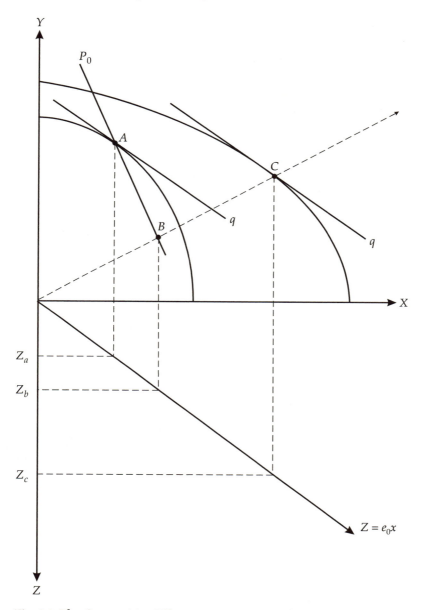

Fig. 2.9. The Composition Effect

sition effect yields an increase in pollution from z_a to z_b. Note that this is positive, because X is the dirty industry.

Next, the movement from B to C is the pure scale effect—it is the effect on pollution of increasing the scale of the economy, while holding the composition of output fixed. That is, along a ray through the origin and through point B, the composition of production is constant. Pollution rises from z_b to z_c via the scale effect.[31]

The increase in pollution due to capital accumulation is therefore partly due to a change in the composition of the economy as it shifts toward dirtier production, and partly due to an increase in the scale of production.

Let us now consider a decomposition of the effects of capital accumulation on pollution using algebra. Differentiating (2.61) logarithmically with respect to K yields an expression for the change in pollution decomposed into scale, composition, and technique effects:

$$\frac{\frac{dz}{dK}}{z} = \frac{\frac{dx}{dK} + \frac{dy}{dK}}{S} + \frac{\frac{d\,(x\,/\,S)}{dK}}{\varphi_x} + \frac{\frac{de}{dK}}{e}. \tag{2.64}$$

There is no technique effect because we held pollution taxes constant by assumption. Hence $de/dK = 0$, and the last term on the right-hand side drops out.

Next consider the composition effect. This is the middle term on the right-hand side of (2.9). First note that $x/S = 1(1 + y/x)$. From the Rybczinski theorem discussed earlier in the chapter, we have $d(y/x)/dK < 0$ because capital accumulation leads to a contraction of Y and an expansion of X. Consequently, the composition effect of capital accumulation on pollution is unambiguously positive:

$$\frac{\frac{d\,(x\,/\,S)}{dK}}{\varphi_x} > 0.$$

This is illustrated in figure 2.9 by the movement from A to B.

---

31. One could alternatively consider the scale effect first, and then the composition effect. As with income and substitution effects, when we consider a discrete change, the magnitude (but not the direction) of the effects will depend on the order in which they are constructed.

To evaluate the scale effect (the first term on the right-hand side of (2.64)), first note that

$$p(1-\alpha)\frac{dx}{dK} + \frac{dy}{dK} = \frac{d\tilde{G}(p, \tau, K, L)}{dK} = r > 0. \tag{2.65}$$

Therefore we can write the scale effect as

$$\frac{dx}{dK} + \frac{dy}{dK} = r + [p^0 - p(1-\alpha)]\frac{dx}{dK} \tag{2.66}$$

$$= r + \alpha\frac{dx}{dK} > 0$$

which is positive because domestic prices equal world prices, $p = p^0 = 1$, and the Rybczinski theorem gives us $dx/dK > 0$.

The key result here is that the composition effect of capital accumulation on pollution is unambiguously positive. This has important empirical implications. We can say little about how we expect pollution to differ across countries if we observe only capital abundance. However, if we control for the scale of the economy and abatement techniques, we would expect that more capital-abundant countries will pollute more because of the composition effect.

Our analysis of the composition effect has focused on capital accumulation. If instead we were to consider growth in the endowment of labor, we would obtain a negative composition effect. We know from the Rybczinski theorem that an increase in the supply of labor will raise the output of the clean good Y and lower the output of the dirty good. Hence x/S falls as L rises, and referring to (2.14), this implies an unambiguously negative composition effect. Therefore, the composition effect of labor accumulation works in the opposite direction to that of capital accumulation.[32]

---

32. The interested reader can show that the scale effect created by growth in the labor force is also necessarily positive as long as the share of pollution charges is not too large relative to the difference across X and Y in factor intensities. Specifically, let s_{kx} be the value share of capital in X production, and s_{ky} the corresponding value share in Y. Then when $s_{kx}/s_{ky} > 1/(1-\alpha)$, scale rises with an increase in L. Note s_{kx}/s_{ky} must exceed 1 since X is capital intensive. The possibility of a negative scale effect arises because we are measuring scale at world prices, rather than world prices adjusted for pollution charges. If firms maximize profits at prices different than we are using to measure scale, the value of output at world prices may fall as a result of factor accumulation just as in the immiserizing growth literature (see Bhagwati 1968). We measure scale at world prices in order to make consistent cross-country comparisons of scale in our empirical work.

Summing up, the composition effect is positive if a shock to the economy leads it to produce a basket of goods that is more pollution intensive on average than it did previously, and negative otherwise. In the model above, this is a simple observation, but in more general models this basic result still holds true.[33]

The Technique Effect: A Change in Emission Intensity

To examine the technique effect, we now consider the effects of a change in pollution policy. Suppose there is an exogenous increase in the pollution emissions tax. From (2.26) we know the producer price for net output is unaffected by this change, but from (2.16) the emissions intensity has to fall. As a result, the net frontier must shift in as more resources are allocated to abatement.[34] The effects of this exogenous policy change are illustrated in figure 2.10. Initially, the economy is at point A, pollution is z_a, and emissions per unit of output are e_0. An increase in the pollution tax increases abatement activity and hence reduces emissions per unit of output (e falls to e_1). The pollution function in the lower part of the diagram shifts up (for any level of x output, there is less pollution). Holding output at A, pollution falls from z_a to z_1. This is the technique effect: a higher pollution tax leads to cleaner production techniques; and, holding the scale and composition of output fixed, this lowers pollution emissions.

The policy change also has two other effects. Note that because the production frontier rotates inward, the final equilibrium is at point C. This movement is comprised of a scale effect (A to B) leading to the further drop in pollution from z_1 to z_b, and the composition effect (B to C) reducing pollution even more to z_c. There is a fall in the scale of output because of increased abatement (which consumes resources). There is a composition effect because the resource cost of further abatement affects the dirty industry disproportionately. As a result, the opportunity cost of producing X rises, and with constant prices, producers shift toward the clean good Y.

To confirm these results, differentiate (2.61) logarithmically with respect to τ to obtain

---

33. See, for example, the discussion of composition effects in Copeland and Taylor 1994.
34. The potential frontier remains in place.

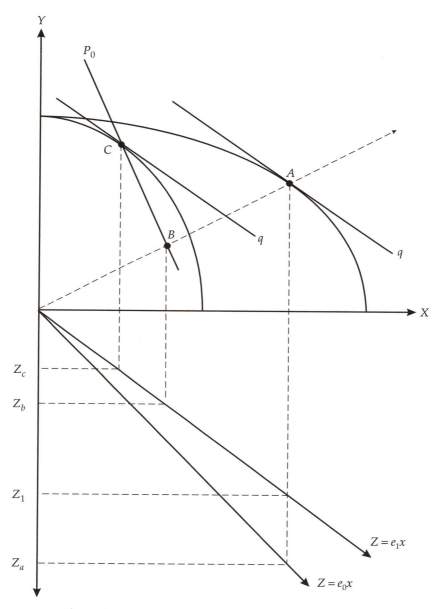

Fig. 2.10. The Technique Effect

$$\frac{\frac{dz}{d\tau}}{z} = \frac{\frac{dx}{d\tau} + \frac{dy}{d\tau}}{S} + \frac{\frac{d\,(x/S)}{d\tau}}{\varphi_x} + \frac{\frac{de}{d\tau}}{e}.$$

Starting with the technique effect, we have from (2.16)

$$\frac{de/d\tau}{e} = -\frac{1}{\tau} < 0.$$

The technique effect is negative because higher taxes reduce the emission intensity.

Next, the composition effect can be signed by noting that

$$\frac{d\,(x/S)}{d\tau} = \frac{d\,[1/(1 + y/x)]}{d\tau} < 0.$$

The sign follows since an increase in the pollution tax leads to a contraction of the X industry and an expansion of Y. This can be confirmed by referring to (2.36). An increase in the pollution tax lowers q^F. This leads to a movement along the potential frontier that reduces the output of F and increases the output of y. Moreover, $x = (1 - \theta)F$ and since $d\theta/d\tau > 0$ (more resources are shifted to abatement as τ rises) and $dF/d\tau < 0$, x unambiguously falls.[35] The composition effect therefore reinforces the technique effect to further reduce emissions.

Finally, the sign of the scale effect is determined by

$$\frac{dx}{d\tau} + \frac{dy}{d\tau} = -z + a\frac{dx}{d\tau} < 0,$$

where the derivation uses the same method we used in obtaining (2.66). Since $dx/d\tau < 0$, the scale effect is negative.

Tightening up pollution policy therefore reduces pollution via three effects: cleaner techniques, a shift in the composition of economic activity toward the cleaner good, and a lower scale of output.

2.4 Endogenous Pollution Policy

So far, we have analyzed the equilibrium of the economy under the assumption that pollution policy is exogenous. In general, we expect pollution policy to be endogenous. In particular, we expect that

---

35. One could also differentiate the full employment and zero-profit conditions to confirm this result.

changes in per capita income will lead to an increase in the demand for environmental quality, and, if governments are responsive, this may lead to a tightening up of pollution regulations. This will be an important component of our analysis. Both trade and growth affect per capita income, and we need to account for possible endogenous policy responses when analyzing their effects on the environment. In addition, endogenous policy differences across countries can themselves be a cause of international trade. This is the well-known *pollution haven hypothesis*, and we will need to understand how pollution policy varies with the economic characteristics of a country in order to fully analyze it.

There are many ways to model endogenous environmental policy. One is to assume that the government is responsive to the preferences of consumers and provides efficient policy. Another is to assume governments respond to interest group pressure. We will make use of both approaches in various parts of the book, but in the main our analysis will assume policy is efficient. This choice is made because the major theories in this area focus on cross-country differences in either income or factor endowments as a basis for trade, whereas much of the recent political economy literature has focused on explaining within-country but across-industry variation in policy. Nevertheless we will investigate the role of interest group pressures in chapter 4 on trade liberalization and discuss them further in our empirical implementation in chapter 7.

At this point, we limit ourselves to deriving the efficient environmental policy. Efficient policy has played a central role in the literature, and all of the political economy approaches tend to build on the analytics of the efficient policy approach. It will also serve as our base case to compare with other scenarios.

The efficient level of pollution is determined by weighing the benefits of pollution against the costs. As we showed earlier, it is helpful to treat pollution (or environmental services) as an input used by producers. A standard tool for analyzing input markets is the demand-and-supply diagram; and we find that it is useful to use such a diagram to illustrate the equilibrium level of pollution. The demand for pollution is a derived demand, as firms in the X sector derive benefits from securing the right to pollute. The "supply" of pollution reflects the policy regime. When pollution policy is optimal, the supply of pollution reflects the aggregate willingness to allow environmental damage. The interaction between these demand and supply side factors determines the equilibrium level of pollution.

The Demand for Pollution

We have already described many features of the demand for pollution. In our previous analysis we fixed the emission intensity for many of our results, and this requires us to fix the pollution tax or permit price τ. For example, when we found higher pollution levels with either balanced factor growth (the scale effect example) or capital accumulation (the composition effect example), implicit in our analysis was an outward shift in pollution demand by the private sector in both these cases. Similarly, when we found that higher pollution taxes reduce pollution, this in effect illustrated that our pollution demand curve has negative slope. Therefore our earlier exercises were very simple characterizations of the derived demand for pollution.

At this point we want to be more explicit about the properties of pollution demand, as well as to introduce a convenient diagram. Starting with a general technology, recall from the properties of the national income function that the inverse demand for pollution is given by[36]

$$\tau = G_z\,(p,\,K,\,L,\,z). \tag{2.67}$$

This defines an implicit function $z = z(\tau, p, K, L)$. We can differentiate and solve for the slope of the pollution demand curve:

$$\frac{dz}{d\tau} = \frac{1}{G_{zz}} \leq 0. \tag{2.68}$$

The slope of the derived demand for pollution is nonpositive because G is concave.[37]

We can say more about pollution demand by recalling pollution is determined by the emission intensity and the output of x. This yields a direct derived demand for the right to pollute as a function of the pollution tax τ, factor endowments, and the price of X.

$$z = e\,(p\,/\,\tau)\,x\,(p,\,\tau,\,K,\,L), \tag{2.69}$$

where e is defined in (2.16) and we have made use of (2.47) to write output as a function of goods prices, taxes, and endowments. The slope of the general equilibrium pollution demand is given by

36. As we indicated earlier, we will suppress the role of the price of p^y in G because we have set $p^y = 1$.
37. For general technology, it is possible that pollution demand may have flat regions. In Copeland and Taylor 2000 we discuss a model with this property.

$$\frac{\partial z}{\partial \tau} = e_\tau x + e x_\tau < 0, \tag{2.70}$$

and hence while (2.68) tells us pollution demand slopes downward, (2.70) identifies the two mechanisms at work in creating the negative slope.

The derived demand for pollution is illustrated in figure 2.11. Pollution demand slopes down for two reasons: first, higher pollution taxes make abatement more profitable, thereby reducing the emissions intensity of production. This is the technique effect. In discrete form this would represent a movement from Z_a to Z_1 in figure 2.10. Second, with greater abatement efforts resources are drawn away from production of final goods and services, and this causes the output of x to fall as producers exit the x industry and move into y. This change is due to both scale and composition effects. And again in discrete terms this is the movement from Z_1 to Z_c in figure 2.10.

Pollution demand shifts in response to changes in factor endowments and goods prices. An increase in the endowment of capital shifts the demand for pollution to the right. To see this, first recall from the production side equilibrium conditions that output X (or F) is only a function of τ through its effect on emissions per unit output. Therefore we could write the direct demand to reflect this:

$$z = e\,(p\,/\,\tau)\,x\,(p,\,\tau,\,K,\,L). \tag{2.71}$$

Then differentiate with respect to K to obtain

$$\frac{dz}{dK} = e\,(p/\tau)\,\frac{dx\,(p,\,\tau,\,K,\,L)}{dK} > 0. \tag{2.72}$$

For a given pollution tax and goods price, an increase in K has no effect on the emission intensity. Therefore, the effect of capital accumulation on the demand for pollution depends on the response of the output of X. But we can now invoke the Rybczinski theorem since e is held fixed when we take this derivative. And hence capital accumulation stimulates output of the capital-intensive dirty good X, and so the demand for pollution rises (the private sector will want to pollute more for any given τ).[38] We illustrate this shift in figure 2.11. For the initial pollution

---

38. Alternatively, we could differentiate (2.67), set $d\tau = 0$, and obtain $dz/dK = -G_{ZK}/G_{ZZ}$. Since $G_{ZZ} < 0$, the result depends on the sign of the cross-derivative G_{ZK}. But since $G_z = \tau$, the term G_{ZK} simply tells us how the inverse demand for pollution shifts in response to an increase in the supply of capital. To sign this, we need to draw upon our knowledge of the structure of technology, as we have done in the text. In our model, because

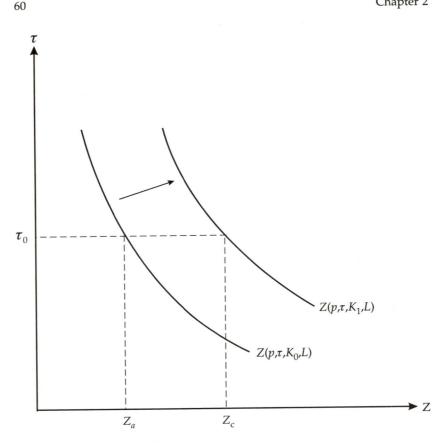

Fig. 2.11. Capital Accumulation

tax τ_0, pollution demand rises from Z_a to Z_c. This is exactly the same as the increase in pollution illustrated in figure 2.9 when we considered an increase in capital.

In contrast to the case of capital, an increase in the endowment of labor shifts pollution demand to the left:

$$\frac{dz}{dL} = e\,(p/\tau)\,\frac{dx\,(p,\,\tau,\,K,\,L)}{dL} < 0. \tag{2.73}$$

This again follows from the Rybczinski theorem.

Finally, an increase in the price of the dirty good shifts pollution demand to the right because abatement becomes relatively more expen-

---

the polluting sector is capital intensive and because the Rybczinski theorem holds, we have $G_{ZK} > 0$, and hence $dz/dK > 0$.

sive, and because factors are drawn into the now more attractive dirty good industry:

$$\frac{dz}{dp} = x \underset{(+)}{\frac{de\,(p/\tau)}{dp}} + e\,(p/\tau) \underset{(+)}{\frac{dx\,(p,\,\tau,\,K,\,L)}{dp}} > 0. \tag{2.74}$$

As discussed earlier, the pollution demand curve can be thought of as a general equilibrium marginal abatement cost curve—it measures the opportunity cost to the economy of reduced pollution emissions. With this interpretation, capital accumulation and increases in the dirty good price raise marginal abatement costs. Hence the outward shift in the derived demand curve discussed above can alternatively be interpreted as an upward shift in the marginal abatement cost curve. Increases in the endowment of labor reduce marginal abatement costs, and hence the inward shift in the derived demand curve can be interpreted as a downward shift in marginal abatement costs.

Finally, the inverse pollution demand curve in (2.67) can also be thought of as a marginal benefit of polluting curve. With this interpretation, we have just shown how changes in endowments and goods prices affect the marginal benefit of polluting. An increase in the price of the dirty good increases the marginal benefit of polluting because the value of the marginal product of emissions is higher. Capital accumulation increases the marginal benefit of polluting because a more capital abundant country is relatively more productive in the dirty industry. And labor accumulation reduces the marginal benefit of polluting because it makes the economy more productive in the clean industry.

Marginal Damage and the "Supply" of Pollution

Let us now find the optimal pollution policy. The demand for pollution as captured by (2.67) measures the marginal benefit of polluting. To determine the optimal pollution policy, we need to balance this against the marginal damage from polluting. Because we have assumed all consumers are identical, the government finds the optimal policy by choosing the pollution level to maximize the utility of a representative consumer subject to production possibilities and private sector behavior.

We start by formulating the government's problem with general preferences and technology:

$$\text{Max } \{V(p, I, z) \text{ s.t. } I = G(p, K, L, z) / N\}, \tag{2.75}$$
$$\text{\scriptsize } z$$

where V is the indirect utility function of a typical consumer. All N consumers are identical, and so each receives the same income.[39] The first-order condition for the choice of pollution is

$$V_P \frac{dp}{dz} + V_I \frac{dI}{dz} + V_z = 0. \tag{2.76}$$

An increase in pollution will in general affect goods prices, income, and environmental damage, and each of these affects the consumer. However, because we are assuming a small open economy in this chapter, changes in domestic pollution will have a negligible effect on world goods prices, and hence $dp/dz = 0$. Using this, and dividing both sides of (2.76) by V_I, yields

$$\frac{dI}{dz} = -\frac{V_z}{V_I}. \tag{2.77}$$

The term on the right-hand side of (2.77) is the marginal rate of substitution between emissions and income; in other words, it measures the typical consumer's willingness to pay for reduced emissions. In the environmental literature, this is referred to as "marginal damage."[40] We denote this by MD, and hence we define

$$MD \equiv -\frac{V_z}{V_I}. \tag{2.78}$$

To further simplify (2.77), use the constraint in (2.75) and the properties of the national income function to obtain

$$\frac{dI}{dz} = \frac{G_z}{N} = \frac{\tau}{N}. \tag{2.79}$$

Substituting (2.79) and (2.78) into (2.77) yields

$$\tau = N \cdot MD. \tag{2.80}$$

The condition (2.80) says that the government should choose pollution

---

39. The government may use either pollution permits or emission taxes. In either case, any revenue accruing to the government is embodied in G as a return to z and is rebated to consumers in lump sum.

40. It is important to make a distinction between the marginal disutility of pollution, $-V_z$ and the marginal willingness to pay for reduced emissions, $-V_z/V_I$. The former has units in "utils," while the latter is a money measure. We have defined marginal damage as $-V_z/V_I$, which is the money measure of the willingness to pay for reduced emissions.

so that the emissions price faced by producers is equal to aggregate marginal damage.

To interpret (2.80), recall that environmental quality is a pure public good (or equivalently, pollution is a pure public bad). The condition (2.80) is simply the Samuelson rule for public goods provision: the government chooses pollution so that firms face an emissions price that is equal to the sum of the marginal damages across all consumers. Notice that this condition holds despite the presence of international trade. That is, when a small country is open to international trade, its efficient pollution policy is simply to internalize the pollution externality and ensure that firms face an emissions charge that is equal to the aggregate marginal damage.[41]

At this point it is instructive to exploit some of the structure (homotheticity and separability) we have put on preferences. Referring to (2.49), we can write (2.80) as

$$\tau = N \cdot [-V_z/V_I] = N \cdot \frac{\beta(p)\,h'(z)}{v'(R)} = N \cdot MD(p, R, z). \qquad (2.81)$$

Recall that $R = I/\beta(p)$ denotes real income. The assumption of homotheticity in goods consumption allows us to write marginal damage as a function of real income, goods prices and emissions: $MD = MD(p, R, z)$.

Next, we can use the national income function to substitute for real income and rewrite (2.81) as

$$\tau = N \cdot MD\,[p, \frac{G(p, K, L, z)}{N\beta(p)}, z]. \qquad (2.82)$$

We can think of (2.82) as the government's general equilibrium supply curve for pollution. It reflects the country's willingness to allow pollution. The pollution supply curve is upward sloping:

This is consistent with the interpretation of marginal damage as a money measure in the partial equilibrium literature.

41. If the Home country is large, then changes in its emission policy may affect world goods prices. This is because an increase in its allowable emissions will stimulate the supply of the dirty good, and if the Home country is sufficiently big, this can push down the world price of the dirty good. Because changes in world prices affect the price at which Home buys and sells goods from foreigners, this effect shows up in the optimal policy rule. That is, if a country is large, then it has market power; and one way to exploit this power is to use pollution policy to try to manipulate world prices. We will discuss this at several points later in the book. See, for example, our discussion of tariff substitution in chapter 7.

$$\frac{dMD}{dz} = MD_z + MD_R R_z \tag{2.83}$$

$$= \frac{\tau}{N} \left[\frac{h''}{h'} - \frac{\tau v''}{v' N \beta} \right] \geq 0,$$

where we have used $G_z = \tau$.[42] The sign of (2.83) follows for two reasons. First holding real income constant, an increase in pollution raises marginal damage given the convexity of $h(z)$. This is the first element in (2.83), and this by itself leads to a non-negative slope. Second, since the increase in z raises real income and v is concave, increases in pollution tend to make environmental quality scarce relative to consumption. This is the second element in (2.83), which also leads to a non-negative slope.

The pollution supply curve also shifts with changes in prices or real income. Consider an increase in real income, holding prices constant. From (2.81) we obtain

$$MD_R = -\frac{v''}{v'} MD \geq 0. \tag{2.84}$$

If v is strictly concave, then MD_R is positive. Marginal damage is increasing in real income because environmental quality is a normal good. If v is linear, then real income gains have no effect on marginal damage.

It is worth considering a simple example to illustrate how pollution policy depends on income. Assume utility takes the following form:

$$V(p, I, z) = \ln \left(\frac{I}{\beta(p)} \right) - \gamma z.$$

Then (2.81) becomes

$$\tau = \gamma N \beta(p) R = \gamma N I = \gamma G.$$

That is, the efficient price of emissions is directly proportional to aggregate income in this example.

Finally, consider a change in relative prices, holding real income constant. This is a pure substitution effect. From (2.81) it is easy to obtain that marginal damage shifts up with an increase in p. Recall that $\beta(p)$

---

42. Note that we have written this as a total derivative because we are allowing the change in z to affect marginal damage through its indirect effect in raising real income. In later chapters we will sometimes employ a construction of pollution supply that holds real income constant. When we hold real income constant, $R_z = 0$, and so from (2.83) the slope of the supply curve is given by MD_z, which depends on the marginal disutility of

is rising in p. As p rises, goods get more expensive relative to environmental quality. At the margin, environmental quality is now more highly valued and the willingness of citizens to supply pollution falls.

Regulatory Equilibrium

The equilibrium level of pollution is determined by the interaction between the pollution demand curve and society's willingness to tolerate pollution as captured by supply:

$$G_z(p, K, L, z) = N \cdot MD\left(p, \frac{G(p, K, L, z)}{N\beta(p)}, z\right). \tag{2.85}$$

This is illustrated in figure 2.12. The efficient level of pollution Z_0 is determined by the intersection of the pollution supply and pollution demand curves. To implement this efficient level of pollution, the government can employ either a pollution tax τ_0 or issue Z_0 marketable permits that would yield an equilibrium permit price τ_0. Any equilibrium that can be implemented with a tax can also be implemented with a permit system.

This figure also makes clear the link between our general equilibrium model and the standard treatment of optimal emissions in partial equilibrium models in environmental economics textbooks. As we noted earlier, pollution demand can be interpreted as the general equilibrium marginal abatement costs, and pollution "supply" is simply marginal damage. That is, optimal pollution emissions are determined by equating marginal abatement costs to marginal damage. The difference is that in our framework, the choice of emissions z also simultaneously determines national income $G(p, K, L, z)$, and all factor prices, such as wages and the return to capital, are fully endogenous. Moreover, our structure allows us to analyze how shocks to the economy as a whole, such as capital accumulation or trade liberalization, will affect pollution via their effects on marginal abatement costs or marginal damage.

2.5 Conclusion

This chapter has set out our general equilibrium pollution and trade model to familiarize the reader with many of the concepts and tools we will use in later chapters. We have drawn quite heavily from trade

---

pollution. The (real income constant) pollution supply curve is horizontal if the marginal disutility of pollution is constant; that is, if $h'' = 0$.

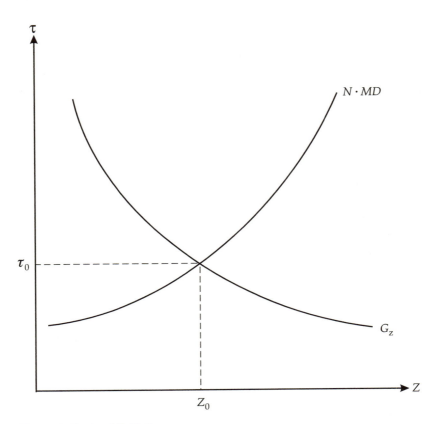

Fig. 2.12. Optimal Pollution

theory, but in the end have developed a simple pollution demand and supply system featuring marginal abatement cost and marginal damage schedules. These constructs should be familiar to environmental economists. We have intentionally kept the model quite simple. This will allow us to focus on issues arising in trading situations in subsequent chapters.

As we progress through the book, we hope it becomes apparent that our framework is well suited to examine the environmental consequences of growth and the impact of trade liberalization. With only slight amendment, it produces canonical models capturing both the pollution haven hypothesis and the factor endowments hypothesis. And as we demonstrate in chapter 7, it yields a parsimonious reduced form suitable for empirical estimation and hypothesis testing.

3 Is There an Environmental Kuznets Curve?

Some environmentalists have entered the debate over the benefits of trade liberalization by turning a classic argument for free trade on its head. Accepting that freer trade promotes growth in real incomes, they argue that this growth is ultimately futile because it will only lead to increased environmental degradation. This has led some skeptics, such as Herman Daly (1993), to question the wisdom of adopting a free trade regime. It has led others to call for a reform of international trading rules to ensure the environment is protected when trade is liberalized.

Proponents of freer trade have countered by suggesting that the link between economic growth and the environment is not that simple. Free trade does raise real income, but it also creates potentially offsetting effects as well. The most important of these is the response of pollution policy to the rising real incomes brought about by trade. If the demand for environmental quality rises with real incomes, then pollution policy will become more stringent as trade liberalization proceeds. Consequently, the impact of trade liberalization on the environment is now far less clear.

In a widely cited paper on the merits of North American free trade, Grossman and Krueger (1993) presented evidence to quantify the relative strength of these opposing effects. Their empirical results showed that air quality at first deteriorates as real incomes rise, but then improves once income per capita exceeds U.S.\$5,000 per year. If this relationship, now dubbed the *environmental Kuznets curve* (EKC),[1] is robust and applies to other forms of pollution as well, it is possible that the

---

1. Since almost all of the academic interest in this area was stimulated by Grossman and Krueger's (1993, 1995) articles, a more accurate label would be the Grossman-Krueger-

real income gains created by free trade may (at least eventually) be good for the environment.

Grossman and Krueger's work spawned a large and still growing literature examining the empirical relationship between per capita income and pollution.[2] Many other studies have found an inverse-U relation between certain types of pollution and per capita income, although the relationship does not hold for all pollutants and may be sensitive to functional form assumptions.[3] Despite the abundance of empirical work confirming, contradicting, or extending Grossman and Krueger's work, very little effort has been expended in linking empirical methods to underlying economic theory. As a consequence, the underlying cause of the EKC relationship is still unknown.

The purpose of this chapter is to investigate the relationship between economic growth and pollution levels within the model developed in chapter 2. We focus on growth here as a precursor to our discussion of trade liberalization in chapter 4. While our overall objective is to investigate the relationship between international trade and a country's environmental quality, the role of economic growth is a key link in this process, as the trade-causes-growth-causes-pollution logic represents one of the primary concerns of many in the environmental community.

In presenting our examination of the theory linking pollution and growth, we develop four major explanations for the EKC. These explanations each provide a link between real income and pollution levels, but they differ in the mechanism responsible for the EKC. By considering each theory in turn, we develop a better understanding of how growth affects pollution, and thus enable the reader to isolate the impact of trade on the environment.

We begin by demonstrating an important, albeit negative result: even within the confines of our simple two-good model, there is no simple relationship between per capita income and pollution. This is because income and pollution are both endogenous variables, and the effect of growth on pollution depends on what causes the growth. This

---

Kuznets curve. We will nevertheless follow the literature and adopt the shorter term with apologies to Grossman and Krueger.

2. The early papers included Grossman and Krueger 1993, 1995; Shafik 1994; and Selden and Song 1994. For recent reviews of the subsequent literature see Cavlovic et al. 2000 and Dasgupta et al. 2002.

3. Hilton and Levinson 1998 contains some of the most convincing evidence of an EKC. Harbaugh, Levinson, and Wilson (2002) examine the sensitivity of the original Grossman and Krueger finding to new data and alternative functional forms.

dependence on the sources of economic growth has been overlooked or at least underappreciated in the current literature because most theoretical models have implicitly or explicitly adopted a one-good framework.[4] As a result, the composition effects created by different sources of economic growth are often rendered mute.

To highlight composition effects, we present a "sources of growth" explanation for the EKC. As we show, if per capita income rises because of an increase in human capital, then we expect pollution to fall as per capita income rises. But if physical capital accumulation causes the growth, then that same economy might instead find pollution rising with per capita income. As a result, even if pollution policy is stagnant and unaffected by changes in real income, the EKC could arise from changes in the sources of growth along the development path. Even though this explanation is congruent with typical views of the development process, a formal treatment appears to be absent from the literature.

The sources of growth explanation is very important to our subsequent analysis. It suggests that income gains brought about by trade may have very different environmental consequences from those brought about by capital accumulation, technological progress, and so on. Therefore, the analogy drawn by some in the environmental community between the damaging effects of growth and those of trade is, at best, incomplete.

The second explanation for the EKC relies on a strong policy response to income gains. To eliminate composition effects, we focus on growth driven by neutral technical progress or factor accumulation. We then show that with efficient and responsive policy in place, the income elasticity of marginal damage is a critical factor in determining the effects of growth on the environment. If the income elasticity of marginal damage rises with income, then pollution can first rise and then fall with neutral growth, thus generating an EKC.

While this income-effect explanation is related to others in the literature (see, for example, Lopez 1994), we explicitly derive a simple reduced form for the EKC and isolate the role of income effects very clearly. Moreover, since our specification gives rise to a closed form solution for pollution solely as a function of income and parameters, it provides microfoundations for the current empirical work on the EKC.

---

4. Note that Stokey (1998) shows that her atemporal one-good model is a reduced form of the many-good model in Copeland and Taylor 1994. However, since tastes and tech-

Our discussion of the income-effect explanation is important because it focuses our attention on the links among income, pollution policy, and pollution levels. These same links are employed in chapter 5 to derive the pollution haven hypothesis. More generally, the link between income and pollution policy appears in all subsequent chapters as reflected in the technique effect.

Closely related to income-effect explanations are theories where "thresholds" limit the responsiveness of pollution policy to income gains at low income levels (Stokey 1998; John and Pecchenino 1994; Jones and Manuelli 1995). In this third explanation for the EKC, pollution at first rises with growth because either the policy process is at first undeveloped or the marginal benefit from abatement too low. Once the threshold has been breached, these theories rely on a strong policy response to income gains to drive pollution levels downward. We present two different threshold models—one based on thresholds in the abatement process, and another arising from fixed setup costs in regulation.

Although there are some differences, both the threshold and the income-effect theories place a large burden of adjustment on technique effects to explain the EKC. Not surprisingly, we show that threshold theories have a close family resemblance to the income-effect explanations.

The threshold theories provide an explanation for countries having no environmental policy at low levels of income. Therefore, they provide partial justification for Chichilnisky's (1994) claim that institutional differences across countries matter for both trade and environmental outcomes.

Finally, we examine an explanation for the EKC based on increasing returns to scale in the abatement technology (Andreoni and Levinson 2001). This explanation is logically distinct from the others in that it arises from an increasing scale of production, and not on factor accumulation causing composition effects, nor income gains driving pollution taxes upwards. Instead, we show that it implies a relationship between the scale of output and the cleanliness of the techniques, with an increased scale of production creating its own technique effect even though pollution taxes remain fixed throughout.

---

nologies are Cobb-Douglas, the share of dirty goods in national income (i.e., our measure of the composition effect) is a constant in her exclusively autarkic analysis.

To examine this explanation, we present an alternative interpretation of our basic model in which abatement is an explicit activity, and then amend our abatement production function to allow for increasing returns to scale. While Andreoni and Levinson presented their theory in the context of an economy with a central planner, we show how one can incorporate increasing returns in abatement into a simple market economy model and maintain the assumption of perfect competition.

The rest of this chapter proceeds as follows. We start in section 3.1 by showing that the EKC is a path traced out by income and pollution as parameters determining growth vary. In the following four sections we then examine each of the explanations of the EKC discussed above and note that they restrict either supply or demand to develop their results. Finally, in our conclusion we sum up by arguing for a new approach to examining the issue of growth and environmental quality.

3.1 Equilibrium Pollution and the Environmental Kuznets Curve

We use the model developed in chapter 2 to examine the relationship between pollution and growth. We assume a small open economy faces given world prices, p, and to simplify notation, we normalize the population so that $N = 1$. Our analysis is purely static, and growth in our context arises from once-and-for-all changes in endowments or technology. This allows us to isolate the fundamental forces at work and is useful in interpreting the empirical work.

As shown in chapter 2, the equilibrium level of pollution is determined by pollution demand, pollution supply, and the economy's budget constraint. We illustrate this system in figure 3.1. Recall that the inverse pollution demand equation is

$$\tau^D = G_z (p, K, L, z) \tag{3.1}$$

and is labeled G^0_z in figure 3.1. Pollution supply is

$$\tau^s = MD \left(p, \frac{I}{\beta (p)}, z \right) \tag{3.2}$$

and is labeled MD_0 in the figure. And the economy's income is labeled G_0 and is determined by

$$I = G (p, K, L, z). \tag{3.3}$$

Equilibrium requires $\tau^D = \tau^S$. Therefore equations (3.1)–(3.3) determine three endogenous variables: τ, I, z. This is illustrated in figure 3.1, with an initial equilibrium at (τ_0, I_0, Z_0).

The EKC literature seeks to estimate a relation between pollution and per capita income. Because the environmental Kuznets curve is a relation between two endogenous variables, I and z, this will be problematic.

From the vantage point of our demand-and-supply system two difficulties immediately present themselves. The first is simply that since income and pollution are each a function of more primitive determinants, why should we expect to find a simple, stable relationship between income and pollution? For example, suppose the initial equilibrium is (Z_0, I_0) in figure 3.1. Now consider increasing K. Then in figure 3.1 pollution demand, pollution supply, and the national income function G all shift. This yields a new equilibrium pair of income and pollution (Z_1, I_1). If we change K again, we get another point in Z, I space; and so on. This will trace out a relation between pollution and income that is driven by changes in the size of the economy's capital endowment. Of course, we could instead vary L and trace out a different relation between pollution and income. And, as well, we could vary parameters in the production or abatement technology (which we have suppressed here) and trace out other paths. Therefore it would be astonishing to find a simple stable relationship between all possible realizations of income and pollution.

The second difficulty is that in many cases income and pollution are determined simultaneously, and hence the current practice of regressing one on the other is of some concern.

To overcome the first difficulty, each of the explanations for the EKC puts strong restrictions on our pollution supply and demand system to generate the required result. These restrictions are of two types. One type of restriction represents what we would call zero restrictions. These are restrictions imposed when assuming either pollution demand or supply is independent of certain factors. For example, to assume that pollution demand shifts right with an increase in the scale of economic activity, but is independent of the composition of this activity, is a zero restriction because it makes the composition of factor endowments irrelevant to pollution demand. These restrictions are typically employed to ensure that pollution is a function of income alone.

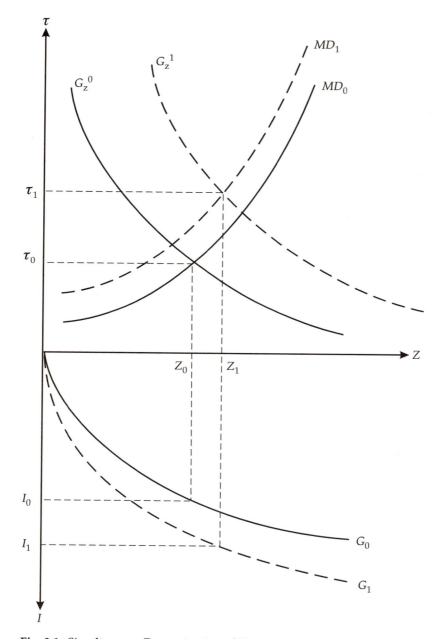

Fig. 3.1. Simultaneous Determination of Emissions and Income

The second are restrictions on preferences or technologies that ensure the desired shape of the income-pollution relationship is obtained. For example, assuming a constant relative risk aversion (CRRA) utility function is such a restriction, as is assuming abatement exhibits increasing returns.

In summary, while theory suggests there may well be a stable relation between pollution and variables such as technology and primary factors of production, and between income and these same variables, there is little reason in general to expect that there will be a simple relation between pollution and income.[5] Therefore, all theories that predict an inverse-U-shaped environmental Kuznets curve must proceed by imposing more structure on the process of growth, as well as by introducing additional assumptions on technology or preferences. We now consider four of the most prominent explanations.

3.2 Sources of Growth

The "sources of growth" explanation for the EKC is frequently mentioned in the literature, but a formal treatment of it appears to be absent. Very simply, suppose that countries grow primarily via capital accumulation in the early stages of development and by human capital acquisition in later stages.[6] If there is no pollution policy at all or if the emission intensity is fixed, then it is relatively easy to show that pollution could at first rise and then fall with growth in per capita income. We start by assuming exogenous or rigid policy and then consider the implications of endogenous policy.

To start, assume the pollution tax is fixed at $\tau = \bar{\tau}$. If we recall (2.16), this implies that the emission intensity is fixed, so we denote it by $\bar{e}$.[7] Pollution demand from (2.69) becomes

$$z = \bar{e}x\,(p,\,\bar{\tau},\,K,\,L), \tag{3.4}$$

5. Some empirical support for this view can be found in the work of Harbaugh, Levinson, and Wilson (2002). They examine the robustness of estimates of the environmental Kuznets curve for SO_2. This was the focus of the original work of Grossman and Krueger (1993) and is one of the most widely cited examples of the existence of an environmental Kuznets curve. They find that the shape of the curve is very sensitive to changes in the time period chosen and the set of countries included in the study. This is highly suggestive of a misspecification of the model, which is exactly what the theory above suggests.
6. An increase in human capital is captured in our model by an increase in the supply of effective labor per person.
7. This includes the possibility that there is no tax at all so that the emission intensity could be $e = 1$.

and income is

$$I = G\,(p,\,K,\,L,\,z),$$ (3.5)

where z is determined endogenously by (3.4).

Now consider growth via capital accumulation alone. Then differentiating (3.4)–(3.5) holding L constant, yields

$$\hat{z} = \varepsilon_{XK}\,\hat{K}$$ (3.6)

and

$$\hat{I} = s_r\,\hat{K} + s_\tau\,\hat{z},$$ (3.7)

where $s_r > 0$ and $s_\tau > 0$ are the shares of capital and emission charges in national income, $\hat{z} = dz/z$, and so on, and $\varepsilon_{XK} > 0$ is the elasticity of X output with respect to the endowment of capital, which is positive by the Rybczinski theorem.[8] Using (3.6) in (3.7) yields

$$\hat{I} = (s_r + s_\tau \varepsilon_{XK})\,\hat{K}.$$ (3.8)

That is, capital accumulation raises both income and pollution. Combining (3.8) and (3.6) yields a relation between pollution and income:

$$\hat{z} = \frac{\varepsilon_{XK}}{s_r + s_\tau\,\varepsilon_{XK}}\,\hat{I}\,.$$ (3.9)
$$(+)$$

There is a positive, monotonic relation between pollution and income when growth occurs via the factor used intensively in the dirty industry.

Alternatively, suppose growth occurs via accumulation of human capital. Then we have

$$\hat{z} = \varepsilon_{XL}\,\hat{L}\,,$$ (3.10)

where $\varepsilon_{XL} < 0$ is the elasticity of X output with respect to the endowment of human capital. Note that $\varepsilon_{XL} < 0$ follows from the Rybczinski theorem of international trade: human capital accumulation stimulates the clean industry Y, which draws resources out of the dirty industry X and lowers pollution. The effect of human capital accumulation on income is

$$\hat{I} = s_w\hat{L} + s_\tau\hat{z} = (s_w + s_\tau\,\varepsilon_{XL})\,\hat{L},$$ (3.11)

---

8. See chapter 2 for a discussion of this theorem. We can apply the Rybczinski theorem in this context because the emission intensity is being held fixed.

where $s_w > 0$ is the share of human capital in national income. Although the coefficient of $\hat{L}$ has both a positive and negative term, the increase in the supply of labor must raise national income, despite the drop in pollution. This follows from looking at the net production frontier. The increase in L shifts out the net frontier, and so, given prices and the fixed emission intensity, income must rise.

Consequently if we combine (3.10) and (3.11), we obtain

$$\hat{z} = \frac{\varepsilon_{XL}}{s_w + s_\tau \varepsilon_{XL}} \hat{L}. \tag{3.12}$$
$$(-)$$

Hence if growth occurs via accumulation of the factor used intensively in the clean industry, there is a *negative* monotonic relation between pollution and income.

A similar result can be obtained even with an endogenous policy response, provided that the income elasticity of marginal damage is not too high. To see this, start with the equilibrium condition for the determination of pollution. That is, equate (3.1) and (3.2) to obtain

$$G_z(p, K, L, z) = MD\left(p, \frac{G(p, k, L, z)}{\beta(p)}, z\right). \tag{3.13}$$

Then differentiating with respect to K and solving for the change in pollution leads to

$$\frac{dz}{dK} = \frac{G_{zk} - MD_R G_k / \beta(p)}{\Delta}, \tag{3.14}$$

where $\Delta = [MD_R G_z / \beta(p)] + MD_z - G_{zz} > 0$.

The first term in the numerator of (3.14) is necessarily positive and reflects the outward shift in pollution demand as the relative attractiveness of dirty good production rises. Recall that $G_z = \tau(p, K, L, z)$, and hence the first term is given by

$$G_{zk} = \frac{\partial \tau(p, K, L, z)}{\partial K} > 0. \tag{3.15}$$

This is the vertical shift in pollution demand created by a change in capital. From our analysis with exogenous policy in chapter 2, we know pollution demand shifts right (and hence upwards) with more capital.

The second term in the numerator of (3.14) represents the induced policy response. This captures the vertical shift in pollution supply when real income changes. The strength of the policy response depends on both the return to a marginal unit of capital (because this gauges how important a change in income more capital represents), and the income elasticity of marginal damage (because this gauges how preferences for pollution versus real consumption adjust at the margin). Using the definition of marginal damage and the properties of the GNP function, we can rewrite (3.14) to highlight these effects:

$$\frac{dz}{dK} = \frac{\tau\,[\varepsilon_{\tau,\,k} - \varepsilon_{MD,\,R}s_K]}{K\,\Delta}, \tag{3.16}$$

where $\varepsilon_{\tau,\,k} = KG_{zK}/\tau$ is the elasticity of the inverse pollution demand with respect to a change in K, $\varepsilon_{MD,\,R} = R \cdot MD_R/\tau$ is the elasticity of marginal damage with respect to real income, and $s_K = rK/I$ is the share of capital in national income.

The sign of (3.16) is in general ambiguous. But if the income elasticity of marginal damage is not too high, then the first term in (3.16) must dominate, and pollution rises with capital accumulation. That is, if an economy accumulates the factor used intensively in its polluting industry, pollution will rise unless the income elasticity of marginal damage is sufficiently strong.

As a special case of this, note that if the indirect utility function were linear in real income, then the elasticity of marginal damage with respect to income would be zero and pollution would necessarily rise with capital accumulation. In this case, pollution supply is unaffected by the change in real income and the result is entirely determined by the demand side. Because pollution demand always shifts upwards with the accumulation of factors used intensively in the dirty industry, pollution rises.

In contrast to the case of capital accumulation, consider the implications of an increase in the supply of human capital (effective labor) in the economy. Then the effect on pollution is given by

$$\frac{dz}{dL} = \frac{\tau\,[\varepsilon_{\tau,\,L} - \varepsilon_{MD,\,R}s_L]}{L\,\Delta}, \tag{3.17}$$

From our analysis with exogenous policy in chapter 2, we know pollution demand shifts left (and hence downwards) with more labor; consequently the first term in (3.17) is negative ($\varepsilon_{\tau,\,L} < 0$). Again the second term represents the effect of the induced policy response representing the positive vertical shift in pollution supply when real income changes. Note that regardless of the strength of the policy response, pollution falls with growth in the clean factor. This is simply because "clean factor" growth stimulates the clean industry at the expense of the dirty industry while raising income levels. Regardless of the policy response, pollution falls. Consequently, if the policy response is not too strong, then differences in the sources of growth at different stages of economic development can provide an explanation for the EKC.

The "sources of economic growth" explanation relies on three key assumptions. First, there is something we can truly identify as a dirty factor so that growth in it stimulates the dirty industry more than it stimulates the clean one. This, together with our model assumptions, ensures a strong composition effect arising from factor growth. Second, the policy response is not too strong. With a weak policy response, technique effects are muted and hence the strong composition effects in our model drive pollution levels. And finally, there is differential accumulation of the two factors over the development path: the factor used intensively in the dirty industry must be accumulated in the early stages of growth, but as the economy gets richer, it switches to accumulating the factor used intensively in the clean industry.

3.3 Income Effects

The most basic and perhaps compelling explanation for the EKC is that its shape reflects changes in the demand for environmental quality as income rises. If environmental quality is a normal good, pollution may at first rise with development but then fall when income levels continue to rise. This theory has been referred to frequently in the literature, although it is rarely spelled out in a full general equilibrium model. Lopez 1994 is one of the early papers to explicitly highlight the role of nonhomothetic preferences with respect to environmental quality in explaining the EKC.

To develop this theory we make three assumptions. First, we focus on neutral growth; that is, technical progress or factor accumulation that is not biased toward either the dirty or clean industry. This restriction neutralizes the sources-of-growth explanation discussed above and amounts to a restriction on the shifts in pollution demand. Second, for convenience, we assume all firms are at an interior solution for abatement purposes.[9] We discuss the importance of corner solutions

---

9. Alternatively we could adopt a specification where the first unit of abatement has an infinite marginal product so that abatement always occurs.

and the possibility of no-abatement equilibria in the next section. Finally, later in this section, we will adopt a specification for utility where the income elasticity of marginal damage is rising in income levels. With these additional restrictions, our pollution demand and supply model generates an income-driven EKC.

We start by considering the effects of neutral technical progress. That is, suppose that for given levels of primary factors (K, L) and emissions z, feasible outputs of both X and Y are shifted up by a factor λ when technology improves. This implies that the national income function can be written as $\lambda G(p, K, L, z)$.[10]

Our analysis will be carried out for a general technology, but it is instructive to consider the implications of neutral technical progress for our more specific technology. In this case, we have

$$
\begin{aligned}
x &= \lambda (1 - \theta) F (K_x, L_x), \\
y &= \lambda H (K_y, L_y), \\
z &= \varphi (\theta) F (K_x, L_x).
\end{aligned}
\tag{3.18}
$$

Although potential output of X increases by a factor λ, pollution emissions will not increase if the allocation of resources to abatement is not changed.

Two interpretations of the effect of technical change on emissions are possible. First, we can think of emissions as being generated by the dirty industry's use of primary factors, so neutral technological change has no effect on potential emissions. This is captured by the last equation in (3.18). Alternatively, we can think of emissions as being proportional to potential output, but emissions per unit output falling because of technical progress.[11] That is, the pollution equation in (3.18) is equivalent to

$$
z = \frac{\varphi (\theta)}{\lambda} \lambda F (K_x, L_x).
$$

Potential output is now λF, but emissions per unit of potential output have fallen to $\varphi (\theta)/\lambda$; and so emissions do not change unless θ changes.

---

10. By applying Hotelling's lemma it is easy to see that for given K, L, and Z, both outputs are scaled up by a factor λ. In the text, we have suppressed the price of y since it is the numeraire, but if we put it back in (with slight abuse of notation), we have $x = \lambda G_{p_x} (p_x, p_y, K, L, z)$ and $y = \lambda G_{p_y} (p_x, p_y, K, L, z)$.
11. Note that this requires neutral technical improvement in abatement *plus* a fall in the ratio of emissions to gross output.

Let us now determine the effect of neutral technical progress on the equilibrium level of pollution. The equilibrium condition for pollution is now:[12]

$$\lambda G_z\ (p,\ K,\ L,\ z) = MD\left(p,\ \frac{\lambda G\ (p,\ K,\ L,\ z)}{\beta\ (p)},\ z\right). \tag{3.19}$$

Differentiating with respect to the technology parameter λ and rearranging yields

$$\frac{dz}{d\lambda} = \frac{\tau\ (1 - \varepsilon_{MD,\ R}\ )}{\varDelta}, \tag{3.20}$$

where $\varDelta > 0$ and $\varepsilon_{MD,\ R}$ is the elasticity of marginal damage with respect to real income. Technological progress shifts both the pollution demand and supply curves. Demand shifts out because the marginal product of pollution rises. This is reflected in the first component of the term in parentheses in (3.20). Supply shifts inward because real income has grown. This captures the policy response to growth. The strength of this shift depends on the income elasticity of marginal damage.

Whether pollution rises or falls with increases in real income depends only on the relative strength of these effects, and from (3.20) we find that if the income elasticity of marginal damage is less than 1, then pollution rises with real income growth; if it is greater than 1, just the opposite occurs. The intuition for this is that neutral technical change shifts up the pollution demand curve in direct proportion to the increase in real income (at the initial pollution level). Whether or not pollution rises or falls depends on whether the willingness to pay for emission reduction rises more or less in proportion to the increase in real income; and this is determined by whether the income elasticity of marginal damage is greater than or less than 1. Notice that this result holds for our general technology embodied in $G\ (p,\ K,\ L,\ z)$ and does not rely on the separability or Cobb-Douglas assumptions of our more specific technology.

Let us now contrast technical progress with growth caused by neutral factor accumulation. That is, suppose that the endowments of capital and labor are both scaled up by a factor λ. In this case, the equilibrium condition for pollution is

---

12. Recall that we have normalized the population to $N = 1$.

$$G_z\,(p,\,\lambda K,\,\lambda L,\,z) = MD\,(p,\,\frac{G\,(p,\,\lambda K,\,\lambda L,\,z)}{\beta\,(p)},\,z). \qquad (3.21)$$

Differentiating with respect to λ yields

$$\frac{dz}{d\lambda} = \frac{\tau\,(s_r + s_w)}{\varDelta}\left[\frac{\tilde{s}_r}{\sigma_{ZK}} + \frac{\tilde{s}_w}{\sigma_{ZL}} - \varepsilon_{MD,\,R}\right], \qquad (3.22)$$

where $\tilde{s}_i \equiv s_i / s_r + s_w$ is the share of factor i in income accruing to primary factors (excluding emission payments), and $\sigma_{ij} \equiv G_i G_j / G G_{ij}$ is the Hicks-Allen elasticity of substitution between inputs i and j in generating aggregate national income.[13]

As in the case of neutral technical progress, both pollution demand and pollution supply shift when there is neutral factor accumulation. The increase in factor supply shifts out the demand for pollution because the marginal product of pollution rises. The supply curve shifts in because real income rises, and the strength of the shift depends on the income elasticity of marginal damage.

The key difference between neutral technical progress and factor accumulation is that the strength of the outward shift in pollution demand depends on the elasticity of substitution between primary factors and emissions in generating national income. Suppose that it is easy to substitute either input for emissions. Then the σ_{ij} are large, and referring to (3.22), this makes it more likely for pollution to fall as the supply of primary factors rises. On the other hand, if it is difficult to substitute primary factors for emissions, then the σ_{ij} are small, and pollution is more likely to rise with factor accumulation.

Lopez (1994) considers the special case where $\sigma_{ZK} = \sigma_{ZL} \equiv \sigma$.[14] In this case, (3.22) simplifies to

---

13. Note that these substitution elasticities reflect substitution possibilities for the economy as a whole—both within *and* across sectors—at a given relative goods price.

14. Lopez argues that this follows from the assumption that both sectors $i = x,\,y$ have constant returns technologies of the form $\varphi^i\,[\,f^i\,(K_i,\,L_i),\,z_i\,]$; that is, they are weakly separable with respect to emissions and other inputs. His claim is that with these assumptions on technology, one can write the national income function as $G\,[p,\,f\,(K,\,L),\,z]$. However, this would imply that the primary factor price ratio is independent of the level of emissions: $w/r = G_f f_L / G_f f_K = f_L / f_K$, which is independent of z. This does not hold even in the simple technology of chapter 2, where increases in the supply of pollution will stimulate X at the expense of Y and lower the w/r ratio. Stronger assumptions, such as identical factor intensities across sectors (or simply assuming a one-sector model) are required to obtain the result. See also Smulders, 2001.

$$\frac{dz}{d\lambda} = \frac{\tau \left(s_r + s_w \right)}{\varDelta} \left[\frac{1}{\sigma} - \varepsilon_{MD, R} \right].$$ (3.23)

If we also restrict ourselves to a model with only one good, then we can obtain a result similar to that for neutral technical progress. Suppose the economy produces only good X, and that X has the specific technology described in chapter 2. Then national income is

$$G \left(p, K, L, z \right) = p z^a F \left(K, L \right)^{1 - a},$$

and we have $\sigma_{ZK} = \sigma_{ZL} = 1$. In this case, factor accumulation will raise emissions if the income elasticity of marginal damage is less than 1, and lower emissions otherwise. To see why this holds, note that

$$G \left(p, \lambda K, \lambda L, z \right) = p z^a F \left(\lambda K, \lambda L \right)^{1 - a} = \lambda^{1 - a} p z^a F \left(K, L \right)^{1 - a}.$$

In this case, factor accumulation at rate λ is equivalent to neutral primary-factor-augmenting technical progress at rate $\lambda^{1 - a}$.[15]

Once we revert to our two-sector model, however, the aggregate elasticities of substitution in (3.22) depend on the differences in factor intensities across sectors. That is, the ability to substitute K and L for emissions in generating national income depends in part on the ability to substitute Y for X production, as well as the ability to substitute K and L for Z at the industry level. Hence even with our simple technologies, we have $\sigma_{ZK} \neq \sigma_{ZL}$ at the aggregate level, and the condition (3.22) applies.

The net effect of factor accumulation on pollution therefore depends on the interaction between the income elasticity of marginal damage and the elasticity of substitution between primary factors and emissions in generating aggregate income. As with neutral technical progress, a higher income elasticity of marginal damage makes it more likely that pollution will fall with growth; however, the critical value of the elasticity depends on substitution possibilities.

Let us now consider the implications of neutral growth for the EKC. Because the EKC has both an increasing and decreasing segment, it is

---

15. This is true if all firms are at an interior solution for abatement purposes, which is what we have assumed in this section. If firms are not abating, then neutral technical progress and factor accumulation have different effects, because $\sigma \neq 1$ once firms are at a corner solution. Factor accumulation raises the no-abatement level of emissions to $F \left(\lambda L, \lambda K \right)$. Neutral technical progress, however, leaves the no-abatement level of emissions unchanged at $F \left(K, L \right)$. If we take into account corner solutions, and compare factor accumulation at rate λ with neutral technical progress at rate $\lambda^{1 - a}$, the demand for pollu-

apparent that the pure income-driven explanation requires either a variable elasticity of marginal damage to generate the required shape, or factor accumulation combined with variable elasticities of substitution.

We focus on the role of a variable elasticity of marginal damage to suggest a possible explanation for the environmental Kuznets curve. If the income elasticity of marginal damage is increasing in income, then at low levels of income, pollution will rise with neutral growth because the policy response is weak. As income rises, the policy response becomes stronger, and if at some point the income elasticity of marginal damage is sufficiently high, pollution will start to fall as neutral growth continues.[16]

Notice that in this scenario, environmental quality is always a normal good, and so the income effect on the demand for environmental quality is always positive. What this theory requires is that the income effect become increasingly strong as growth proceeds.

A CARA Example

To illustrate the income-effect theory, consider the following example, which generates a closed form solution for an EKC. Suppose we adopt a standard constant absolute risk aversion sub-utility function for the consumption component of utility (v), so that indirect utility is given by

$$V(p, I, z) = c_1 - c_2 e^{-R/\delta} - \gamma z, \tag{3.24}$$

where $\delta > 0$ (and $R = I/\beta(p)$ is real income as usual), and where for simplicity we have assumed a constant marginal disutility of pollution.

Also for simplicity, let us assume a one-good model. By assuming the economy is specialized in producing the dirty good X, we eliminate any role for composition effects. This will clearly differentiate our results from those of the sources-of-growth explanation.

With these assumptions, national income is

$$I = p\lambda z^{\alpha} F(K, L)^{1-\alpha}, \tag{3.25}$$

---

tion (and the corresponding shifts in demand) in the two cases will coincide as long as $z \leq F(K, L)$.

16. If growth is driven by factor accumulation, this explanation requires that the aggregate substitution elasticities between emissions and primary factors do not change enough to offset the effects of the changes in the income elasticity.

where λ is a shift parameter.[17] Inverse pollution demand, which is just the value of the marginal product of emissions, is

$$\tau^D = a p \lambda z^{\alpha-1} F(K, L)^{1-\alpha} = \frac{a}{z} I. \tag{3.26}$$

Pollution demand is downward sloping and shifts out as income rises.

Pollution supply is just marginal damage, which we determine from the utility function:

$$\tau^s = MD = -\frac{V_z}{V_I} = \frac{\gamma \beta (p) \delta}{c_2} e^{R/\delta}. \tag{3.27}$$

Pollution supply is flat for any given real income R because we assumed constant marginal disutility of pollution in (3.24). But as z rises, I (and hence R) rises via (3.25), so pollution supply slopes up when plotted as a function of z. In addition, referring to (3.25) again, pollution supply shifts back as λ rises, because environmental quality is a normal good in this utility function.

If we equate pollution demand and supply, then (3.26) and (3.27) yield a simple reduced form relation between pollution and real income:

$$z = \frac{a c_2}{\gamma \delta} R e^{-R/\delta}. \tag{3.28}$$

That is, we have a simple closed form solution for the environmental Kuznets curve.

This curve is illustrated in figure 3.2. If we choose $\delta = 5,000$, this function can generate a curve that is much like that estimated by Grossman and Krueger (1993) for sulfur dioxide. The slope of the environmental Kuznets curve in (3.28) is

$$\frac{dz}{dR} = \frac{z(\delta - R)}{R\delta}. \tag{3.29}$$

For low income ($R < \delta$), the curve slopes upward; and for high income ($R > \delta$), it slopes down. It reaches a peak at $R = \delta$.

Note that because both the level and responsiveness of marginal damage will differ across pollutants, we should expect very different EKCs for different pollutants. If preferences have the form in (3.24),

---

17. Because we are assuming a one-good model with the elasticity of substitution between z and F equal to 1, and focusing on the case where active abatement occurs,

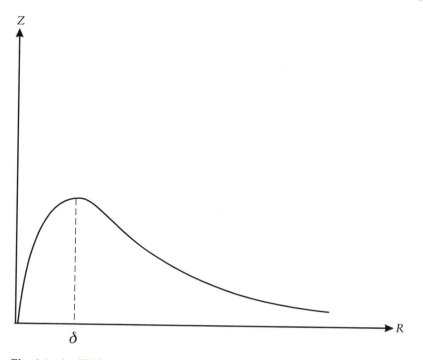

Fig. 3.2. An EKC Generated by Income Effects

we might expect δ to be low for very damaging pollutants, such as contaminated drinking water; but it might be high for carbon emissions because damage is uncertain and delayed.

To check that our results with this example are consistent with (3.20), note that for our utility function (3.24), the elasticity of marginal damage with respect to real income is

$$\varepsilon_{MD, R} = \frac{R}{\delta}.$$

That is, $\varepsilon_{MD, R} < 1$ for $R < \delta$, and $\varepsilon_{MD, R} > 1$ for $R > \delta$. Our result in (3.20) showed that pollution rose or fell with neutral technical progress depending on whether the income elasticity of marginal damage was greater than or less than one; and that is exactly what we have found here with our example.

---

we can interpret growth as being driven either by factor accumulation or by technical progress.

Income-Effects Theory: Discussion

Any theory of the EKC requires some force to eventually more than fully offset the scale effect of growth. In the "sources of growth" explanation, a very strong composition effect (created by clean factor growth) outweighed the scale effect. In the income-effect explanation, it is primarily a technique effect that does this. At low incomes, pollution initially rises with growth because increased consumption is valued highly relative to environmental quality. As income rises, the willingness to pay for environmental quality rises, and increasingly large sacrifices in consumption are made to provide greater environmental benefits. In models with only one good, the reduction in emissions driven by tighter policy is the only force that can eventually lower pollution as growth proceeds. In the more general two-good model presented earlier, the technique effect may be reinforced by a composition effect: tighter policy not only reduces emission intensities, but also encourages the private sector to shift production toward the clean good.

The extent to which composition effects contribute to the adjustment depends on consumer tastes if we are in an autarky setting (since they determine how relative prices will change with supplies) or on openness to trade in an open economy setting. While we have deferred our investigation of international trade until the next chapter, it should be apparent that there is scope for a larger composition effect in a trading world. This is because a tightening of policy in one country encourages dirty good production to relocate to other countries. Because we have a small open economy model, this mechanism is always implicit when we discuss the effects of growth in our two-good model.

3.4 Threshold Effects

Several papers explain the environmental Kuznets curve by using a model with threshold effects in either abatement or environmental policy. Threshold effects can arise in either the political process as in Jones and Manuelli 1995, or in terms of abatement activity as in John and Pecchenino 1994 and Stokey 1998. In general, threshold effects lead to a very different relationship between income and pollution during early stages of development than in later stages. In the early stage, pollution may be unregulated entirely, or regulation may have little impact on the profitability of abatement. Consequently, pollution rises with output in the early stages of development. When income is sufficiently high, however, abatement activity begins, and pollution may fall with further increases in income. After the threshold has been breached, these models still require assumptions on tastes or technologies to ensure that pollution declines once regulation or abatement begins in earnest.

We will illustrate how threshold effects can generate an environmental Kuznets curve with two different models. The first, the *abatement threshold model*, is based on Stokey 1998 and relies on threshold effects in the abatement process. The second, the *policy threshold model*, relies on a threshold effect in the policy process.

The Abatement Threshold Model

Recall from figure 2.2 that in our model, firms will not find it cost effective to abate if the pollution tax is below a critical level. Consequently, our model predicts no abatement when the pollution tax is sufficiently low because firms are at a corner solution in their choice of production techniques. Moreover, we have also seen that the pollution tax is increasing in income. Consequently, the no-abatement solution occurs only at low levels of income. As income rises, the pollution tax rises, leading to a flatter isocost line in figure 2.2, and at some point (point A in the figure) firms begin to abate. At this point, the analysis of the previous section becomes relevant. If the income elasticity of marginal damage is greater than 1, then pollution falls as growth continues.

To illustrate this more clearly, we will again suppose that the country produces only good X, so that income is

$$I = pz^\alpha F(K, L)^{1-\alpha}. \tag{3.30}$$

for $z \leq F(K, L)$. In addition, we will focus on growth driven by factor accumulation, so that the level of pollution rises with growth in the absence of abatement. And finally, we adopt the commonly used constant relative risk aversion utility function:[18]

$$V(p, I, z) = \frac{[I/\beta(p)]^{1-\eta}}{1-\eta} - h(z) \text{ with } \eta \neq 1. \tag{3.31}$$

With this utility function, the income elasticity of marginal damage is constant and equal to η. Given our earlier results, we can then conclude

18. See for example Stokey 1998 and Copeland and Taylor 1994. Copeland and Taylor use the limiting case where $\eta = 1$.

that when firms are abating, pollution rises with growth if $\eta < 1$, and pollution falls with growth if $\eta > 1$. If we take the limit as η approaches 1—which represents log utility—then the income elasticity of marginal damage is 1 and pollution is entirely unaffected by growth. Scale effects perfectly offset technique effects.

If we solve for the reduced form relation between income and pollution as in the previous example (that is, assuming for simplicity that only X is produced and that $h(z) = \gamma z$), then we obtain

$$z = \frac{\alpha}{\gamma} R^{1-\eta} . \tag{3.32}$$

We have plotted three examples of this relation in figure 3.3. With this utility function, pollution is either flat or else monotonically increasing or decreasing in income. With neutral growth and an interior solution to the firm's abatement problem, there is no environmental Kuznets curve with this utility function. By adopting this specification, we ensure that income effects alone cannot generate an EKC. And hence threshold effects must be responsible for any EKC found.

To derive the EKC we start by determining the region where no abatement occurs. By differentiating (3.30), we obtain the pollution demand curve in the region where abatement does occur:

$$\tau = G_z = \alpha p \left(\frac{F(K, L)}{z} \right)^{1-\alpha} . \tag{3.33}$$

This slopes down as usual (z rises as τ falls), but (3.33) is valid only for $z \leq F$, since emissions cannot exceed potential output. At $\tau = \alpha p$, we have $z = F$, and further reductions in τ do not lead to further increases in emissions. Conversely, for $\tau < \alpha p$, small *increases* in the pollution tax do not lead to reductions in emissions. That is, as we saw in (2.15), firms will not abate if

$$\tau < \tau^* \equiv \alpha p. \tag{3.34}$$

In this region, we have $z = F$, and so the pollution demand curve is vertical for $\tau < \tau^*$.

With our CRRA utility function, pollution supply is given by

$$\tau^s = -\frac{V_z}{V_I} = \gamma \beta (p)^{1-\eta} I^\eta.$$

If income is sufficiently low, the pollution supply curve intersects the pollution demand curve in its vertical region. This occurs if

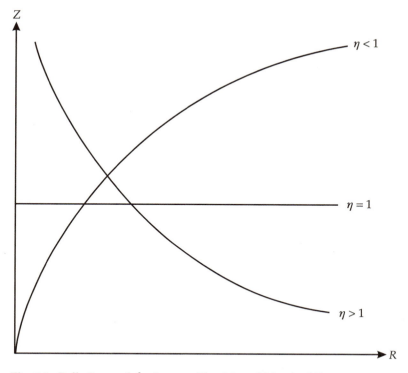

Fig. 3.3. Pollution and the Income Elasticity of Marginal Damage

$$I < I^T \equiv \left[\frac{\alpha p}{\gamma \beta \, (p)^{1-\eta}} \right]^{1/\eta} , \tag{3.35}$$

in which case there is no abatement. Pollution is equal to output and therefore proportional to both nominal and real income:

$$z = F \, (K, L) = \frac{I}{p} = \frac{\beta \, (p)}{p} R.$$

In this region, increases in income raise the demand for environmental quality, but the willingness to pay for pollution reduction (marginal damage) is less than the marginal abatement cost. Consequently, an increase in income does not lead to a technique effect to offset the scale effect of growth.

However, once potential output is sufficiently high, the threshold is breached and pollution is determined by the usual interior solution. We saw in the last section that pollution in that case is given by (3.32). Consequently, we have

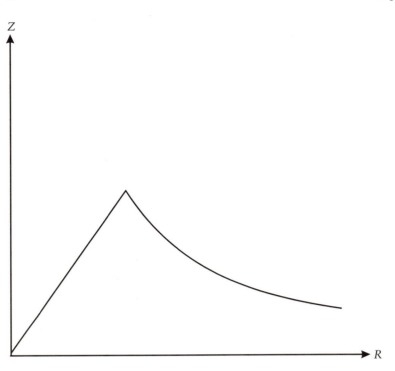

Fig. 3.4. The Abatement Threshold Model

$$
z = \begin{cases} \dfrac{\beta\,(p)}{p}\,R & \text{if } pF\,(K,\,L) < I^{T} \\[2ex] \dfrac{\alpha}{\gamma}\,R^{1-\eta} & \text{if } pF\,(K,\,L) \geq I^{T} \end{cases}.
$$

This is graphed in figure 3.4 for the case where $\eta > 1$. Pollution rises to a peak, which occurs at the threshold income I^{T}. Beyond that point, pollution falls if the income elasticity of marginal damage is sufficiently high, which requires $\eta > 1$.

This example illustrates that threshold effects alone are not sufficient to explain the EKC phenomena. Even after the threshold is crossed and abatement occurs, pollution will still rise if $\eta < 1$. It would remain constant if $\eta = 1$. We need, as in Stokey 1998, the assumption of a quickly declining marginal utility of real income.

It should be clear that the EKC explanations based on threshold and income effects bear a close family resemblance. Both rely on a strong policy response to income gains as development proceeds, but they differ in their explanations for the rising segment. The threshold-effect theory predicts a period of long inactivity in private sector responses to ever tightening pollution policy; the income-effect theory predicts that the abatement intensity rises continuously as policy tightens.

We have illustrated the abatement threshold model for the case where the economy produces only one good. Once we consider a model with more than one good, the abatement threshold effect is less compelling as an explanation for the EKC. To see why, consider our standard two-good model, and suppose that in the absence of any pollution regulation, the economy is diversified in production. Suppose also that income is low, so that (3.35) holds. There is no abatement, and so the economy will produce somewhere along the potential production frontier.

Let us now consider the pollution demand curve. Starting at the point where $\tau = 0$, a small increase in the pollution tax will not lead to any abatement because the economy is below the abatement threshold. However, the pollution tax will nevertheless act as a tax on the output of the dirty good, and production will move away from X toward Y along the potential production frontier. As X production falls in response to the increased pollution tax, the demand for pollution falls. Consequently, when the economy has more than one good (and emission intensities differ across goods), the pollution demand curve slopes down even when there is no abatement. As we discussed in chapter 2, the pollution demand curve will in general slope down for two reasons: a technique effect and a composition effect. Higher pollution taxes can reduce pollution either by reducing emission intensities or by shifting the composition of output toward the cleaner good. When the economy is below the abatement threshold, the technique effect is absent; but with multiple goods, the composition effect is still operative.

Since the pollution demand curve slopes down in the two-good model, the effect of growth on pollution when the economy is below the abatement threshold will depend on the relative magnitudes of the shifts in pollution demand and supply, as it did in the income-effects model of the previous section. This further underscores the strong linkage between explanations of the EKC based on threshold effects and those based on income effects.[19]

---

19. The abatement threshold effect still has a role to play in a multigood model, as it leads to a kink in the pollution demand curve—once the abatement threshold is

The Policy Threshold Model

Although the abatement threshold model discussed above generates a threshold effect in pollution abatement, governments are still able to influence the level of pollution by using policy to affect the composition of economic activity, even when income is very low. An alternative possibility is that there is a threshold effect in policy activity itself. That is, when either income is low or environmental problems are not too serious, governments may not find it worthwhile to set up any regulatory apparatus at all. This can generate a simple explanation for the EKC that applies equally well to models with one or many goods.

We can capture the idea of a policy threshold effect quite simply by assuming a fixed cost of regulating. We adopt the same basic simplifying assumptions as above—we assume that utility is given by (3.31), and that the economy produces only good X. (We will discuss the implications of more than one good at the end of the section.)

The simplest way to introduce a fixed regulatory cost in our general equilibrium framework is to assume that regulatory services require a fixed amount of primary inputs $(\bar{K}, \bar{L})$. This diversion of resources away from production reduces the potential output that can created by the private sector in the regulatory regime to

$$F^R \equiv F(K - \bar{K}, L - \bar{L}).$$

Consequently, the cost to the economy of setting up a regulatory regime can be measured by the drop in potential output $\bar{F}$, which is determined by

$$\bar{F} \equiv F(K, L) - F(K - \bar{K}, L - \bar{L}).$$

Finally, to simplify notation, we choose units of X so that $\beta(p) = 1$. Because the economy produces only good X, this means that real income is simply

$$R = x.$$

The government has two choices—it can either incur a fixed cost and regulate pollution, or it can not regulate at all and allow pollution to

---

breached, the economy can reduce pollution via both technique and composition effects. That is, the elasticity of substitution between emissions and primary factors will change at this point, and this may potentially have some implications for the shape of the EKC. However, we leave the analysis of the implications of the abatement threshold effect in a multiple-good model for future researchers to consider.

be fully demand determined. The government chooses the option that leads to the highest utility for the representative consumer. To solve the government's problem, we therefore need to find the utility under each of the two options.

First consider the regulatory option. Once the regulatory system is set up, the government chooses pollution in the usual way by setting the demand for pollution equal to marginal damage:

$$G_z(p, K, L, z) = MD(p, R, z).$$

This can be solved for pollution z^R, and output x^R, and therefore yields a utility level in the regulatory regime of V^R. Referring to (3.32), pollution is

$$z^R = \frac{\alpha}{\gamma} R^{1-\eta}. \tag{3.36}$$

If we substitute (3.36) into (3.31), we can write utility as

$$V^R = \left[\frac{1}{1-\eta} - \alpha \right] R^{1-\eta}. \tag{3.37}$$

That is, we can write utility simply in terms of real income R.

Suppose that $\eta > 1$. As we saw above, this assumption is needed for pollution to fall after the threshold is breached. Then it is instructive to write (3.37) as

$$V^R = -\frac{1 + \alpha(\eta - 1)}{(\eta - 1) R^{\eta - 1}}.$$

As one would expect, utility is increasing in real income. Note that because utility is a negative number here, utility rises as V decreases in absolute value. As R approaches infinity, utility monotonically increases toward zero.

Finally, we need to determine real income in terms of primitives. Real income is determined by

$$R = z^\alpha (F^R)^{1-\alpha}.$$

And using (3.36), this becomes

$$R = [(\alpha/\gamma)^\alpha (F^R)^{1-\alpha}]^{1/[1 + (\eta - 1)\alpha]}.$$

Real income is determined by potential output and by the fixed regulatory cost. It is straightforward to show that $dR/dF > 0$; that is, real income increases as potential output F rises.[20] This implies that utility is monotonically increasing in F, as we have illustrated in figure 3.5.

Next consider the government's other option. It can choose not to regulate. In this case, there is no abatement, and so real income is just equal to potential output ($R = F$) and pollution is directly proportional to output ($z = F$). Consequently, using (3.31), utility in the no-regulation option (V^N) is

$$V^N (p, I, z) = - \left[\frac{1}{(\eta - 1) F^{\eta - 1}} + \gamma F \right].$$

We have plotted V^N in figure 3.5. Notice that as F rises, V^N first rises and then falls. In the limit, as F gets large, V^N approaches $-\infty$.

The government chooses the option that yields highest utility. As long as the fixed cost $\bar{F}$ is sufficiently high, we initially have $V^N > V^R$. But at some point, as potential output increases, V^R rises above V^N. At this point, it is cost effective to set up an environmental regulatory apparatus. We denote the threshold level of F by F^T. For $F < F^T$, there is no regulation and pollution is proportional to output. Once the threshold is reached, regulations are introduced and pollution is given by (3.36). Pollution falls as income rises under our assumption that $\eta > 1$.

The reduced form relation between real income (net of fixed regulatory costs) and pollution implied by this model is

$$z = \begin{cases} R & \text{if } F(K, L) < F^T \\ \dfrac{\alpha}{\gamma} R^{1-\eta} & \text{if } F(K, L) \geq F^T. \end{cases}$$

We have plotted this in figure 3.6. This yields a Kuznets-like relationship between income and pollution, although it differs somewhat from the previous model. Pollution first rises monotonically with real income. When the threshold is reached, environmental regulations are introduced and pollution drops discretely. In addition, real income drops discretely because firms devote resources to abatement, moving net output below potential output. This model has an overshooting feature. Both income and pollution rise to a peak, and then once the country decides to confront its environmental problems, both drop. Eventually as F continues to expand, real income surpasses its former peak, but pollution continues to fall.

---

20. Real income also increases in F if $\eta < 1$.

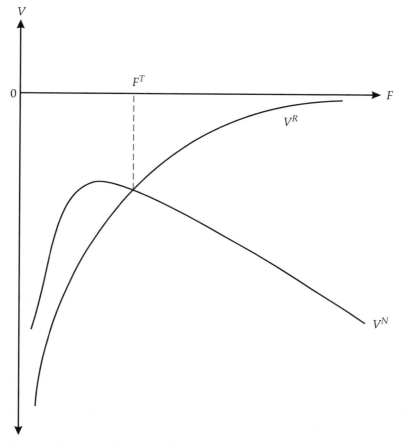

Fig. 3.5. Deriving the Policy Threshold

As was the case with the abatement threshold model, a threshold alone is not enough to generate an environmental Kuznets curve in the policy threshold model. If the income elasticity of marginal damage is less than or equal to 1, pollution will continue to rise even after the threshold is surpassed. Threshold theories rely on a strong policy response to further increases in income in order to generate a continuing decline in pollution after the threshold is breached.

In comparing the two threshold theories, both predict an initial period of no abatement, followed by an introduction of abatement and declining pollution. The policy threshold model, however, differs in that it predicts no policy at all until income is sufficiently high. Policy is always present in the other model. Consequently, the policy thresh-

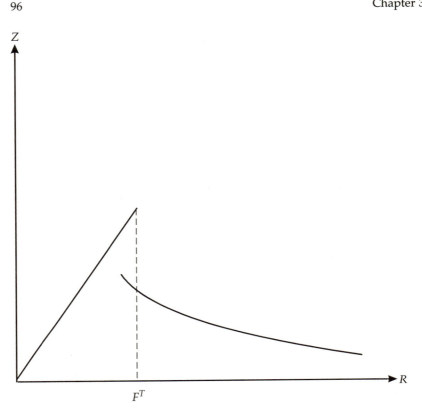

Fig. 3.6. The Policy Threshold Model

old model predicts a discrete drop in pollution once the threshold is breached, while the abatement threshold model predicts a smoother transition.

The other major difference between the two models is that the policy threshold model generalizes straightforwardly to the case of multiple goods, while the abatement threshold model does not. In the policy threshold model, the fixed cost of pollution regulation precludes any pollution policy at low levels of income. Consequently, even when there are multiple goods, income growth generates neither technique nor policy-induced composition effects to offset the scale effects of growth until the threshold is reached. In contrast, when there are multiple goods in the abatement threshold model, income-induced increases in pollution taxes induce composition effects that work against the scale effects of growth.

3.5 Increasing Returns to Abatement

The last explanation we investigate is based on increasing returns to scale. Andreoni and Levinson (2001) argue that increasing returns in the abatement technology could be responsible for the shape of the EKC found in some of the empirical literature. The argument is simply that in larger and richer economies, the optimal scale of operation is larger and this higher scale creates efficiencies in abatement. These efficiencies then make abatement more profitable even if pollution policy is stagnant and unchanging.

Andreoni and Levinson develop this explanation within a one-good, endowment model with a central planner. In that context it is not made explicit whether the scale economies in abatement apply at the firm level or at an industry-wide basis. We show how one can model increasing returns in the abatement technology in a simple way in a competitive market economy. To do so, we adopt a formulation with industry-wide external economies of scale in abatement. This captures the flavor of their analysis while simultaneously generalizing it to a competitive market economy.

To proceed, we adapt our model from chapter 2. We amend our pollution demand and supply analysis in three ways. First, we need to be more explicit about the abatement technology, rather than keeping it in the background as we have done thus far. We do so to reformulate the abatement technology to incorporate increasing returns. Second, we fix the pollution tax to distinguish this explanation from the income-effect explanation. This restriction ensures the pollution tax remains constant in the face of real income growth. In addition, to remove threshold-effect explanations, we set the pollution tax high enough so that abatement is always optimal. Finally, to distinguish this explanation from the sources-of-growth explanation, we assume exogenous growth in our economy's potential output F, and let our economy specialize in the dirty good. These assumptions rule out any role for composition effects.

With these restrictions in hand, we now reconsider abatement. Recall from (2.6) that if no abatement occurs, each unit of output generates one unit of pollution. That is, with no abatement, F units of pollution are generated. If the firm abates, then it allocates a fraction θ of its inputs to abatement activity. As we discussed previously, we can equivalently think of the firm as producing F units of gross output and allocating θF of these units to abatement. Let $x^A = \theta F$ denote the amount of (potential) gross output redirected to abatement. Actual pollution emitted can therefore be written as

$$z = F - a\,(F,\,x^A),\tag{3.38}$$

where a defines the abatement function. That is, we define abatement to be the amount by which pollution is reduced from its potential. In our model, the abatement function is

$$a\,(F,\,x^A) = F\,[1 - (1 - \theta)^{1/a}] = F\,[1 - (x^A\,/\,F)^{1/a}].\tag{3.39}$$

To confirm this, apply (3.38) to the above and obtain

$$z = (1 - \theta)^{1/a}\,F\tag{3.40}$$

which is the pollution function we specified in (2.7) and (2.11).

Notice that our abatement technology has constant returns to scale. If we scale up F and x^A by a factor $\lambda > 0$, then using (3.39), we have

$$a\,(\lambda F,\,\lambda x^A) = \lambda a\,(F,\,x^A).$$

We now want to modify the abatement technology to allow for the possibility of increasing returns to scale. A simple way to do this, while at the same time maintaining the assumption of competitive markets, is to model the increasing returns as an external economy of scale. That is, for a given level of aggregate abatement activity, each individual firm perceives constant returns to scale, but as the aggregate scale of abatement rises, each individual firm's abatement productivity increases.[21]

This type of assumption is widely used in the literature on agglomeration.[22] A variety of factors can lead to productivity increasing with industry size. For example, if there are knowledge spillovers across firms, then individual firms have a larger knowledge pool to draw upon as the industry expands and so they will be more productive. In addition, a larger industry can allow a larger set of specialized interme-

---

21. This is a standard method of modeling increasing returns in the international trade literature (see Markusen and Melvin 1981; Ethier 1982; and Helpman and Krugman 1985).

22. Markusen (1989) shows how to give the external economy model more explicit microfoundations using a monopolistic competition market structure for abatement. In applying his model to our context, we could suppose that abatement activities are produced by specialized firms, and that abatement costs fall as firms have access to a wider variety of specialized abatement services. If each individual firm producing specialized abatement services faces a fixed cost, then a larger market will be able support a wider

diate suppliers of components and technology to emerge. We have not explicitly modeled the role of intermediate suppliers here, but one can show that the reduced form of such a model behaves very much like a model with external economies of scale.[23]

Overall, the assumption of external economies of scale captures the idea that productivity improves with the scale of the industry, but because individual firms perceive constant returns, we can maintain our assumption of a competitive market structure.

We have to distinguish between an individual firm i's abatement and aggregate abatement. Suppose then that an individual firm's abatement A_i is given by

$$A_i = A^\delta a (F_i, x_i^A), \tag{3.41}$$

where A denotes aggregate abatement in the economy, the function a has constant returns to scale, and $0 < \delta < 1$. We will use the same function a as before, as given in (3.39). Because a has constant returns, we can rewrite (3.41) as

$$A_i = A^\delta a (1, \theta) F_i, \tag{3.42}$$

where we have not used a subscript for θ because in equilibrium all firms choose the same θ (recall they all face the same prices). Summing both sides of (3.42) over all firms i and rearranging yields aggregate industry abatement:

$$A = [a (1, \theta) F]^{1/(1-\delta)}, \tag{3.43}$$

where F is industry output.

Notice that in the aggregate we have increasing returns to scale in abatement. If we scale up industry-wide abatement activity by a factor $\lambda > 1$, we obtain

$$A (\lambda F, \lambda x^A) = \lambda^{1/(1-\delta)} A (F, x^A), \tag{3.44}$$

which indicates increasing returns because $0 < \delta < 1$. Also note that if $\delta = 0$, we revert back to our standard constant returns model.

With the abatement technology specified, we now consider the equilibrium level of pollution. The profit maximization problem for a typical firm is

---

variety of specialized abatement services. Markusen shows that such a model behaves in a way that is very similar to a model with external economies of scale.
23. See Markusen's (1989) model of intermediate suppliers and compare it with the external economies model of Markusen and Melvin (1981).

$\pi_i = p(1 - \theta) F_i - wL_i - rK_i - \tau(F_i - A_i).$

Using (3.39) and (3.41), we have

$\pi_i = p(1 - \theta) F_i - wL_i - rK_i - \tau F_i (1 - A^\delta [1 - (1 - \theta)^{1/\alpha}]).$

We assume there are many firms so they treat aggregate abatement as given when they maximize profits. The first-order condition for the choice of θ is

$$pF_i = \frac{\tau A^\delta}{\alpha} (1 - \theta)^{(1 - \alpha)/\alpha} F_i.$$

The marginal cost to the firm of increasing the fraction of resources allocated to abatement (θ) is pF_i. The marginal benefit is the pollution tax savings as more pollution is abated. This is the term on the right-hand side. Notice that for $\delta > 0$, the marginal benefit of shifting resources to abatement is increasing in industry-wide abatement, A. This is the increasing returns effect. With a larger industry, the abatement technology is more productive, so the marginal benefit of putting resources into abatement is higher.

While we have adopted a profit maximization approach here rather than the cost minimization detailed in chapter 2, the formulations are identical. For example, using (3.45) and (3.40), we find emissions per unit of net output given by

$$e = \frac{z}{x} = (\alpha p/\tau) A^{-\delta}, \qquad (3.46)$$

which the reader should compare to (2.14). Therefore, emissions per unit output depend on the pollution tax and goods price, but also on aggregate abatement. Since $\delta > 0$, it should be clear that even with a fixed tax and given price, emissions per unit of output can fall with aggregate abatement. This is, of course, how this explanation will generate a technique effect in the face of static pollution policy.

To solve for the equilibrium level of abatement, we can rearrange (3.45) to obtain one relationship between θ and A:

$$A = \left(\frac{\alpha p/\tau}{(1 - \theta)^{(1 - \alpha)/\alpha}} \right)^{1/\delta} \qquad (3.47)$$

This is plotted in figure 3.7, where we have called it the *optimality condition*. This condition gives the firm's optimal level of abatement inten-

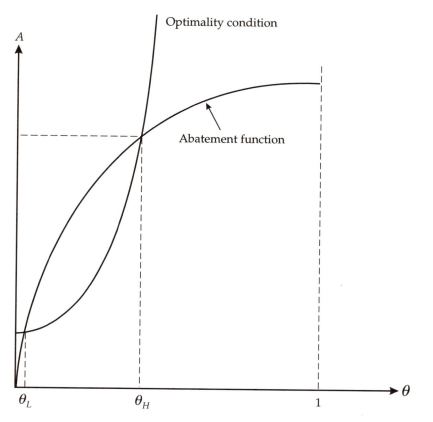

Fig. 3.7. Abatement with Increasing Returns to Scale

sity, θ, for every given level of industry-wide abatement, A. Notice that θ is increasing in A.

As aggregate abatement rises, firms allocate a higher fraction of their resources to abatement because abatement is more productive. For future purposes we should also note that points above this curve would represent unexploited opportunities to abate (since A is higher than that specified in (3.47)).

Another relation between A and θ is given by the abatement technology. Use (3.43) and (3.39) to obtain

$$A = [F(1 - (1 - \theta)^{1/\alpha})]^{1/(1-\delta)}. \tag{3.48}$$

This has also been plotted in figure 3.7 (where it is labeled *abatement function*).

We restrict ourselves to situations where the pollution tax is sufficiently high to encourage some abatement. Notice the curves in figure
3.7 intersect twice: at θ_L and at θ_H. As is often the case in models with
increasing returns to scale, there are multiple equilibria. However, the
equilibrium at $\theta = \theta_L$ is unstable with respect to small perturbations of
abatement by firms.

To see this, suppose we start at $\theta = \theta_L$. Note that aggregate abatement
is always given by the technologically imposed abatement function,
but deviations of firm behavior from profit maximization can move us
off the optimality condition. With this in mind, suppose some firm
abates a little more. Then from the abatement function, A rises. But we
are now above the optimality condition, and hence given the higher
A, abatement is more productive, so all other firms will want to abate
more as well. Consequently, small deviations from $\theta = \theta_L$ will move
us away from this low abatement equilibrium. In addition, this same
adjustment process ensures that in the neighborhood of $\theta = \theta_H$ small
deviations in abatement are self-correcting.

We can now consider the impact of growth on pollution. We want
to demonstrate how increasing returns can generate an environmental
Kuznets curve in a way that is distinct from the mechanism in the previous three explanations we discussed. To do so, as noted above, we
assume that there is a fixed pollution tax that does not vary with
growth. In our previous three explanations, it would be impossible for
neutral growth to reduce pollution with a fixed pollution tax.

Start at the equilibrium in figure 3.7 denoted by $\theta = \theta_H$. Consider an
increase in the scale of both factor endowments; this raises F. Then
from (3.48) it is easy to ascertain that the abatement function shifts upwards. Using figure 3.7, we can conclude that both aggregate abatement, A, and θ rise. The optimality condition is independent of F and
hence is unchanged. For a given pollution tax, firms increase the fraction of resources they allocate to abatement because abatement becomes more productive as the size of the economy expands. To find
the effect on pollution, note that pollution is

$$z = [1 - A^\delta (1 - (1 - \theta)^{1/\alpha})] F. \tag{3.49}$$

where the bracketed term is emissions per unit of (gross) output. When
F rises and we hold the emission intensity fixed, pollution rises. This
is the scale effect. Since we have specialized to a one-good model, there
is no composition effect. But from our analysis above, we know that
aggregate abatement rises, as does firm-specific abatement. Conse-

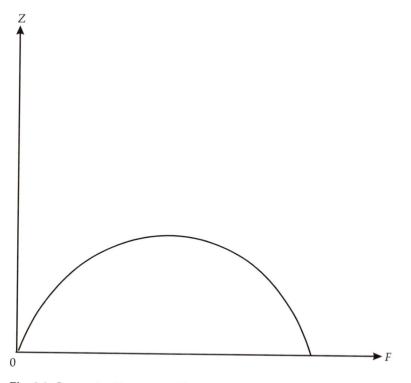

Fig. 3.8. Increasing Returns to Abatement and the EKC

quently, emissions per unit output (in either gross or net terms) fall. That is, the scale effect of growth creates its own technique effect. This tends to reduce pollution.

The interaction between the scale and technique effects yields an environmental Kuznets curve as illustrated in figure 3.8. To confirm the shape of the curve, refer to (3.49). Notice that when F is zero, pollution is zero. So pollution is low when the economy is small. From figure 3.7 we know that for small F, A is initially low because the economy is small, and so pollution is positive. However as F rises, A rises without bound, and so at some point pollution falls to zero. Hence increasing returns alone can generate an environmental Kuznets curve.

As in all theories of the EKC, the model needs some force to offset the increase in pollution driven by the scale effect of growth. In the increasing returns model, the increase in scale creates its own technique effect as a larger market leads to increased productivity in abatement.

3.6 Conclusion

We began this chapter by noting that even within our very simple two-good model, there is in general no consistent relationship between per capita income and pollution. The equilibrium level of pollution is set by the interaction of both pollution demand and pollution supply, and without further restrictions the equilibrium level of income and pollution are unlikely to trace out an EKC. Therefore, to derive an EKC, we need to impose further restrictions on our demand-and-supply system. To illustrate this, we developed the four major explanations of the EKC by adding to or restricting our basic model. Each of these explanations gives center stage to either scale, technique, or composition effects; and each imposes different restrictions on either pollution demand or pollution supply to do so.

In the income-effects and threshold theories, we imposed restrictions on the growth process to eliminate composition effects and then adopted a utility function ensuring that the marginal value of consumption, relative to environmental quality, falls with income. This explanation works by restricting the possible shifts in pollution demand, and then ensuring pollution supply shifts are sufficiently strong. As a consequence, this theory predicts rising pollution taxes and abatement levels as society places greater and greater value on a clean environment. And it associates the declining portion of the EKC with a strong policy response to income growth.

But two other theories generate an EKC while assuming no policy response at all. Neither the "sources of growth" explanation nor the increasing returns explanation requires a policy change to generate an EKC. In both of these cases, the results follow from assumptions we made on how pollution demand responds to growth, because the fixed pollution tax eliminates movement in the pollution supply curve.

The sources-of-growth explanation exploits the strong composition effects affecting pollution demand when factor accumulation takes different forms. Combining these composition effects with an assumption on the sequencing of dirty versus clean factor growth yields the result.

In the increasing returns theory, composition effects play no role and pollution demand shifts only with the scale of output. The scale effect is eventually more than offset by a technique effect, which is itself driven by the increase in scale. The fall in emission intensity is not due to policy changes (since we held the pollution tax fixed), but rather is driven by the increase in abatement productivity arising from the increased scale of abatement activity. In both the increasing returns and the sources-of-growth explanations, the finding of the EKC is consistent with no change in policy as growth proceeds.

The chapter contains several lessons relevant to the trade and environment debate. The first is simply that empirical evidence of an EKC is not necessarily an indication of a strong policy response to income gains. Unless we can rule out the increasing returns or sources-of-growth explanation, policy responses are not necessary for the EKC. And therefore evidence of an EKC is not evidence for policy response. In addition, an active and responsive pollution policy is not sufficient to ensure pollution falls, since both the threshold and income-effect theories rely on a strong policy response. As we demonstrated, unless the income elasticity of marginal damage is sufficiently large, policy tightens with economic growth but pollution still rises.

The EKC literature has, however, been very useful in highlighting the role of income effects in influencing environmental quality. As we will see in the following chapters, income effects—and in particular, the strength of the income elasticity of marginal damage—will play a pivotal role in our analysis of the effects of trade on the environment.

A second lesson is that while income is surely an important determinant of pollution policy, it is not the only determinant of pollution levels. Per capita income plays an important role because it determines policy, which in turn determines the techniques of production. However, the effects of per capita income must be considered in tandem with the determinants of composition and scale of the economy, such as relative factor abundance and production capacity. By focusing exclusively on the role of income in determining pollution, this literature has neglected these other potentially important factors.

A final lesson concerns future research efforts in this area. The original Grossman and Krueger discovery of the EKC was made possible by their inspired choice of a reduced form methodology linking pollution to income levels. Given the difficulties in obtaining good cross-country data, the number of pollutants involved, and the overall purpose of their research—this empirical strategy was brilliant. It created a large literature examining data and questions that were previously left unexplored.

But if we are to ask more detailed questions of the pollution data, we will need different methods. And if we are to base policy recommendations on empirical work we will need to unpackage the Grossman and Krueger finding to identify the causal forces at work. The finding of the EKC is a perfect example of measurement far ahead of theory. The theoretical explanations that have been offered are ex post rationalizations for an empirical result. There has so far been little attempt to use theory to guide the empirical work, nor to use evidence to distinguish between the different theories.

In contrast, the model of chapter 2 steps back from the EKC mindset to develop a theory determining the equilibrium level of pollution as a function of a relatively few factors. This chapter has shown that in order to move from this theory to the EKC explanations, we need to impose severe restrictions on both pollution supply and demand. This begs an important question: why should empirical research in this area continue to estimate such highly restricted models?

In chapter 7 we present an alternative method by estimating a reduced form of the model in chapter 2. Our purpose is to estimate international trade's environmental effects, but this necessitates some control for other possible determinants and a consideration of economic growth. The methods we employ in chapter 7 will not always be useful or available, as they do require much more information. Hence in some situations the EKC methodology may retain its usefulness. But clearly diminishing returns has set in with a vengeance.

4

Trade Liberalization and Environmental Quality

Very few issues in recent years have been as hotly debated as the environmental consequences of trade liberalization. Environmentalists point to examples such as the Maquiladora zone in Mexico, where trade with the United States led to a heavy concentration of industry that contributed to a deterioration in local environmental quality. Trade has also been implicated in unsustainable harvest rates in tropical rainforests (because of trade in timber), threats to species such as elephants (because of trade in ivory), worsening air quality in parts of China (due to export-led growth), as well as numerous other environmental problems.

In contrast, free trade advocates point to examples of improvements in air and water quality over the last three decades in Japan, the United States, and Europe, and argue that the increases in income generated by trade have helped these countries afford the regulatory costs needed to obtain better environmental quality. In addition, they argue that environmental problems are best dealt with by using good environmental policy, and that restrictions on trade are an inefficient and unreliable way to protect the environment.

In this chapter, we begin our analysis by asking what are the effects of trade liberalization on environmental quality in a small open economy. We study both positive and normative issues—we examine both how trade liberalization affects the level of pollution in a country, as well as how it affects the welfare of a representative consumer.[1] We

---

1. The welfare effects of trade liberalization in the presence of pollution have been one of the major themes of the literature on trade and the environment, and our normative results in this chapter reflect a synthesis of earlier work. Early work on the welfare effects of trade liberalization under various assumptions about the policy regime include Baumol 1971; Pethig 1976; Siebert 1977; Asako 1979; Anderson 1992; Copeland 1994; and

also consider how the effects of trade liberalization may vary if the government is politically motivated. Throughout this chapter, we treat world prices and the trade pattern as exogenous: the country either exports or imports the dirty good, and we treat this as given. The next two chapters focus on multicountry models where the pattern of trade is endogenous and affected by a country's policy and factor endowments.

We examine two types of policy regimes: rigid policy that remains constant in the face of the changed conditions brought about by exposure to international trade; and flexible policy that adjusts when trade liberalization occurs. We can think of a rigid policy regime as a proxy for an analysis of the short run. In contrast, a flexible policy regime may be a useful way of thinking about long-run outcomes. When considering flexible policy, we investigate the impacts of trade liberalization both in cases where pollution policy is guided by a benevolent social planner, and where policy reflects the wishes of a politically motivated government. The analysis of rigid policy allows us to examine the implications of trade liberalization when policymakers are either slow to respond to changed conditions, or forced to adjust slowly because of the fixed emission-to-output ratios embedded in much of a nation's existing—and slowly changing—capital stock.

We make extensive use of our pollution demand and supply framework to present our analysis. This framework is quite easy to use, employs well-known concepts of income and substitution effects, and is easily modified to include the additional motivations arising from political economy considerations. The advantage of this approach is that it focuses directly on the link between trade liberalization and a change in pollution levels. In settings where pollution policy is rigid, knowledge of the impact of freer trade on pollution levels is key to determining welfare impacts. In regimes where pollution policy is flexible, the demand-and-supply approach allows for a neat decomposition and identification of the potentially offsetting forces at work.

Our results reflect two common themes. First, the effect of trade liberalization on environmental quality depends on the comparative ad-

---

others. This literature has also been heavily influenced by the literature on trade policy in the presence of distortions—see Dixit 1985 for the standard treatment.

The analysis of how trade liberalization affects environmental quality in the presence of endogenous pollution policy has received much less attention. Lopez (1994) and Rauscher (1997) consider these issues, although with a focus somewhat different from ours.

vantage of the liberalizing country. Trade liberalization often has dramatically different effects for dirty good importers and dirty good
exporters. This has important implications for the empirical work we
pursue later in the book: there is no reason to expect the effects of trade
on the environment to be similar across all countries.

Second, the normative implications of trade liberalization differ
quite dramatically across policy regimes. If policy is flexible and the
policymaker acts to fully internalize pollution externalities, then freer
trade is welfare-improving. On the other hand, if policy is rigid and
does not adjust to fully internalize externalities, then freer trade can
lead to welfare losses. Whether such losses occur depends on the stringency of a country's pollution policy, its comparative advantage, and
the types of instruments used to control pollution.

If pollution policy is too weak and trade stimulates the polluting
sector, then the income gains generated from freer trade can be more
than offset by the costs of increased environmental degradation. A
country with weak environmental policy can therefore lose from trade
liberalization if it has a comparative advantage in the dirty good. However, trade can be beneficial in the presence of weak environmental
policy if a country has a comparative advantage in the clean good. In
that case, freer trade relieves pressure on the environment as producers
shift out of the formerly protected dirty industry to take advantage of
export opportunities elsewhere in the economy.

Excessively *stringent* environmental policy can also lead to losses
from freer trade. In this case losses occur not because of environmental
damage, but because the excessively stringent environmental policy
can lead to real income losses when the country is exposed to freer
trade.

We also find that the effects of trade on the environment may be
muted if governments are politically motivated. Pollution supply then
depends on the distribution of income across groups in society and
their relative importance in the government's objective function. As
trade liberalization proceeds, politically motivated governments may
try to use environmental policy to shelter favored groups from the
competitive pressures of trade. This tempers the pollution consequences of trade liberalization.

The rest of this chapter proceeds as follows. In section 4.1 we introduce the concept of trade frictions and show how a change in trade
frictions affects domestic prices differently for importers and exporters. Following this, sections 4.2–4.4 study the positive and normative

consequences of trade liberalization when pollution policy is rigid. We examine both the case where emission intensities are fixed, and the case where the number of emission permits is in fixed supply. In section 4.5 we investigate the effects of trade liberalization when pollution policy is guided by a welfare-maximizing social planner. We consider a politically motivated government in section 4.6. Section 4.7 sums up.

4.1 Trade Frictions

Trade liberalization is a reduction in trade barriers. There are many types of trade barriers in the world today. Some—such as shipping and communication costs—arise from natural or market-induced factors; while others—such as tariffs, customs agency fees, and a host of other regulations—are imposed by governments.

In much of the literature, the standard trade barrier analyzed is a tax on trade, such as a tariff or export tax. We explicitly consider tariff reductions later in this chapter. However, in most of our analysis, we do not want to focus on the details of a particular barrier to trade. Instead, we want to capture in a simple way the effects of increased trade opportunities. To do so, in most of our analysis we model trade barriers very simply by introducing a parameter that measures what we refer to as *trade frictions*. We assume that these trade frictions create a wedge between domestic and foreign prices but do not create government revenue, and we construct our measure in such a way that an increase in trade frictions moves a country closer to its autarky equilibrium. We will refer to a reduction in trade frictions as a trade liberalization. By construction then, trade frictions capture the essential trade-reducing feature of all trade restrictions but without the complication of carrying along revenue effects in the derivations.

Specifically, we adopt the simple "iceberg" model of trading costs, introduced by Samuelson (1954). If an importer wants to receive a unit of X from a foreign country, then $1 + \rho$ units of the good must be shipped from the foreign country (where $\rho \geq 0$).[2] The additional ρ units of the good (which "melt" in transit) can be thought of as the cost of

---

2. With this formulation, a fraction $1/(1 + \rho)$ of the goods shipped from a source arrive at their destination.

trading a unit of X.[3] With this approach, trading consumes real resources, and so constitutes a real "friction" that inhibits trade.[4]

As we show in subsequent sections, the effect of trade liberalization
on the environment depends on whether the home country imports or
exports the polluting good, and so we will allow for each possibility.

First suppose that Home imports X. Then to acquire 1 unit of X from
abroad, which will sell at domestic price p^d, Home must purchase 1 +
ρ units at the world price p to cover the cost of the good itself, plus
trading costs. Hence the domestic price of X is given by

$$p^d = p\,(1 + \rho). \tag{4.1}$$

Note that because of competition in goods markets, domestic producers of X will also receive a price of $p\,(1 + \rho)$ for their output. Hence
trade barriers raise the relative price of the import-competing good at
home for both consumers and producers.

On the other hand, if Home exports X, then a foreign exporter want-
ing 1 unit of the good to sell at the world price p must acquire 1 + ρ
units from the home country at the home price p^d. Hence if X is exported, we have

$$p^d = p\,/\,(1 + \rho). \tag{4.2}$$

Trade barriers tend to reduce the domestic price of the export good
relative to world prices.

For both importers and exporters of the dirty good, an increase in
trade frictions tends to reduce trade and move countries back toward
their autarky equilibrium.

Trade liberalization in this framework corresponds to a fall in trade
frictions ($d\rho < 0$). It is important to keep in mind that while trade liberalization always corresponds to a fall in trade frictions, the effect of
this on the domestic price of the dirty good depends on whether the

---

3. For simplicity, we assume there are no trade barriers for the numeraire good. This
does not affect the qualitative results: with transport costs for both goods, trade liberalization will continue to stimulate production of the good in which the country has a
comparative advantage. This will generate the composition effect that drives the results
of this chapter.

4. The advantage of this approach is that it yields a real resource cost of trading but
avoids explicitly modeling the details of the transportation and communication technologies, or government regulations that generate the cost. Moreover, by focusing on the
real resource costs of trade, rather than revenue-generating policies such as tariffs, we
avoid the complications of carrying along the revenue effects of trade policies.

country is a dirty good exporter or importer. Trade liberalization reduces the domestic price of the import good and increases the domestic relative price of the export good.

4.2 Trade Liberalization with Rigid Pollution Policy

To begin our analysis of trade liberalization, we consider the simple
case where government policy holds the emission intensity of production fixed. If the government uses pollution taxes, this is equivalent to
holding the pollution tax measured in terms of the dirty good (τ/p^d)
constant, because from (2.16), this implies that the emissions intensity
is constant.[5] This scenario is both instructive and realistic. It is instructive because it simplifies the analysis by ruling out a technique effect.
It is realistic because pollution regulation tends to target emissions intensities, rather than overall emissions.

Fixing emission intensities in the face of trade liberalization has the
effect of eliminating one possible channel of adjustment. As with
growth, we can decompose the effects of trade liberalization into scale,
composition, and technique effects. For convenience, we reproduce the
decomposition from (2.62) here:

$$\hat{z} = \hat{S} + \hat{\varphi} + \hat{e}. \tag{4.3}$$

With fixed emission intensities, trade liberalization will generate both
scale and composition effects (the first two terms in (4.3)); but there
will be no technique effect (the last term in (4.3) will drop out).

First consider the case where X is *imported*, so that the domestic price
is initially $p^d = p(1 + \rho)$. Trade liberalization corresponds to a *fall* in ρ,
which reduces the domestic relative price of X. This is illustrated in
figure 4.1. Starting from point A, a trade liberalization reduces the domestic consumer and producer price of X. Production moves from
point A to C, and pollution falls from Z_a to Z_c. This change in pollution

---

5. More directly, we could just assume that the government uses emission intensities as
the regulatory instrument, and that these are held constant. The results on the effects of
trade on pollution would be same as we present here; the results on the welfare effects
of trade liberalization would be similar, but differ slightly because as we have noted,
one cannot implement the first-best outcome with an emission intensity restriction as
the policy instrument. This means that there would be an additional second-best aspect
to the results because of the use of an inefficient instrument: not only may pollution be
too high or low, but the abatement costs to achieve the equilibrium level of pollution
would not be minimized. We prefer to focus on the pure effects of too tight or too weak
policy by assuming that a tax is used to implement the policy.

can be decomposed into a composition effect (A to B) that lowers pollution from Z_a to Z_b, and a scale effect (B to C) that raises pollution from Z_b to Z_c. These two effects move in opposite directions in the case illustrated. As noted above, there is no technique effect in this example by assumption.

In figure 4.1, the scale effect is positive and tends to increase pollution.[6] Trade leads to an increase in the efficiency of production (measured at world prices), and this leads to more output, and hence more pollution.[7]

The composition effect is driven by the change in relative prices, which cause producers to shift toward the good whose relative price increases with trade. Because protection is being removed from the polluting good in figure 4.1, dirty good production falls, and clean good production rises. Therefore, if the economy has a comparative advantage in the clean good, then the composition effect of trade liberalization tends to reduce pollution.

The composition effect is critically important in determining the effects of trade liberalization. In our simple model where only one good pollutes, the composition effect always dominates the scale effect, because the economy moves along the production frontier, which has an unambiguous effect on the output of the polluting good.[8] Trade liberalization causes an economy to focus its production on goods in which it has a comparative advantage. If the economy has a comparative ad-

---

6. The scale effect will be positive if the share of emission charges in costs is sufficiently small.

7. It is important to emphasize that although trade liberalization induces a movement along the production frontier, and not a shift in the frontier, it nevertheless generates a scale effect. In order to compare pollution levels across countries we need to account for cross-country differences in the scale of production. This necessitates a quantity index valuing outputs at common reference prices. As a result, any movement along a production frontier must generate both composition and scale effects. *Any* sensible definition of scale yields this same result.

8. More generally, if both goods pollute, then it is possible that the scale effect could dominate the composition effect. That is, pollution can rise even if the composition of output shifts toward the cleaner good. To see this, suppose that Y is less pollution intensive than X (emissions per dollar of output are lower), but that the production frontier is heavily skewed toward the Y axis. Suppose also that initially, the X sector is heavily protected and the economy produces mostly X and not much Y. An elimination of trade barriers will cause the economy to move along the production frontier toward Y. But because the frontier is heavily skewed toward Y, this leads to a large increase in the output of Y, and hence a large scale effect. Consequently, although the composition of output is shifting toward the cleaner good, the large scale effect can lead to an increase in pollution.

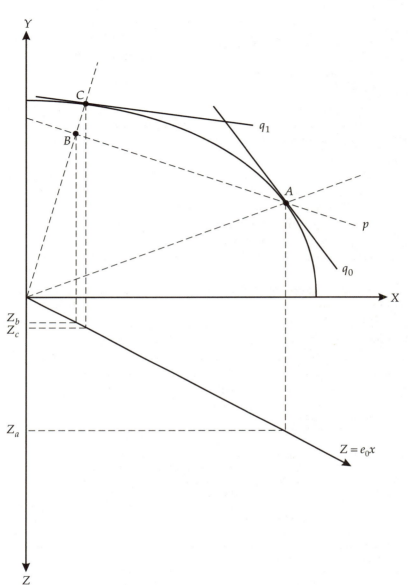

Fig. 4.1. Trade Liberalization with a Fixed Emission Intensity

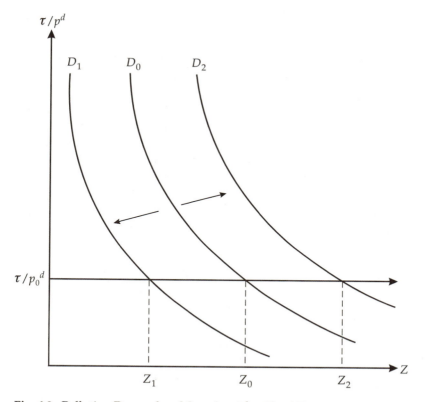

Fig. 4.2. Pollution Demand and Supply with a Fixed Emission Intensity

vantage in clean goods, as in this example, and if emission intensities are rigid, then trade liberalization is good for the environment because it induces a shift away from dirty good production.

The pollution demand and supply diagram provides an alternative illustration of this result. Because we want to focus on the case of fixed emission intensities, it is convenient to draw the supply and demand curves as functions of τ/p^d. With e fixed, τ/p^d is held constant by the regulator, and hence the pollution supply curve is a flat line determined by the current fixed level of e. This is illustrated in figure 4.2.

Recall that pollution demand is given by

$$\tau^d = G_z (p^d, 1, K, L, z), \tag{4.4}$$

where we have made explicit the role of the previously suppressed price of Y (1) as one of the arguments. To plot the curve, we need to rewrite our pollution demand in terms of τ/p^d. To do so, we divide both sides by p^d, and use the linear homogeneity of G_z to obtain

$$\frac{\tau^d}{p^d} = G_z\left(1, \frac{1}{p_d}, K, L, z\right). \tag{4.5}$$

As usual, the demand curve slopes down ($G_{zz} \leq 0$) both because lower pollution taxes increase emission intensities, and because lower pollution taxes encourage expansion of the dirty industry.

The initial equilibrium is at Z_0 in figure 4.2. Now consider the effect of trade liberalization. Since we are assuming that X is imported, a reduction in trade barriers lowers the relative price of X, or equivalently raises the relative price of Y. This is shown in (4.5) by the fact that the relative price of Y, which is $1/p^d$, rises when p^d falls. Hence the derived demand for pollution shifts left from D_0 to D_1 in figure 4.2. Pollution falls from Z_0 to Z_1. This is another way of illustrating the same change that we had previously illustrated in figure 4.1 as the movement from A to C.

Next consider the case where X is *exported*. In this case, the domestic price is initially $p^d = p/(1 + \rho)$. Trade liberalization now causes p^d to rise. Producers shift toward the dirty good. As before, there is a positive scale effect, which tends to increase pollution, but now the composition effect also tends to increase pollution, as the share of the dirty industry in GDP rises. That is, if a country has a comparative advantage in the dirty good, then the scale and composition effects reinforce each other. For given emissions intensities, trade liberalization raises pollution. In figure 4.2, if X is exported, trade liberalization leads to an increase in the derived demand for pollution from D_0 to D_2, raising the equilibrium level of pollution to Z_2 if emissions intensities are fixed.

In summary, with fixed emissions intensities, the composition effect is critical in determining the effects of trade liberalization on the environment. If trade stimulates the polluting sector, pollution tends to rise; but if it stimulates the clean sector, pollution tends to fall. Moreover, the sign of the composition effect is ultimately determined by a country's comparative advantage. If a country has a comparative advantage in clean industries, then it is the clean industries that expand with trade; and conversely, if it has a comparative advantage in polluting industries, then the dirty industries expand with trade.

Trade Liberalization with a Fixed Supply of Pollution Permits

In the above example, emission intensities were unresponsive to trade liberalization, because they were fixed by government policy. In this section, we suppose instead that the government uses marketable pollution permits and holds their supply fixed while trade is liberalized. Earlier, we noted that the first-best pollution policy could be implemented with either a pollution tax or a pollution permit system, and we illustrated the equivalence of these two systems as a method of implementing the first best. But if we hold policy instruments fixed in the face of shocks to the economy, this equivalence breaks down, as we demonstrate here.

Figure 4.3 illustrates the demand and supply for pollution in the presence of a fixed supply of pollution permits Z_0. The demand curve is given by (4.5), and the supply curve is vertical because of the fixed supply of permits. If X is imported and we liberalize trade, then as in the case of pollution taxes, the derived demand for pollution will fall from D_0 to D_1 as producers shift toward the clean industry. However, because of the fixed supply of pollution permits, total pollution does not change. Instead the relative price of a pollution permit drops because τ/p^d falls. This in turn leads to an increase in emissions intensity.[9]

Referring to our decomposition in (4.3), we can conclude that the scale effect tends to increase pollution, but this is dominated by a stronger composition effect, which leads to a fall in the derived demand for pollution. The scale and composition effects are exactly offset by a technique effect, as the market-induced decline in the relative price of a pollution permit leads to a reduction in abatement activity.

If instead X is exported, the polluting industry expands with trade liberalization, leading to an increase in the derived demand for pollution to D_2 in figure 4.3. In this case, the scale and composition effects work together to increase pollution. But the fixed pollution quota increases the real pollution tax to τ/p^d_2, leading to an decrease in emissions intensity. The ensuing technique effect exactly offsets the scale and composition effects, ensuring that pollution is again unaffected by the trade liberalization.[10]

An important implication of this analysis is that the effects of trade on the environment in the presence of unresponsive government pol-

---

9. In contrast to the case of fixed emission taxes, the fall in the price of pollution permits acts as a stimulus to the X industry. That is, trade liberalization in the presence of fixed emission permits leads to a smaller shift toward Y production than in the case of fixed emission taxes.

10. The increase in the price of emission permits raises the costs of X production above the level that would be realized under a fixed emission tax regime. Consequently, if we compare a tax and permit regime where the initial level of pollution is the same, the expansion of the X industry is smaller under a permit regime than under a tax regime.

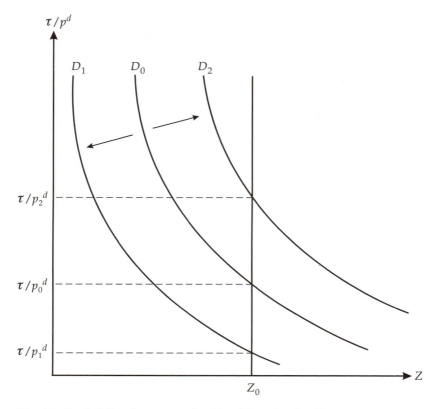

Fig. 4.3. Trade Liberalization with a Fixed Supply of Pollution Permits

icy depend on the type of regulatory instruments used. With rigid pollution taxes or emissions intensities, the environmental effects of trade liberalization may be substantial. But if pollution quotas are in place, the environmental effects of trade liberalization are negligible.

Welfare Effects of Trade Liberalization with Rigid Policy

We now consider the welfare effects of trade liberalization. Recall from equation (2.49) in chapter 2 that our indirect utility function can be written as

$$V (p^d, I, z) = v (I / \beta (p^d)) - h (z), \tag{4.6}$$

where p^d is a function of the trade barrier ρ, and $I/\beta (p^d)$ is real income R. As in chapter 3, we have normalized the population to $N = 1$.

Totally differentiating (4.6) yields

$$dV = V_{p^d} \, dp^d + V_I \, dI + V_z \, dz = V_I \left(\frac{V_{p^d}}{V_I} \, dp^d + dI + \frac{V_z}{V_I} \, dz \right), \tag{4.7}$$

where $V_I = v'/\beta > 0$ is the marginal utility of income. Recall that income is given by

$$I = G\,(p^d,\, K,\, L,\, z),$$

so that

$$dI = x dp^d + \tau dz. \tag{4.8}$$

Using (4.8), Roy's identity, and our definition of marginal damage, we can rearrange (4.7) to find

$$\frac{dV}{V_I} = -\, m dp^d + [\tau - MD\,(p^d,\, R,\, z)]\, dz, \tag{4.9}$$

where recall that $m = x^c - x$ denotes net imports of X.

From (4.9) notice that trade liberalization has two effects on welfare. First, there is the standard gains-from-trade effect captured by the first term in (4.9) $(-mdp^d)$,[11] and second there is the effect of a change in pollution on welfare. This is captured by the second term.

The gains-from-trade effect is always positive. To see this, note that if Home imports X, then $m > 0$, and the domestic price of X falls with trade liberalization. Hence $-mdp^d > 0$. On the other hand if Home exports X, then $m < 0$, but the domestic price of X rises with trade liberalization. Once again $-mdp^d > 0$. This is just the standard result: if there are no other distortions in the economy, then trade liberalization is necessarily welfare-improving in a representative agent economy because it increases purchasing power and therefore allows consumers to increase their goods consumption.

The second term in (4.9) measures the effect on welfare of any changes in pollution induced by trade liberalization. The welfare effect of a change in pollution depends on whether the marginal value of another unit of pollution to firms, τ, is lower or higher than the marginal damage suffered by citizens from another unit of pollution, $MD\,(p^d,\, R,\, z)$. If pollution policy is too lax ($\tau < MD$), then any increase in pollution ($dz > 0$) tends to lower welfare; that is, $[\tau - MD\,(p^d,\, R,\, z)]\, dz$

---

11. The gains-from-trade effect here reflects the reduction in the real resource cost of trading, and hence is essentially a terms-of-trade improvement. This is different than the

< 0. Alternatively, if the marginal value of pollution to firms, τ, is greater than marginal damage MD (p^d, R, z), then increases in pollution are welfare improving.

Welfare Effects of Trade Liberalization with Rigid Emission Intensities

So far, we have seen that trade liberalization generates both a gains-from-trade effect and an environmental effect. The gains-from-trade effect is always positive, but the environmental effect can be negative if trade liberalization stimulates the polluting industry. Therefore, changes in pollution can therefore potentially undermine the benefits of trade liberalization and lead to losses from trade.

To see this, suppose that emission intensities are constant, and regulation is lax so that $\tau < MD$ (p^d, R, z). Then if Home exports X, pollution, as we saw above, rises with trade liberalization. Because pollution policy is too lax, this increase in pollution tends to reduce welfare; that is, $[\tau - MD]\,dz < 0$. The net effect of trade liberalization on welfare is therefore ambiguous. The costs of increased pollution have to be compared with the benefits of increased goods consumption. If pollution is sufficiently damaging, then the pollution costs will dominate and trade liberalization will reduce welfare.

On the other hand, it is also possible that trade liberalization may yield a double dividend by reducing pollution as well as generating increased consumption. If Home imports X, then trade liberalization in the presence of a fixed pollution tax causes pollution to fall. In this case, with weak pollution regulation $(\tau < MD)$, the economy gains from reduced pollution $(\tau - MD)\,dz > 0$ as well as from the increased consumption arising from the standard gains from trade.

Finally, it is worth pointing out that an economy can also potentially suffer a loss from trade liberalization if pollution policy is excessively stringent. In this case, $\tau > MD$, so that a decrease in pollution tends to *decrease* welfare. This is because when the pollution tax is too high, the ensuing distortion in the economy leads to emission intensities that are too low (which is harmful because of the excessively high abatement costs) and insufficient output in the dirty good sector (which is harm-

---

standard "volume of trade" effect (see Dixit 1985) arising from tariff reduction. We will discuss the tariff reduction case below.

ful because of the loss of income from X production). A decrease in pollution will exacerbate this distortion.

To see this, suppose a country imports the dirty good. Then, as we saw above, trade liberalization will reduce pollution ($dz < 0$). With excessively stringent pollution policy, $\tau > MD$, and so $(\tau - MD)\,dz < 0$. Referring to (4.9), we see that the cost from lower pollution works against the standard gains-from-trade effect; and if it is sufficiently strong, welfare can fall.[12] Intuitively, when pollution taxes are too high, the economy is losing potential income because the X sector is too small. If the country imports X, then trade barriers tend to stimulate the X sector, and this helps to offset the excessive pollution regulation. Once these trade barriers are eliminated or reduced, the country loses income as the X sector contracts.

Tariff Reductions

Although our focus is on reductions in trade frictions rather than the effects of reform of specific trade policies, it is useful to compare our results with those for tariff reform.[13]

We will consider the case of a dirty good importer.[14] With an ad valorem tariff t on imports of X in place, the domestic price of X is $p^d = p\,(1 + t)$, and the welfare effect of tariff change is again given by (4.7). Income of our representative consumer now includes tariff revenue, and so we have

$$I = G\,(p\,(1 + t),\ K,\ L,\ z) + tpm. \tag{4.11}$$

Differentiating (4.11), yields[15]

$$dI = pxdt + \tau dz + tpdm + pmdt. \tag{4.12}$$

Substituting (4.12) into (4.7) yields

---

12. If the country instead exports the dirty good, and pollution taxes are too high, then trade liberalization increases pollution and therefore raises welfare because $(\tau - MD)\,dz > 0$, which reinforces the standard gains from trade.
13. See Siebert 1977, and Copeland 1994 on the effects of tariff reduction on pollution; and Dixit 1985 for the standard analysis of the effects of tariff reform more generally.
14. For a dirty good exporter, one could either consider a tariff on Y, or an export tax on X. By the Lerner symmetry theorem, the two policies are equivalent. If there is an export tax t on X, then the domestic price of X is $p\,/\,(1 + t)$. It is then straightforward to consider the effects of a reduction in trade barriers. A reduction in the export tax will reduce the trade distortion but stimulate pollution.
15. Recall that we are treating world prices as exogenous.

$$\frac{dV/dt}{V_1} = tp \frac{dm}{dt} + [\tau - MD\,(p^d,\, R,\, z)] \frac{dz}{dt}, \tag{4.13}$$

where $dm/dt < 0$. Note that a fall in tariffs ($dt < 0$) will have the same qualitative effect on pollution as a fall in trade frictions ($d\rho < 0$), since both will lead to a fall in the producer price of X for a dirty good importer, and so both lead to a fall in pollution. That is, the second term in (4.13) behaves in the same way as the second term in (4.9).

Hence the difference between a reduction in trade frictions and a reduction in tariffs lies in the difference in the trade distortion term (the first term in (4.13)). In both cases, a reduction in the trade barrier reduces the trade distortion, but the magnitude of the effect differs in the two cases.

With a trade friction, importing consumes real resources. With a fall in trade frictions, the economy can acquire imported goods at a lower opportunity cost, and so the reduction in trade barriers is like an improvement in the terms of trade (even though the world price is fixed). From (4.9), the change in the trade distortion is given by $-mdp^d = -mpd\rho$. Hence a fall in trade frictions ($d\rho < 0$) generates real import cost savings that are proportional to the initial volume of trade.

Tariffs, on the other hand, create a distortion because consumers and producers face prices that do not reflect true opportunity costs. However, importing does not consume real resources, and so the actual cost to the economy of importing a good is simply the world price. The difference between what consumers pay and what is paid to foreigners is tariff revenue and is captured by the government (and assumed here to be rebated to consumers). Hence the key problem with a tariff is simply that imports are too low. The value to the economy of a reduction in the tariff is measured by the benefit of increased imports, which is the size of the gap between domestic and foreign prices (tp) multiplied by the change in imports. In the literature, this is known as a *volume of trade effect*.[16]

Consequently, the magnitude of the benefits created by a fall in trade distortions depends on the type of trade barrier in place.[17] However, the main point we want to emphasize is simply that trade liberaliza-

---

16. See Dixit 1985 for an exposition.
17. This means that in order to perform a cost-benefit analysis of trade liberalization, one would have to take care in modeling the specific trade distortions being eliminated. The magnitude of the benefits from reducing trade distortions will differ across instruments.

tion creates two types of effects: a change in pollution and reduction in the trade distortion; and there is a trade-off between these two effects for a dirty good exporter. The net effect of this trade-off may vary across the type of trade barrier, but the direction of the two effects is the same whether we consider trade frictions or tariffs.

Welfare Effects of Trade Liberalization with Rigid Emission Quotas

Next consider the effects of trade liberalization when pollution regulation takes the form of a binding aggregate pollution quota. In this case, trade must always raise welfare, even when marginal damage is high and pollution regulation is lax. As long as the pollution quota is binding, pollution does not change with trade liberalization ($dz = 0$), and hence we have $[\tau - MD(p^d, R, z)]\, dz = 0$. That is, in the presence of binding pollution quotas, trade liberalization cannot exacerbate environmental distortions. If we refer to (4.9), this leaves only the standard gains from trade, which as we have already shown must be positive.[18]

4.3 Trade Liberalization with Flexible Pollution Policy

We now consider the effects of trade liberalization when pollution policy is flexible and determined by a welfare-maximizing social planner. The policymaker now has the ability to raise or lower pollution in response to freer trade, and so the effect on pollution levels depends on the strength of the policy response. The policy response, in turn, depends on the trade-offs consumers make between consumption and environmental quality.

To consider this issue in more detail we must derive the policy response. Recall that the equilibrium condition determining the efficient level of pollution is

---

18. See Falvey 1988 and Copeland 1994. Falvey makes the general point that piecemeal reform in the presence of binding quotas can prevent harmful distortions from being exacerbated. Falvey did not consider pollution, but presented a model with multiple trade distortions and showed that if binding import quotas were in place, the loosening up of any import quota would be welfare improving (in contrast, in the presence of multiple tariffs, the reduction of one tariff may exacerbate trade distortions in other sectors). Copeland (1994) compared tariff reform in the presence of pollution taxes and quotas and showed that trade policy reform in the presence of pollution quotas was welfare improving. The result is also generalized to the case of multiple goods and multiple pollutants.

$G_z (p^d, K, L, z) = MD (p^d, R, z),$

where we have again normalized the population (N) to unity. Trade liberalization corresponds to a change in ρ, which in turn affects the domestic price, p^d.

$$\frac{dz}{d\rho} = \frac{dz}{dp^d} \frac{dp^d}{d\rho}$$

Since we have modeled trade barriers as a trade friction, a fall in trade barriers has the same effect on the economy as a change in the world price.[19] Consequently, to understand the effects of trade liberalization on pollution, we need to know how the policymaker responds to changes in the price of the dirty good. We will therefore first spend some time analyzing dz/dp^d, without specifying whether the change in p^d comes from a change in ρ or a change in the world price p. As well as a key step in our analysis of trade liberalization, the analysis of the response of pollution to changes in p^d will be useful later when we study the response of pollution to exogenous changes in world prices.

Effects of an Increase in the Price of the Dirty Good on Pollution

Totally differentiating and rearranging, we obtain an expression for the change in pollution in response to a change in the price of the dirty good:

$$\frac{dz}{dp^d} = \frac{G_{zp} - MD_p + \frac{m}{\beta (p^d)} MD_R}{\Delta}, \tag{4.14}$$

where $\Delta \equiv MD_z + MD_R R_z - G_{zz} > 0$.

An increase in the price of the polluting good has three effects on pollution. First, recall that $G_z = \tau$ is the inverse derived demand for pollution. Hence the term $G_{zp} > 0$ in (4.14) reflects the upward shift in the derived demand for pollution as the domestic price of the dirty good rises. This is a combined scale and composition effect, as producers shift out of the clean good and into the polluting good.

---

19. If instead we model trade barriers as a tax on trade, then a fall in trade barriers has an effect that is different than the effect a fall in the world price has, as we discussed earlier. We will note below how this would affect the analysis of the effects of trade

The next two terms in (4.14) capture the policy response arising from the change in relative goods prices. The policy change has two terms: a substitution effect and an income effect. The substitution effect is given by $-MD_p$. Recall that MD is marginal damage, or the willingness to pay for reduced pollution. As the price of consumption goods rises, environmental quality becomes cheaper relative to consumption, and hence the willingness to pay for environmental quality rises via this substitution effect. To confirm this, note from (2.34) that[20]

$$MD\ (p^d,\ R,\ z) = \frac{\beta\ (p^d)\ h'\ (z)}{u'\ (R)}.$$ (4.15)

Differentiating, and using Roy's identity we find that

$$MD_p = \frac{\beta_p MD}{\beta} = \frac{\tau x^c}{I} > 0,$$ (4.16)

where x^c is domestic consumption of x. The consumer substitution effect $(-MD_p)$ in (4.14) is therefore negative. This tends to increase the pollution tax, which reduces pollution.

The last term in (4.14) is the income effect, the sign of which depends on whether the country is an importer or exporter of the polluting good. If the country imports the polluting good, then $m > 0$, and an increase in the domestic price of X worsens its terms of trade, leading to a reduction in national income.[21] This reduces the demand for environmental quality, and therefore tends to lower the pollution tax and increase pollution. On the other hand, if the country exports the polluting good $(m < 0)$, then an increase in the price of X raises national income. This increase in income then increases the demand for environmental quality, leading to a higher pollution tax, and a decline in pollution.

It is useful to rewrite (4.14) in elasticity form. Note that $G_{zp} = \partial \tau^D / \partial p$; that is, G_{zp} measures the increase in the willingness of producers to

---

liberalization on pollution. The only difference is the magnitude of the income effect of trade liberalization.

20. To verify that this is indeed a pure substitution effect, note that the expenditure function dual to (2.34) can be written as $E\ (p,\ u,\ z) = \beta\ (p)\ \varphi\ (u,\ z)$. Hence $E_{zp} = \beta_p \varphi_z = (E_p / \varphi)\ (E_z / \beta) = x^c \tau / I$, since $I = E$, $\tau = E_z$, and $x^c = E_p$ is consumption of X from Shephard's lemma.

21. Recall that since p^d depends only on the world price p and the trade friction ρ, which is modeled as a real trading cost, a change in domestic price yields a real change in the opportunity cost to the economy of X, and hence is a terms of trade effect. If instead we modeled the trade barrier as a tariff, then we have to be more careful in distinguishing

pay for the right to release a given level of emissions z. This allows us to rewrite (4.14) as

$$\frac{dz}{dp^d} = \frac{\tau}{p^d \Delta}\left[\varepsilon^D_{,p} - \varepsilon_{MD,p} + \frac{p^d m}{I}\varepsilon_{MD,R}\right].$$ (4.17)

The net effect of an increase in the price of the polluting good on pollution is ambiguous in general, as it depends on the strength of the income and substitution effects. We can better understand when pollution rises or falls by exploiting the production structure of our model given by (2.2) and (2.8).

As a first step in interpreting (4.17), we show that the shift in the demand for pollution always dominates the substitution effect in consumption. That is, $\varepsilon_{\tau^D,p} - \varepsilon_{MD,p} > 0$. To see this, first note that $\varepsilon_{\tau^D,p} > 1$. This follows because an increase in p^d will stimulate x. Hence for given z, we must have a fall in the emissions intensity e.[22] But since $e = ap^d/\tau$, this requires an increase in τ/p^d; that is, $\varepsilon_{\tau^D,p} > 1$. Next, use (4.16) to obtain

$$\varepsilon_{MD,p} = \frac{p^d}{\tau}\frac{\partial MD}{\partial p} = \frac{p^d x^c}{I} \le 1.$$ (4.18)

That is, $\varepsilon_{MD,p}$ is equal to the share of good x in consumption, which cannot exceed 1. Putting this together yields $\varepsilon_{\tau^D,p} - \varepsilon_{MD,p} > 0$. Hence, referring to (4.17), we see that if there were no income effect, an increase in the price of the dirty good would raise pollution. The sign of dz/dp^d therefore hinges on the strength and direction of the income effect.

The direction of the income effect is determined by a nation's trade pattern. If the country imports the polluting good ($m > 0$), then an increase in the price of the dirty good lowers the country's real income. This reduces the demand for environmental quality, and hence the income effect shifts out pollution supply. Pollution unambiguously rises when the price of the dirty good rises.

On the other hand, if the country exports the polluting good ($m < 0$), then real income rises with an increase in p^d. This increases the demand for environmental quality and induces the policymaker to

---

between domestic and world price changes when discussing terms of trade effects. We discuss the effects of tariff liberalization on pollution below.
22. We treat z as given here because $\varepsilon_{\tau^D,p} = (p/\tau)(\partial\tau^D/\partial p)$; that is, we are asking how much the demand curve shifts up in response to an increase in p for given z.

tighten pollution policy. In this case, the income effect works against the outward shift in pollution demand and tends to reduce pollution. With a very strong income effect, it is possible that pollution may fall even though the price of the dirty good rises.

Although the response of pollution to an increase in the price of the dirty good is ambiguous for a dirty good exporter, the ambiguity arises only when the income effect is strong. We can be more precise about what "strong" means by noting that if $\varepsilon_{MD,R} \leq 1$, then (4.17) is non-negative:

$$\frac{dz}{dp^d} \geq \frac{\tau}{p^d \Delta} \left[\varepsilon^D_{,p} - \varepsilon_{MD,p} + \frac{p^d m}{I} \right] = \frac{\tau}{p^d \Delta} \left[\varepsilon^D_{,p} - \frac{p^d x}{I} \right] \geq 0,$$

where the first inequality follows because $m < 0$ for a dirty good exporter; and the next two steps follow by using (4.18), and noting that $m = x^c - x$, and that $\varepsilon_{\tau^D,p} > 1$. Consequently, as long as the income elasticity of marginal damage is less than 1, an increase in the price of the dirty good will lead to an increase in pollution even with a benevolent social planner setting policy.

Effects of Trade Liberalization on Pollution

Let us now use these results to complete our analysis of trade liberalization in a regime where the government sets pollution policy efficiently. First suppose that Home imports X, as in figure 4.4. For a dirty good importer, $p^d = p(1 + \rho)$. Trade liberalization reduces the trade friction ρ and so lowers the domestic price of X; that is,

$$-\frac{dp^d}{d\rho} < 0.$$

Trade liberalization stimulates the industry in which the country has a comparative advantage (the clean good) and contracts the other industry (dirty good production). We showed above that a change in the price of the dirty good has an unambiguous effect on pollution for a country that imports the dirty good—a fall in the price of the dirty good will unambiguously reduce pollution. However, it is worth reviewing the forces that lead to this result.

Trade liberalization leads to a contraction of the dirty good industry, and this shifts in the derived demand for pollution from D_0 to D_1. If the pollution tax were held fixed, pollution would drop from Z_0 to Z_2.

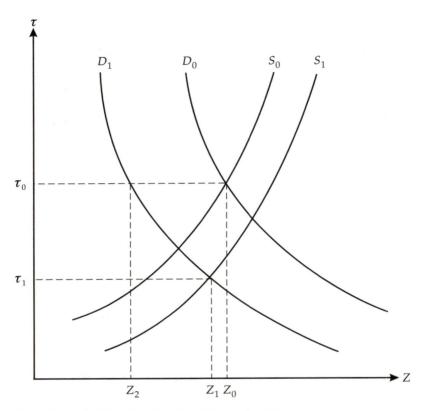

Fig. 4.4. Trade Liberalization for a Clean Good Exporter

However, with an optimal policy response, the pollution tax responds in three ways.

First, there is a movement down along the marginal damage curve S_0, as trade liberalization relieves pressure on the environment. Because consumers can import the polluting good, less is produced at home, and the government can afford to ease up on pollution regulations.[23] This dampens the demand-induced fall in pollution.

Second, there are two shifts in the marginal damage curve (one down and one up) arising from the substitution and income effects in policy. As the price of the dirty good falls, consumers want to substitute away from environmental quality toward consumption, and this leads the policymaker to increase pollution (the *MD* curve shifts

23. The magnitude of this effect shows up in the denominator in the equations above.

down). This further dampens the demand-induced fall in pollution. But as we showed above, the shift in the producers' demand for pollution always dominates this consumer substitution effect, so the pollution supply curve shifts down by less than the shift in the pollution demand curve. The net effect of the shift in the pollution demand curve and the substitution-induced shift in the supply curve is therefore to reduce pollution. In addition, there is another shift in the marginal damage curve coming from the income effect. For a dirty good importer, the fall in the price of the dirty good raises real income, and this causes the MD curve to shift up. This reinforces the fall in pollution. That is, for a dirty good importer, trade liberalization unambiguously reduces pollution.[24]

Now suppose instead that Home exports X. This is illustrated in figure 4.5. Trade liberalization will stimulate the polluting industry if the country is a dirty good exporter; that is, in this case $p^d = p/(1 + \rho)$ and so a fall in trade frictions ρ leads to an increase in p^d. As we saw in the previous section, an increase in the price of the dirty good has an ambiguous effect on pollution for a dirty good exporter, but pollution will rise as long as the income elasticity of the demand for environmental quality is not too high.

To see this, first note that for a dirty good exporter, trade liberalization shifts out the derived demand for pollution from D_0 to D_1. With a fixed pollution tax, this would increase pollution to Z_2. However, this increase in pollution is dampened via a technique effect that is driven by two forces. First, as the polluting industry expands, increased pressure is placed on the environment, and the economy moves up the marginal damage curve S_0. The optimal response is to tighten pollution regulations. In addition, the marginal damage curve shifts up from S_0 to S_1, because both the substitution and the income effects lead to an increased demand for environmental quality. This leads to a further

---

24. Whether trade liberalization leads to a net inward or outward shift in pollution supply depends on the strength of the income effect. If $\varepsilon_{MD, R}$ is not too large (in particular, if $\varepsilon_{MD, R} \leq 1$), then

$$- \varepsilon_{MD, p} + \frac{p^d m}{I} \varepsilon_{MD, R} \leq - \varepsilon_{MD, p} + \frac{p^d m}{I} = - \frac{px^c}{I} + \frac{p^d m}{I} = - \frac{px}{I} \leq 0.$$

Referring to (4.17), this means that if $\varepsilon_{MD, R} \leq 1$, then the policy response shifts the pollution supply curve down. This is the case illustrated in the figure where the net policy response has shifted the pollution supply curve outward from S_0 to S_1. But as we showed above, the policymaker will not perversely increase pollution: policy merely dampens the trade-induced reduction in pollution demand. In figure 4.4, the net effect of trade on pollution is illustrated as the fall from Z_0 to Z_1.

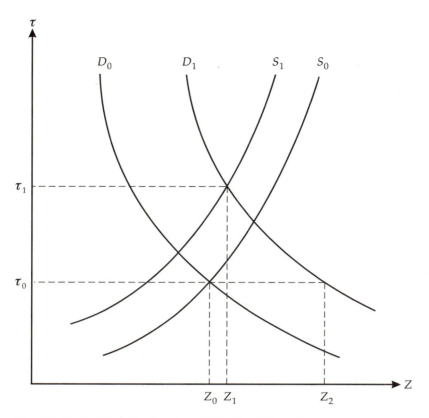

Fig. 4.5. Trade Liberalization for a Dirty Good Exporter

tightening of pollution regulations. The pollution tax will unambiguously increase (from τ_0 to τ_1 in the figure). Pollution will also increase (from Z_0 to Z_1 in the figure), provided that the income elasticity of the demand for environmental quality is not too strong. As we showed above, a sufficient condition for pollution to rise is that $\varepsilon_{MD, R} \leq 1$.[25]

---

25. If the trade barrier instead took the form of a tariff, then the expression for the effect of a change in the tariff on pollution, dz/dt, would have a form similar to (4.14), except that the income-effect term would be multiplied by the elasticity of imports with respect to an increase in the tariff. That is, letting t denote the ad valorem tariff and recalling that with tariffs, we have $R = G + tpM$, we obtain

$$\frac{dz}{dt} = \frac{\tau}{p^d \Delta} \left[\varepsilon_{\tau^D, p^d} - \varepsilon_{MD, p^d} - \frac{p^d m}{I} \varepsilon_{MD, R} \, \varepsilon_{m, t} \right] p,$$

where $\varepsilon_{m, t} \leq 0$ is the elasticity of imports with respect to a change in the tariff. If the country imports the dirty good, then pollution unambiguously falls as the tariff falls,

To summarize, when pollution policy is efficient and fully responsive, the effects of trade liberalization on environmental quality depend both on a country's comparative advantage and on the strength of the policy response. Trade liberalization will always reduce pollution for a dirty good importer. Trade liberalization will raise pollution for a dirty good exporter unless the income elasticity of the demand for environmental quality is high. This means that the effects of trade on the environment tend to be somewhere between those for the two rigid policy regimes (fixed emission intensities and fixed overall quotas) we analyzed previously. In comparison with the fixed emission intensity regime, the presence of efficient and flexible policy tends to dampen (but not reverse) the demand-driven effects of trade on the environment. And in comparison with the fixed overall quota regime, an efficient policymaker will allow some adjustment in pollution levels to reflect changes in the opportunity cost of emissions induced by trade-induced changes in domestic goods prices.

Welfare Effects with a Social Planner

Finally, let us consider the welfare effects of trade liberalization when a social planner regulates pollution policy. The welfare effects of trade liberalization were derived in (4.9), which we reproduce here:

$$\frac{dV}{V_I} = - mdp^d + [\tau - MD\,(p^d,\,R,\,z)]\,dz. \tag{4.19}$$

When policy is optimal, we have $\tau = MD\,(p^d,\,R,\,z)$, and hence we have

$$\frac{dV}{V_I} = - mdp^d > 0.$$

We are left with just the gains-from-trade effect.[26] If pollution externalities are fully internalized, trade must always increase welfare. Trade

---

which is the same result we obtain with trade frictions. If the country exports the dirty good, then a sufficient condition for pollution to rise is that $|\,\varepsilon_{MD,\,R}\varepsilon_{m,\,t}\,| \leq 1$. That is, the magnitude of the income effect of tariff reduction depends on the elasticity of imports with respect to a change in the tariff. This is because the magnitude of the increase in real income depends on the magnitude of the fall in the tariff distortion, which depends on the volume of trade. The substitution effects of trade liberalization on pollution depend only on the change in the domestic prices, and so have similar effects whether they are driven by changes in tariffs or trade frictions.

26. If instead, trade barriers take the form of tariffs, we are left with the standard volume of trade effect, which measures the benefits of the reduced tariff distortion. This must

may lead to an increase in pollution if the economy has a comparative advantage in pollution, but this reflects an optimal trade-off between environmental quality and consumption. Prior to trade, the policymaker chooses pollution levels to reflect domestic willingness to pay for environmental quality. With trade liberalization, if a country has a comparative advantage in polluting goods, then it can obtain higher prices for these goods in export markets than at home. This means that the opportunity cost of preserving the environment has risen, as consumers are now able to obtain more from foreigners from the exploitation of their environment than they are willing to pay to preserve it. The policymaker responds by allowing increased exploitation of the environment. Provided all externalities are fully internalized, this must improve welfare.

This is an important result because it emphasizes that the presence of pollution alone does not reverse the standard argument that a country can gain from trade. As long as externalities are internalized, firms face prices that reflect true opportunity costs of all of their activities, including their impact on the environment.[27] Consequently, standard gains-from-trade theorems apply, whether or not pollution rises or falls with trade. The possibility of losses from trade due to environmental problems requires a combination of both the presence of pollution and inefficient environmental policy.

4.4 The Political Economy Motive

Up until this point, we have assumed that all domestic agents are identical. Government policy simply reflected the preferences of a representative consumer. If, however, consumers have different incomes (because of different factor endowments) or different preferences, then the government must balance the interests of different consumers when choosing environmental policy. In particular, the government may employ pollution policy to affect the distribution of income. For example, pollution taxes may be set lower than their Pigouvian levels if the factors employed in the dirty industry are politically powerful. When trade is liberalized, governments may attempt to use pollution policy to shield favored interest groups from the competitive pressures of in-

be non-negative, and hence we obtain the same qualitative result: tariff reform in the presence of efficient pollution policy is welfare improving.

27. This is one of the key insights from the literature on trade policy in the presence of distortions. See Dixit 1985.

creased trade. This political motive for pollution policy introduces an additional channel through which freer trade can affect the environment. In this section, we develop a simple extension of our model to illustrate the implications of this possibility.

Suppose there are two groups in society differing only in factor ownership. The two groups are labeled Greens and Browns. Browns primarily own physical capital and Greens primarily own human capital. Rather than adopting an explicit voting or lobbying model, we assume the government chooses pollution to maximize a weighted sum of each group's preferences.

This simple representation has two benefits. First, it captures the idea that governments value utility gains of some groups more than others. Second, it allows us to model an interaction between political economy motivations for pollution policy, and typical income-based motivations.[28]

Let I^i denote the aggregate factor income accruing to type i agents, where $i = g$ denotes "Green" and $i = b$ denotes "Brown." That is, I^g is total income accruing to all Greens. There are N^i identical agents of each type, and hence each agent's factor income is I^i/N^i. Let $V^i \equiv V(p^d, I^i/N^i, z)$ denote the preferences of a type i agent. As noted above, we assume preferences are identical, but that factor ownership differs across agents. The government chooses its policy instruments to maximize its objective, which we take to be a weighted sum of the utilities of the two types of agents. The government's objective, W, is

$$W = \lambda V^g + (1 - \lambda) V^b, \tag{4.20}$$

where λ is the weight put on Greens and $1 - \lambda$ is the weight on Browns.[29]

It is important to emphasize that political economy considerations alone need not alter any of our analysis. To see this, suppose the gov-

28. Many political economy models, such as Grossman and Helpman 1994, adopt preferences that are quasi-linear. As a result, the indirect utility function is linear in income, implying $\varepsilon_{MD, R} = 0$. Such a setup rules out a role for income gains to determine pollution policy. While some recent models of political economy allow for more general preferences, their results are hard to characterize analytically. Our approach sacrifices some of the richness arising from the microfoundations of the more sophisticated political economy models, but allows us to capture income-induced changes in the demand for environmental quality.

29. The weights λ may depend on the numbers of each type of agent, but because we do not vary population, we do not make this explicit. For example, if $\lambda = N^g/N$, the government's objective is utilitarian.

ernment can use lump-sum transfers as well as choose pollution. Letting T be an aggregate transfer from Greens to Browns, the government's problem is

$$\operatorname*{Max}_{z,\,T} \left[\lambda V \left(p^d, \frac{I^g - T}{N^g}, z \right) + (1 - \lambda) V \left(p^d, \frac{I^b + T}{N^b}, z \right) \right].$$

The first-order condition for the choice of the transfer implies

$$\frac{\lambda}{N^g} V^g_I = \frac{(1 - \lambda)}{N^b} V^b_I. \tag{4.21}$$

The government uses transfers to equate the politically weighted marginal utilities of income. Next, the first-order condition for the choice of pollution yields

$$\frac{\lambda V^g_I}{N^g} [I^g_z - N^g MD^g] + \frac{(1 - \lambda) V^b_I}{N^b} [I^b_z - N^b MD^b] = 0, \tag{4.22}$$

The government now weighs the trade-off between pollution and income made by the private agents, but also considers the different weights it places on the different agents. The condition (4.22) looks more complicated that those we have obtained previously, but if we use (4.21), then (4.22) reduces to

$$I^g_z + I^b_z = N^g MD^g + N^b MD^b \tag{4.23}$$

National income is simply $I = I^b + I^g$, and recall that $\tau = I_z$. Consequently, (4.23) is equivalent to

$$\tau = N^g MD^g + N^b MD^b, \tag{4.24}$$

which is just the standard Samuelson rule. Therefore we have shown that, regardless of the weights placed on the two types of agents, the government chooses pollution so that the pollution tax is equal to the (unweighted) sum of the marginal damages across all agents. Pollution policy is efficient, and our previous analysis continues to apply.

The key insight here is that a politically motivated government must weigh both the benefits and costs of its income redistribution policies. Consequently, such a government will want to minimize the cost of raising the income of a favored group. If lump-sum transfers are available, the government's income redistribution objectives will be carried out entirely with lump-sum transfers, and pollution policy will be implemented efficiently. The reason for this is that lump-sum transfers introduce no new distortions, but deviating from the Samuelson rule introduces inefficiencies into the economy. Consequently, the government will rely exclusively on lump-sum transfers for its income redistribution objectives. Another way of looking at this is to note that if the government holds the utility of Greens at a given fixed level, then it can raise the utility of Browns higher if it relies on lump-sum transfers than if it manipulated pollution policy to try to favor Browns. This is a simple application of the well-known policy-targeting rule.[30]

The result that pollution policy will not be manipulated for political gain when lump-sum transfers are available is not specific to our model, but is also true in many political economy models. To obtain the result that pollution policy will be manipulated for political gain, most political economy models proceed by restricting the set of available policy instruments.[31] Typically, these models assume that the only policy instrument available to governments is pollution policy.[32] That is, not only are lump-sum transfers ruled out, but so are output subsidies, differential taxes on factor income, and other policies. For the purposes of illustrating how our results would be changed by standard political economy considerations, we will follow the literature and rule out all other policy instruments except for pollution policy.[33]

Suppose, then, that the government's only policy instrument is the level of pollution. Then it chooses z to maximize (4.20), which yields (4.22). Because there are no lump-sum transfers available, (4.21) is no longer relevant, and hence the politically weighted marginal utilities of income in (4.22) are not generally equal. The government must weigh marginal gains by both Greens and Browns when deciding pollution policy.

To see the types of trade-offs involved and how pollution policy can be used to redistribute income, consider the effects of an increase in pollution on a type i agent. Let φ^i denote the fraction of national income accruing to group i; that is

$$I^i = \varphi^i I, \qquad i = g, b, \tag{4.25}$$

where $\varphi^g + \varphi^b = 1$. Then the effect of an increase in pollution on the utility of a typical agent in group i is

---

30. See Dixit 1985.

31. Grossman and Helpman (1994) note that there may be incentives to precommit to the use of inefficient instruments in order to influence the outcome of the political equilibrium.

32. See, for example, Fredriksson 1997 and Aidt 1998.

33. We are also assuming that trade barriers cannot be manipulated to influence the distribution of income. The motivation for this assumption is that trade barriers are constrained by international trade agreements.

$$\frac{dV^i}{dz} = V^i_I \left[\frac{\varphi^i \tau + I\varphi^i_z}{N^i} - MD^i \right]. \qquad (4.26)$$

A change in pollution has three effects on indirect utility. First, each unit of pollution generates τ additional units of national income. A typical consumer of type i gets a fraction φ^i / N^i of national income, and so gets an income gain of $\tau \varphi^i / N^i$. In addition, the change in pollution tax will alter the distribution of national income. This is captured by the term $I\varphi^i_z / N^i$. This term will differ in sign for Greens and Browns. An increase in pollution will stimulate capital-intensive polluting industries and raise the return to capital. This will reduce the fraction of national income accruing to Greens and raise the fraction of income accruing to Browns. Consequently, $I\varphi^g_z / N^g < 0$ and $I\varphi^b_z / N^b > 0$. This means that Browns will pressure the government to raise pollution by more than Greens would like. And finally, an increase in pollution harms the environment, and the cost of this to each agent is measured by their marginal damage.

The government's optimal pollution tax will balance these various effects and will reflect the weights given to the different groups. It can be found by using (4.26) to simplify (4.22) and then solving for τ. This is somewhat messy in general, and so for clarity, we will present a special case, where the elasticity of marginal utility with respect to income is a constant equal to 1. That is, we adopt the utility function we have used previously in some of our examples:

$$V^i = \ln \left(\frac{I^i / N^i}{\beta (p)} \right) - h (z). \qquad (4.27)$$

In this case, (4.22) simplifies to[34]

$$\tau = N^g MD^g + N^b MD^b + I \left[\frac{\lambda - \varphi^g}{\varphi^g \varphi^b} \right] \varphi^b_z, \qquad (4.28)$$

where, recall, $\varphi^b_z > 0$ because an increase in pollution redistributes income toward Browns, and λ is the weight given to Greens, who have a share of national income given by φ^g.

To understand the impact of political economy elements entering the pollution tax determination, compare (4.28) with (4.24). The Samuelson rule has been modified by the addition of the last term in (4.28), which reflects the income redistribution motive of the government. If Greens'

---

34. Note that with this utility function, $N^g MD^g + N^b MD^b = h'(z) I$.

share of national income is below the weight placed on their utility by the government, then $\lambda > \varphi^g$ and the last term in (4.28) is positive. The pollution tax τ will be distorted above aggregate marginal damage because this will redistribute income toward Greens. Alternatively if Greens' share of national income is above their weight λ, then pollution taxes will be distorted below aggregate marginal damage so that the government can redistribute income toward Browns.

Let us now consider how political economy elements can influence the way in which trade liberalization affects pollution. Let MD denote aggregate marginal damage, and note that with our utility function, we have

$$MD \equiv N^g MD^g + N^b MD^b = h'(z) \, G \, (p^d, K, L, z).$$

The equilibrium level of pollution is determined by the intersection of pollution demand and supply, where supply now reflects political economy motives:

$$G_z \, (p^d, K, L, z) = \tau = MD + I \left[\frac{\lambda - \varphi^g}{\varphi^g \varphi^b} \right] \varphi^b_z. \tag{4.29}$$

We wish to consider the impact of a change in trade fictions on pollution. Suppose we start from a point where the income distribution is initially optimal without any manipulation of pollution policy, so that initially $\lambda = \varphi^g$. That is, we can think of the economy as initially in a long-run policy equilibrium where the government has used other instruments to achieve its income redistribution objectives. Suppose, though, that when trade is liberalized, the only instrument available to the government is pollution policy. In this case we have

$$\left. \frac{dz}{d\rho} \right|_{\lambda = \varphi^g} = \frac{\left[\dfrac{\tau}{p^d} \left(\varepsilon_{,p} - \dfrac{px}{G} \right) + \left(\dfrac{I\varphi^b_z}{\varphi^g \varphi^b} \right) \left(\dfrac{d\varphi^g}{dp^d} \right) \right] \dfrac{dp^d}{d\rho}}{\Delta}. \tag{4.30}$$

For clarity, first suppose that the county is a dirty good exporter, so that freer trade raises the domestic price of the dirty good. The change in pollution is determined by three broad forces affecting pollution demand and supply: substitution effects, income effects, and politically motivated redistributive effects.

First, there are the conventional substitution and income effects that we have analyzed previously. This is the term

$$\frac{\tau}{p^d}\left(\varepsilon_{\tau, p} - \frac{px}{G}\right) > 0.$$

As we discussed previously, when the income elasticity of marginal damage is equal to 1, as it is with the utility function (4.27), the substitution effect in production always dominates and an increase in the price of the dirty good leads to an increase in pollution in the absence of political effects. Hence the conventional determinants of supply and demand together generate an increase in pollution for a dirty good exporter.

The last term in (4.30) reflects political economy influences. An increase in the domestic relative price of X lowers real income for Greens and raises real income for Browns. Hence a trade liberalization that raises the relative price of the dirty good redistributes income away from Greens toward Browns; that is, referring to (4.30),

$$\left(\frac{I\varphi_z^b}{\varphi^g \varphi^b}\right)\left(\frac{d\varphi^g}{dp^d}\right) < 0.$$

Since the income distribution was originally optimal, the government will attempt to dampen this loss of income for Greens. With pollution policy the only instrument available, the only way to compensate Greens for the effects of trade liberalization is to reduce pollution. That is, the political economy effect tends to shift the pollution supply to the left as the government raises the pollution tax to partially undo the income distributional changes brought about by freer trade. Since this shift left would lower pollution, the political economy elements in this case tend to work against the more conventional determinants. For a dirty good exporter, the pollution-increasing effects of freer trade are dampened by the political economy motives of the government as it attempts to restore the original (and assumed optimal) income distribution.

Now consider a dirty good importer. Freer trade leads to a fall in the domestic price of the dirty good, and the conventional demand and supply effects tend to reduce pollution. But a fall in the price of the dirty good redistributes income away from Browns. The government responds to this political economy concern by shifting its pollution supply outward—that is, it dampens the trade-induced fall in pollution to cushion Browns from the competitive pressures of freer trade.

Overall we have shown that if the government responds to political pressures, then the effects of freer trade on the environment may indeed be influenced by political motives. If the income distribution is initially optimal (from the government's perspective), then we have shown that political economy motives lead the government to dampen the response of pollution to freer trade. This will partially insulate the losers from freer trade from increased international competition and tend to make pollution less responsive to freer trade than our simple representative agent model would predict.

4.5 Conclusion

Is free trade bad for the environment? One answer is that it depends on the policy regime: free trade does not causes environmental problems; bad environmental policy causes environmental problems. With the appropriate environmental policy regime in place, freer trade need not have any adverse effects on the environment. However, this may not be the most relevant question to ask. If we are willing to accept trade-offs between real income and environmental quality, then a trade liberalization that raises pollution and lowers environmental quality may well be welfare-enhancing. A trade liberalization that lowers pollution may be welfare-reducing. One of the primary messages of this chapter is that a trade liberalization that lowers pollution is not necessarily good, nor is one that raises it necessarily bad.

With efficient environmental policy, the classic case for free trade in a small economy emerges unscathed.[35] This is true whether pollution is regulated by taxes or an emission permit system, and true even though trade may lead to more pollution.

Although freer trade is always welfare-improving with efficient policy in place, we may still be interested in its effect on environmental outcomes. As we have shown, the effects of trade on the environment depend on a country's comparative advantage, and on the strength of income and substitution effects. If the income elasticity of the demand for environmental quality is not too high, then we expect that trade will improve the environment in countries with a comparative advantage in clean goods, and worsen the environment in countries with a comparative advantage in dirty goods. The trade-induced increase in

---

35. With heterogeneous agents, trade will typically benefit some agents at the expense of others, both via its effects on income distribution and via its effects on pollution levels. The argument that trade liberalization is welfare-improving in such an economy relies on the presence of lump-sum transfers—that is, the gainers can afford to compensate the losers. See Dixit and Norman 1980 for a discussion of standard gains-from-trade results.

pollution in dirty good exporters arises because the increase in potential income from polluting industries raises the opportunity cost of marginal improvements in the environment.

In reality, trade occurs between countries that have imperfect environmental policy even in the long run. If we do not reform environmental policy when we liberalize trade, then trade liberalization may well exacerbate environmental problems. In some cases, the effects can be severe; in others further trade can be benign. The net result depends both on a country's comparative advantage and on the policy instruments in place.

The case of fixed emission intensities is probably not an unreasonable approximation of actual environmental policy in many countries, at least in the short run. With fixed emission intensities, we expect that trade liberalization will reduce production-generated pollution in countries with a comparative advantage in clean goods, and increase production-generated pollution in countries with a comparative advantage in dirty goods. If emission intensities are both rigid and too lax, trade liberalization may indeed be bad for the environment and welfare in dirty good exporters. The increased environmental damage may more than offset the income gains from trade.

In some cases, rigid environmental policy can actually help to insulate a country's environment from the effects of freer trade. When there are rigid and binding pollution quotas in place, free trade must raise welfare even if the existing policy is excessively lenient. There are two ways to interpret this result. One is to take the model literally and think of policy as fixing the number of permits and then auctioning them off. Alternatively we could imagine that for every fixed level of emission permits there is a resulting level of ambient concentrations within cities in the country. Therefore, putting a ceiling on ambient concentrations in metropolitan areas is much like having a fixed pollution quota. And as we have shown, liberalizing trade in this case will always bring benefits.

Therefore a safe pro-free-trade position would be one where we measure the level of environmental quality prior to trade and require governments provide no worse than that after trade. While this is a safe position, it is of course not costless. It may be the case that the individuals in this country would prefer the trade-off of more real income for lessened environmental quality.

If governments are responsive to the environment, but also responsive to pressure groups, there is an additional channel through which trade can affect the environment. These political economy elements have an impact that differs across countries according to their trade pattern. For example, suppose politically powerful groups are concentrated in the industries that produce dirty goods. If this country imports the dirty good, then trade liberalization will lower the returns to dirty good producers. To compensate them, the government may lower its pollution tax. Alternatively, if the dirty good is exported, the government may instead raise its pollution tax and lower pollution. This suggests that political economy motives may act so as to dampen the environmental effects of trade liberalization.

A key question for policymakers is whether trade policy should be conducted under the premise that environmental policy will be available to deal with any environmental problems exacerbated by free trade; or instead whether an explicit second-best approach should be adopted in which trade policy is conducted in a framework that recognizes the failures of environmental policy. The costs of the former depend on the impact a trade liberalization will have on pollution levels, and as we have emphasized repeatedly, this in turn depends upon a nation's comparative advantage. Therefore, in the next chapter we start to investigate the determinants of comparative advantage.

5   Pollution Haven Models of International Trade

In 1986, the barge *Khian Sea* left Philadelphia carrying 15,000 tons of incinerator ash. After being thwarted by strict local environmental regulations and public hostility toward hazardous waste sites in the United States, a waste contractor sent the barge off to look for a country with weaker environmental regulations. The search was ultimately futile, as all attempts to unload the cargo in foreign ports (mainly in low-income countries) were rebuffed.[1] But for many environmentalists, this well-publicized odyssey was just one more example of how international trade allows a rich country to avoid responsibility for the environmental consequences of its high consumption by shifting its pollution to another country.

In fact, only a rather small fraction of global waste is traded. But waste itself need not be shipped for trade to shift pollution from rich to poor countries. Instead, trade may encourage polluting production processes to move to regions with weak environmental policy. Rather than reducing consumption or increasing abatement activity, rich consumers can have both a clean environment and affluent consumption by importing pollution-intensive goods from elsewhere. In other words, trade may create pollution havens. Pockets of polluting industries may emerge in countries with weak environmental policy, while the rest of the world enjoys a clean environment by specializing in environmentally benign production activities.[2]

---

1. Eventually the cargo mysteriously disappeared, with much speculation that it was dumped at sea.
2. This chapter will focus on pollution havens induced by relatively weak environmental policy. Copeland and Taylor (1999) consider an alternative channel through which trade can result in a country having both low income and a concentration of dirty indus-

The purpose of this chapter is to investigate the economic logic be-hind pollution havens. We define a pollution haven as a region or coun-try with a concentration of pollution-intensive activity that has been in-duced by pollution policy that is weak relative to its trading partners.[3]

We first demonstrate how differences in pollution policy create a basis for trade. We consider not only cases where policy differences are exogenous, but also cases where they arise endogenously.[4] We show how pollution havens can arise when countries differ in income levels, when there are differences in institutions and when countries differ in their environments' carrying capacity. We focus on two key questions throughout the chapter. First, is trade driven by environmental policy differences necessarily bad for the environment? Second, what are the welfare effects of this trade—do rich countries benefit at the expense of poor countries?

Pollution haven models rest on two assumptions. The first is that differences in pollution regulation are a key determinant of production

---

try, even in a world with *ex ante* identical countries. If pollution from one industry harms another industry, then even in the absence of policy, the clean industry has an incentive to move away from the dirty industry. Trade can facilitate this separation of incompati-ble industries and lead to a concentration of dirty industry in one country. Moreover, because of the negative production externality, an expansion of the dirty industry lowers productivity in the clean industry and so in some cases, the country with a high concen-tration of dirty good production may suffer a real income loss from trade.

3. We consider both cases where pollution policy is efficient and where it is inefficient. Some authors prefer to use the term *pollution haven* only for cases where pollution policy is inefficiently low; that is where the shadow price of emissions is below marginal dam-age. We prefer to focus on the more general issue of trade driven by differences in pollu-tion policy, regardless of its efficiency. In addition, we will focus on pollution havens created by international trade and do not study foreign investment in this chapter. It is also possible for differences in pollution policy to cause foreign investment flows, and indeed one of the concerns of some environmentalists during the debate on NAFTA is that American firms in polluting industries would shift some of their capital to Mexico because of its weaker environmental regulations. Capital mobility would tend to amplify some of the effects that we study in this chapter. See Rauscher 1997, chap. 3, for a simple general equilibrium model where there is no trade, but where pollution policy induces capital movements. Markusen, Morey, and Olewiler (1995) study the issue in a partial equilibrium model with imperfect competition. Copeland (1994) investigates capital mo-bility in a small open economy model and shows how it amplifies output and pollution responses to pollution tax changes.

4. Pethig (1976) has perhaps the earliest pollution haven model—he considers the role of exogenous regulations in influencing trade patterns. Chichilnisky (1994) considers ex-ogenous differences in institutional capacity as a motive for trade—in her model, North internalizes environmental externalities while South does not. Copeland and Taylor (1994, 1995) consider endogenous income-induced policy differences as a motive for

costs and hence industry location. The second is that differences in regulation arise from inequality in the world distribution of income because protection for the environment is a normal good.[5] Of these, only the first is subject to much controversy. And hence in chapters 6 and 7, we will consider other motives for trade.

In this chapter we limit ourselves to models where trade is driven *only* by differences in policy to isolate the pollution haven effect. We eliminate other motives for trade by assuming that countries have identical technology, preferences, and capital/labor ratios. In reality, countries of course differ in many dimensions, and in chapter 6, we consider theoretical models that allow countries to differ in relative capital abundance.

To examine the pollution haven hypothesis more closely, we begin in sections 5.1 and 5.2 by considering trade driven by exogenous policy differences. Exogenous policy differences are useful to consider because they may be a reasonable approximation to short-run behavior, and because they provide us with some of the tools needed later in the chapter. Not surprisingly, we demonstrate that the country with weaker policy exports the dirty good and increases its dirty good output when trade is liberalized.[6] We also find, however, that the effects on pollution depend not just on the stringency of policy, but also on the type of policy instrument used. If trade is driven by exogenous differences in pollution taxes or emission intensities, then pollution rises in the country with weaker environmental policy and falls in the other country. In contrast, if trade is driven by differences in binding (and enforced) aggregate pollution quotas, then trade does not harm the environment.

We consider endogenous differences in pollution policy in section 5.3. We start with the most often cited reason for policy differences— income inequality at the country level. If two countries differ only in

---

trade. Rauscher (1997, chap. 5) also considers trade between countries where policy is endogenous.

5. It is well known that the world distribution of income is highly unequal. For a recent analysis of trends, see Bourguignon and Morrison 2001. There is a variety of evidence that environmental quality is a normal good, ranging from amenity value studies using hedonic techniques to contingent valuation studies. For direct evidence linking pollution regulation to income levels, see Hilton and Levinson 1998 and Pargal and Wheeler 1996.

6. This result relies on the absence of production externalities. Brander and Taylor (1997) show that this seemingly obvious result can be easily overturned if lax environmental policy leads to resource depletion in the long run.

their per capita income, then we find that the richer country will have more stringent pollution standards. Trade will therefore create a pollution haven in the poor country. Pollution rises in the poor South and falls in the rich North. Nevertheless, if pollution externalities are fully internalized, both countries must gain from trade, despite the increase in pollution in the poor country.

In section 5.4 we examine the impact of trade-induced pollution havens on world pollution levels. One of the concerns emanating from the pollution haven hypothesis is that trade not only allows Northern consumers to escape the pollution consequences of their own consumption, but also raises world pollution. As we show, these concerns may be justified. We demonstrate that world pollution can rise with trade even in situations where income growth in autarky would leave country and world pollution levels unchanged. The reason for the difference between the effects of growth and trade on global pollution is that trade reallocates the dirtiest good production to the country with weakest emission standards. This world composition effect tends to raise world pollution.

In section 5.5, we consider trade that arises from differences in assimilative capacity across countries. If all countries have efficient pollution policy in place, we demonstrate that pollution-intensive production will be drawn to the country with the most resilient environment because marginal damage is lower for any given level of physical pollution discharge. Trade leads to a concentration of polluting activity in the country with weaker policy, and so in this sense creates a pollution haven. But in this case, trade is good for the global environment, because it shifts polluting activity to the country with a more resilient environment.

Finally, in section 5.6, we consider the implications of differences in institutional capacity across countries as a motive for trade. If countries are otherwise identical, but one has institutions to regulate the environment, while the other has no such institutions, then trade will take place between these countries. Exogenous differences in institutional capacity can yield trade patterns very similar to our North-South model where income differences create asymmetries endogenously. This type of example has been used in the literature before, and there is often a presumption that the country that lacks pollution regulations will lose from trade. We show that this is indeed a possibility, but not a necessary outcome. Using a simple example, we show that even when these economies are otherwise identical—and hence would not trade in a first-best world where both have active policy—both may gain from trade.

5.1 Exogenous Policy Differences: Rigid Emission Intensities

We start by considering the implications of exogenous differences in pollution policy across countries. We divide the world into two regions—North and South—who together determine world prices. Each region is composed of many identical countries; that is, they have the same endowments, preferences, and technologies.[7] The only difference between regions is the stringency of their pollution policy. If pollution policies were identical across regions, then there would be no trade. Our objective here is to investigate the pure effects of trade induced by pollution policy. We continue to assume pollution has only local effects—it does not spill over international borders.

Recall that Y is the numeraire, so that $p_y = 1$, and denote the relative price of X by p. Let an asterisk (*) denote Southern variables. Therefore, τ denotes North's pollution tax, and τ^* denotes South's pollution tax (each measured in terms of good Y). Measured in terms of good X, the pollution taxes are τ/p and τ^*/p^*.

As our first example of exogenous policy differences, we assume that emission intensities are held constant.[8] From (2.16) in chapter 2, the emission intensity is $e = \alpha p/\tau$. This means that we are assuming each country holds constant the pollution tax measured in terms of X as trade is liberalized.

We assume that North has stricter pollution policy than South. Therefore, emissions intensities are higher in the South than in the North:

$$e < e^* \tag{5.1}$$

---

7. One can also think of this as a simple two-country model. We adopt the regional formulation, with each region having many identical countries, because we want to eliminate any strategic motive for manipulating pollution policy to influence a country's terms of trade.

8. As in chapter 4, when assuming that emission intensities are held constant, we continue to assume that they are implemented with pollution taxes, so that we are equivalently assuming that pollution taxes measured in terms of good X are held constant. One could do a similar analysis by assuming either that emission intensities themselves are the policy instrument and are held constant, or that the pollution taxes measured in terms of good Y are held constant. Qualitatively similar results will be obtained. We prefer the approach in the text because it yields the cleanest exposition.

From (2.16), this implies that

$$\frac{\tau}{p} > \frac{\tau^*}{p}. \tag{5.2}$$

And since both North and South will face the same prices in trade, this means Northern pollution taxes are always higher than Southern $\tau > \tau^*$.[9]

Other than (5.1), we make no restrictions on the levels of e or e^*. For example, we could have $e^* = 1$, with Southern firms not abating at all. And pollution policy may be either stricter or weaker than is optimal in either or both countries. Much of the concern over pollution havens arises from a belief that the South's current level of regulation is too low. While we will focus on that case, we will also examine other possibilities.

Comparative Advantage

To determine the North-South trade pattern, we need to determine autarky goods prices. As is common in the international trade literature, we do this by employing the relative supply and demand for goods. We assume that both regions have the same utility function as defined in chapter 2:

$$V(p, I, z) = v[I / \beta(p)] - h(z). \tag{5.3}$$

Because preferences over goods are identical and homothetic, the demand for X can be written as $b_x(p)I$, and the demand for Y as $b_y(p)I$, where the b_i depend only on p,[10] and I is national income for the relevant region. Note that b_x is decreasing in p, and b_y is increasing in p. The demand for X *relative* to Y must be independent of income, and we can write this as

$$RD(p) = \frac{b_x(p)}{b_y(p)}, \tag{5.4}$$

where $RD'(p) < 0$. Moreover, because preferences are identical across regions, the relative demand curve is the same in each country. This common relative demand is illustrated in figure 5.1 as the curve labeled RD.

---

9. Note it will also mean that pollution abatement costs as a fraction of value-added will always be higher in North than in South.
10. Note that the role of p_y has been suppressed since we set $p_y = 1$.

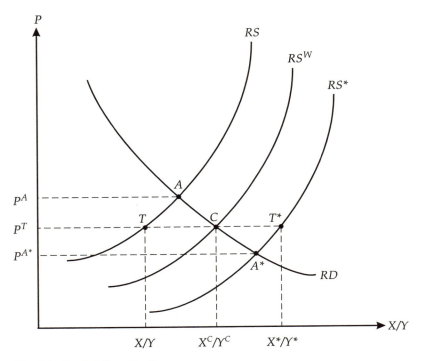

Fig. 5.1. Trade Liberalization

Next, we need to determine the relative supply curves for each country. To this end, we employ (2.21) and (2.43)–(2.46) to write equilibrium outputs as functions of endowments, the relative price of X, and the emissions intensity e:[11]

$$x = x\,(p, e, K, L),\qquad\qquad\qquad\qquad\qquad\qquad\quad (5.5)$$
$$y = y\,(p, e, K, L).$$

Because we have constant returns to scale, the supplies can be written as functions of K/L:

$$x = Lx\,(p, e, K/L, 1),\qquad\qquad\qquad\qquad\qquad\qquad (5.6)$$
$$y = Ly\,(p, e, K/L, 1).$$

The supply of X relative to Y (which we denote RS) is now obtained by dividing:

---

11. Note that we have previously written outputs as functions of the pollution tax, which is the policy variable. However, note from (2.43)–(2.46), that we can solve for outputs as a function of θ, which from (2.21) is equivalent to writing outputs as a function of e.

$$RS\,(p,\,e,\,K/L) = \frac{x\,(p,\,e,\,K/L,\,1)}{y\,(p,\,e,\,K/L,\,1)}\,. \tag{5.7}$$

Relative supply is increasing in p (that is, $RS_p > 0$). To verify this, use figure 2.2 and recall that holding e constant fixes the net production possibilities frontier in this diagram. Therefore, an increase in p raises the net producer price $q = p\,(1 - \alpha)$, and producers move along a given (net) frontier to produce relatively more X and less Y. Therefore, holding e constant, an increase in p stimulates X and contracts Y, yielding a standard upward sloping relative supply curve.

We can now compare the relative supply curves for our two regions. We have assumed North and South have the same endowments, and hence K/L is the same across regions. But North's pollution policy is stricter. Differentiating (5.7) with respect to the emissions intensity yields

$$\frac{\partial RS}{\partial e} > 0. \tag{5.8}$$

since an increase in the emissions intensity stimulates the X industry and contracts Y. This was illustrated in figure 2.5, where we investigated how a change in emission intensity, holding world prices constant, altered production of X and Y. We showed that a reduction in emission intensity led to a reduction in the relative supply of X. Therefore a region with the stricter pollution policy (i.e., lower e) produces relatively less X for any given p.

In figure 5.1, we have drawn the relative supply curve for the North, the South, and the world. From our analysis above we know North's relative supply, RS, must lie above and to the left of South's relative supply, RS^*, as illustrated. The world relative supply curve is just a weighted average of the relative supply curves of North and South because

$$RS^W = \frac{x + x^*}{y + y^*} = \frac{x}{y}\left[\frac{y}{y + y^*}\right] + \frac{x^*}{y^*}\left[\frac{y^*}{y + y^*}\right] = \lambda RS + (1 - \lambda)\,RS^*. \tag{5.9}$$

where $\lambda = y/(y + y^*)$.

We can now compare autarky prices. Since relative demand RD is independent of income, it is the same in both autarky and trade. Consequently, autarky relative prices are determined by the intersection of a region's relative supply with the common RD, as shown. From the intersections at A and A^* we can now conclude the autarky relative price of X is higher in the North than in the South:

$$p^A > p^{A*}, \qquad\qquad\qquad\qquad\qquad\qquad (5.10)$$

where A denotes autarky.

The intuition is straightforward. Because North taxes pollution more heavily, relatively less of the polluting good is produced there. The ensuing relative scarcity of X in turn pushes up its relative price. Therefore, using autarky relative prices as our guide, South has a comparative advantage in the dirty good and North a comparative advantage in the clean good.

International Trade

Figure 5.1 illustrates how differences in pollution policy alone can generate trade. If North and South had the same pollution policy, the relative supply curves of the two regions would coincide, autarky prices would be identical, and there would be no trade. With differences in pollution policy, X is relatively expensive in the North. The country with the stricter pollution policy has a comparative advantage in the clean good, and this will generate trade. Northerners will import X from the South, and Southerners will import Y from the North.

To illustrate the trading equilibrium, note that in free trade, the world relative demand must be equal to world relative supply. The equilibrium free trade relative price of X is p^T, which lies between the two autarky prices. Consumption is at point C.

In the North, trade leads to a decline in the relative price of X from p^A to p^T and an ensuing fall in X/Y. In figure 5.1, this change in North's production is captured by the movement down along its relative supply curve from A to T. It is apparent from our earlier use of figure 2.2 that not only does relative supply of X fall, but the overall production of the dirty good falls, while the overall production of the clean good rises. In the South just the opposite occurs.[12] The relative price of X rises from P^{A*} to P^T, which stimulates the polluting industry at the expense of the clean industry. As illustrated, South moves upwards along its supply curve from A^* to T^*. Similarly, Southern production of X rises, while that of Y falls. Therefore, free trade leads the South to change the composition of its output toward specialization in dirty good production.

---

12. Trade creates both composition and scale effects but no technique effect (because we assume e is held fixed). For both North and South the change in pollution is determined by the direction of the composition effect; scale effects either work in the same direction as the composition effect (for the South) or are small relative to the composition effect (for the North).

While outputs in North and South move in different directions as a result of trade, consumption ratios must converge as shown from A and A^* to C. Since preferences are identical and homothetic, and since consumers in both regions face a common world price in free trade, consumption ratios must be the same in free trade, as indicated by point C with X^C/Y^C. Therefore, trade in commodities must make up for the gap between consumption and production ratios. Since North's relative production of X/Y is less than its consumption X^C/Y^C, North is importing X and exporting Y; conversely, since Southern relative production of X/Y is higher than X^C/Y^C, it exports X and imports Y. We have found a pollution haven pattern of trade.

What happens to pollution? If we use (5.5), pollution demand can be written as a function of e, world prices, and endowments:

$$z = ex\,(p, e, K, L).\tag{5.11}$$

Since e is held fixed by our assumption of rigid policy, pollution supply is flat. That is, the economy is willing to supply an unlimited amount of pollution as long as production occurs with emissions per unit output fixed at e. Therefore, the exogenous emission intensity e together with pollution demand in (5.11) determines equilibrium pollution z.

Because emissions intensities are unaffected by trade, pollution must move in the same direction as does dirty good output. From figure 5.1 we know that p falls with trade for the North. This shifts its pollution demand inwards and lowers pollution. Conversely, p rises with trade in the South. This shifts its pollution demand outwards and raises pollution. Hence we conclude that when trade is motivated only by exogenous differences in emission intensities, pollution rises with trade in the country with weak pollution policy (here the South), and falls in the country with strict pollution policy (here the North). Trade induced by pollution policy differences creates a pollution haven in the country with weaker policy.[13]

The Welfare Effects of Trade

To examine the welfare consequences of trade, we proceed much as we did before when we considered trade liberalization in chapter 4. Indirect utility for our representative consumer is given by (5.3). Totally differentiating and rearranging, we obtain

---

13. World pollution will also rise in some circumstances. See our example in section 5.4.

$$\frac{dV}{V_I} = - mdp + [\tau - MD\,(p,\,R,\,z)]\,dz. \qquad (5.12)$$

where m is imports of X. Although we are considering a discrete change in the trade regime, the above expression applies at all points along the path from autarky to free trade, and can therefore be used to infer the welfare effects of trade liberalization.

Trade liberalization has two impacts on consumer welfare: there are standard gains from trade ($-mdp$); there is the welfare effect of the change in pollution $((\tau - MD)\,dz)$. Both countries obtain increased consumption opportunities via the standard gains from trade, but because pollution falls in the North and rises in the South, the net welfare effects of trade liberalization may be different across the two countries.

First consider the North. In the North, $m > 0$ since the dirty good X is imported. And moreover, $dp < 0$, since the price of X falls with trade liberalization in the North. Hence $-mdp > 0$, reflecting standard gains from trade along the trade liberalization path.

The second effect of trade liberalization in the North is that pollution falls. If pollution regulation in the North is too weak, so that $\tau < MD$, then North obtains a double dividend from trade liberalization: it gains access to cheaper Southern supplies of X, and its environmental quality improves. Hence North must gain from trade. If instead, North's pollution regulation is efficient, then the fall in pollution has no first-order welfare effects. However, North still reaps consumption gains from trade. The only possibility for North to lose from trade is if regulation was too tight to begin with. If $\tau > MD$ at the autarky level of pollution, then the reduction in pollution created by trade would actually lower Northern welfare, but again this would need to be set against the typical gains from trade.

Let us now turn to the South. South achieves standard gains from trade via access to higher prices in Northern markets for exports of its X production. Since South exports X, we have $m < 0$; and since the price of X rose in the movement from autarky to trade, we have $dp > 0$. Therefore, the gains-from-trade term given by $-mdp > 0$ is necessarily positive here as well.

But pollution rises in the South. Hence if South's pollution tax is below marginal damage ($\tau < MD$), we have $(\tau - MD)\,dz < 0$. The increased pollution tends to lower Southern welfare. South will lose from trade liberalization if the damage from increased pollution more than offsets the benefits of increased goods consumption. This will happen if environmental damage is severe enough and the shift in Southern production large enough.[14]

We conclude that if trade is driven only by exogenous differences in emission intensities, then trade may indeed create a pollution haven in the country with weaker pollution regulations. The country that becomes a pollution haven may lose from trade if pollution is sufficiently damaging, while the country with stricter pollution regulations gains both from increased consumption and improved environmental quality. Losses from trade arise from trade shifting the composition of output in the South toward dirtier industries.[15]

5.2 Exogenous Policy Differences: Marketable Permit Systems

In the previous section, relatively weak pollution taxes (or emission intensities) led to the creation of a pollution haven, trade-induced environmental degradation, and possible welfare losses from trade. In this section, we again consider trade between regions that differ only in their environmental regulation, but now consider a pollution permit system. Once again, differences in policy alone will create trade, but in contrast to the case of pollution taxes, trade will always be welfare improving and need not cause any increased environmental damage.

The Pollution Permit Market

North and South are assumed to be identical except for differences in the allowed level of pollution.[16] Each country implements its pollution policy by issuing a fixed number of pollution permits. We assume that North has a more restrictive pollution policy than South, and hence with a permit system this implies

$$z < z^*, \tag{5.13}$$

where z and z^* represent the inelastic permit supplies available in North and South respectively.

---

14. Alternatively, if Southern regulation was either overly stringent or just stringent enough, then the South must gain from trade.
15. The empirical literature contains many studies examining changes in the composition of dirty good output in developing countries. See, for example, Low and Yeats 1992; Mani and Wheeler 1997; and Xu 1999.
16. Pethig (1976) briefly considers a model where exogenous differences in the supply of pollution permits determined trade.

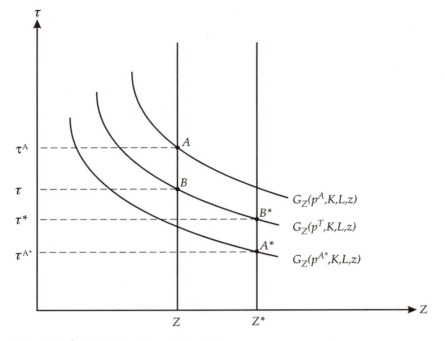

Fig. 5.2. The Pollution Permit Market

The demand for permits comes from firms who must buy a pollution permit for each unit of pollution emitted. Because North and South are identical except for their supply of pollution permits, both North and South share the same pollution demand curve.

This policy regime is illustrated in figure 5.2. In the figure we have drawn three pollution demand curves together with North's and South's (inelastic) pollution supplies. These demand curves differ because they are evaluated at different prices: $p^{A^*} < p^T < p^A$.

We need to derive the relative supply and demand for goods to determine the pattern of trade. As before, relative demand, RD, is the same across countries because preferences over goods consumption are identical and homothetic. To determine relative supply, we have to ask how the supply of X relative to Y will differ between North and South for any given level of the world price p that is common across countries.

Referring to figure 5.2, consider first the "middle" pollution demand curve indexed by the price p^T. Suppose both countries face the same given world price p^T. Then since North and South have identical pollution demands, equilibrium in the permit markets would occur at points B and B^* in North and South, respectively. The market clearing equilibrium permit prices would be τ and τ^*. North's permit price must exceed the South's because North's supply of pollution permits is smaller. Therefore, using (2.16), we can conclude that $e < e^*$. North's emissions per unit of output are less than South's. We can therefore again employ (5.8) to conclude that when both countries face the goods price p^T, North's relative supply is to the left of South's.

Since a similar analysis holds for any given p, we conclude that for any given goods price p, North's relative supply of goods lies to the left of South's. Consequently, the relative supply and demand curves look much the same as in figure 5.1.[17]

Comparative Advantage, Trade, and Welfare

Using figure 5.1, we conclude that the autarky relative price of a dirty good is higher in the North than in the South. South's abundance of pollution permits creates a basis for trade. Consequently, when trade opens, South will export dirty goods and North will export clean goods. Free trade has led the South to shift the composition of its output toward the dirty good, while the composition of North's output shifts toward the clean good. On the surface, it looks like trade is generating a pollution haven in the South.

A key difference from our earlier analysis, however, is the effect of trade on pollution. With a fixed supply of pollution permits, Northern and Southern pollution levels are unaffected by trade. With trade, the derived demand for pollution falls in the North and rises in the South. But unlike the case of fixed taxes, there is no change in the level of pollution in either country as long as the pollution quotas are binding. Instead of a change in pollution, there is a convergence in pollution permit prices.

We can illustrate this convergence in figure 5.2 with a slight reinterpretation of the diagram. Let p^A and p^{A^*} denote the autarky relative prices of X in North and South, respectively, and let p^T denote the equilibrium free trade price. Northern pollution demand falls as trade liberalizes because North has a comparative advantage in the clean good.

---

17. The relative supplies are not identical to those we found before. With e fixed, pollution levels increase as we move up each country's relative supply; with z fixed, emissions per unit of output falls as we move up each country's relative supply. This has no bearing on our results here.

This can be represented by shifting the highest pollution demand in this figure—indexed by p^A—to the middle one indexed by p^T. With trade, the real price of a pollution permit falls in the North, as the X industry contracts there. Emissions per unit of output in the North rise with trade. Similarly, autarky prices were lower in the South prior to trade, and hence its pollution demand shifts out with trade. This can be represented by the shift from the lowest pollution demand indexed by p^{A*} to the one indexed by p^T. In the South the real pollution tax rises as the X industry expands there. It is interesting to note that even though South's composition of output moves toward more dirty good production, its techniques of production become cleaner. Similarly, although North sheds dirty goods in trade, its pollution per unit of output rises with trade and its techniques become dirtier.

The welfare consequences of trade follow directly from (5.12). Because the supply of permits is fixed, we have $dz = 0$. Hence for both North and South we have

$$\frac{dV}{V_I} = -m\,dp > 0. \tag{5.14}$$

That is, the only effect of trade liberalization on welfare is via the standard gains from trade.[18] In the North, $m > 0$ since X is imported, and $dp < 0$, since the price of X falls with trade. Hence $-m\,dp > 0$, and North gains from trade. The South also gains because it exports X and the price of X rises there with trade.

Rigid Policy: Summary

Our analysis with rigid policy, although simple, has produced several results worth reinforcing. First, one important lesson is that trade induced by different and inefficient policy across regions need not be harmful to the environment in either country. It is not just the stringency of the policy that matters, but also the type of policy. Trade in the presence of policies such as rigid pollution taxes or restrictions on emissions intensities can potentially be harmful because pollution may

---

18. The effects of trade liberalization in the presence of pollution quotas was discussed in chapter 4, and the references there are relevant here as well. The result that trade liberalization does not exacerbate pollution distortions in the presence of pollution quotas is similar to Falvey's (1988) result that a trade liberalization in one sector does not exacerbate trade distortions in sectors protected by import quotas. Copeland (1994) stud-

rise with trade. But if pollution policy instead caps allowable emissions, then even if these caps are very lax, trade cannot increase harm to the environment as long as the caps are binding and enforced. In fact, trade will raise welfare by equalizing marginal production costs across regions.[19]

A second observation is that dirty industry migration can be a partial remedy for environmental policy failures. Note that in the pollution permit case, the South was already a pollution haven prior to trade in the sense that it had higher pollution than North because of weak environmental policy. And when trade barriers fell, South's relatively lax policy induced trade, which attracted even more dirty industry to the South. But this trade did not harm the environment; instead it raised welfare. Trade is welfare improving in this case precisely because environmental policy was distorted. To see this, note that in this example trade only occurs between regions because of differences in pollution policy. Because these regions are otherwise identical, they should choose identical policies in the first best equilibrium, and hence there would be no trade. The policy-induced trade here is a second-best welfare-improving response to inefficient pollution policy. Trade in this case creates gains because it improves allocative efficiency without harming the environment.

A third lesson is that international trade has a very different impact on these countries because of their differences in comparative advantage. In the North, the derived demand for pollution falls with the advent of trade, while in the South it rises. Consequently, trade per se does not have a unidirectional impact on pollution levels. Consequently, empirical work trying to identify the impact of trade on pollution flows needs to distinguish between dirty good exporters and dirty good importers. In addition, our simple pollution permit example

---

ies the interaction between trade distortions and pollution distortions and finds that pollution quotas help to prevent pollution distortions from being exacerbated by trade.

19. The result that welfare gains from trade liberalization are guaranteed when pollution policy is implemented with quotas, but not guaranteed when taxes are used, does *not* imply that pollution quotas are necessarily superior to pollution taxes. We are dealing here with a second-best world where we attempt to alleviate one distortion (trade barriers) while at the same time doing nothing proactive about other distortions (pollution). If pollution policy could be simultaneously reformed, then the distortion exacerbation issue would not arise. In addition, we are abstracting from other issues, such as uncertainty, information asymmetries, and market power, that influence the relative efficiency of taxes and quotas. See Weitzman 1974 for an analysis of the choice between taxes and quotas.

showed how the South may alter the composition of output toward dirty goods, export dirty goods in trade, and be dirtier than the North (both pre- and post-trade) but still gain from trade. A simple empirical finding that the composition of South's production is becoming dirtier over time does not mean the South loses from trade—even if the South is known to have extremely lax pollution regulations.

A final point of note concerns the relationship we found between the price of pollution permits and the pattern of trade. In the permit trade case, figure 5.2 shows how trade in final goods drives pollution permit prices closer together. This occurs because in autarky the South is relatively abundant in pollution permits and scarce in productive capacity. This difference makes pollution a relatively cheap input in the South and productive capacity more expensive. Instead of trading pollution directly, the South exports goods that embody pollution services intensively and by doing so they substitute trade in goods for direct trade in pollution services. Therefore trade raised the value of pollution services in one economy and lowered them in another thereby moving emission per unit output closer together. That is, international trade has led to a partial harmonization of emission intensities.

5.3 Endogenous Pollution Havens

We now examine the emergence of pollution havens in a world where pollution policy is flexible. We adopt a specification where North-South income differences lead to different pollution policies. That is, exogenous income differences will create endogenous differences in pollution policy and a motive for trade.

Perhaps the most important reason for examining the implications of flexible policy is that analysis of trade liberalization with rigid policy is incomplete. If the differences in environmental policy that create pollution havens are ultimately driven by differences in income, and if freer trade affects national incomes, then we would expect that there would be a feedback from the change in trade regime to environmental policy. In this section, we want to capture this feedback effect.

While it is relatively easy to generate a North-South pattern of trade by assuming exogenous policy differences, endogenous policy creates two new problems. The first is simply that countries may have a motivation to manipulate pollution policy in an attempt to improve their terms of trade (for example a country importing X might try to lower the world price of X by reducing its pollution tax to stimulate the supply of X).[20] We will assume this difficulty away by adopting assumptions that render our country small in world markets.[21] That is, we assume that North and South are each composed of many small countries; and for simplicity, we assume that countries within each region are identical.

The second problem is the simultaneity of policy formation and trading outcomes: policy differences create trade, but trade alters policy. This simultaneity can easily lead to a mess of uninformative algebra. In our earlier work (Copeland and Taylor 1994), we avoided this by adopting a set of simplifying functional form assumptions on production and utility. While that analysis was useful, some of the assumptions ruled out possibilities that we would now like to explore. In the present chapter, we adopt more general functional form assumptions.[22]

To ensure that income differences are the only basis for trade, we assume regions differ in the most minimal way. We let North's endowments be larger than South's by a factor $\lambda > 1$: that is, $K = \lambda K^*$, $L = \lambda L^*$. Since we have already normalized their (common) populations to one, $\lambda > 1$ implies North's workforce is more highly skilled than South's. Our assumption renders North uniformly richer than South without introducing additional motivations for trade. Moreover, it dovetails nicely with part of our analysis in chapter 6, where we take the opposite tack by assuming that incomes are identical and countries differ only in the composition of their factor endowments.

The Pattern of Trade

To generate predictions on the pattern of trade we start by examining the effects of income differences on relative pollution taxes. Although

---

20. Tariffs are the first-best instrument to use to target the terms of trade. However, if there is a free trade agreement that precludes the use of trade policy, then large countries may look to other sorts of policy to use as a substitute for trade barriers. There is a large literature examining the strategic manipulation of tariffs and/or pollution policy in order to influence the terms of trade. Markusen (1976) is the seminal work in this area—he considered first- and second-best policies in a simple general equilibrium trade model with pollution. In the 1990s, a number of papers examined strategic environmental policy in models with imperfect competition using an adaptation of the Brander-Spencer (1985) model. Early papers exploring this approach were Barrett 1994; Conrad 1993; Kennedy 1994; and Ulph 1996. See Ulph 1997 for a review of this work.
21. In Copeland and Taylor 1995 we explicitly consider the effects of trade liberalization in the context of large countries that actively affect their terms of trade.
22. However, we restrict ourselves here to a model with two goods, whereas we considered a continuum of goods in Copeland and Taylor 1994.

we are considering a world with endogenous world prices, each country is assumed to be small in the world economy and has no market power in trade. Therefore, it treats world prices as beyond its influence and hence its pollution tax is simply given by (2.81):

$$\tau = \frac{\beta\,(p)\,h'\,(z)}{v'\,[R]} = MD\,(p,\,R,\,z).\tag{5.14}$$

Countries choose environmental policy to internalize pollution externalities. Because marginal damage is increasing in real income, the country with the higher income has a greater willingness and ability to pay for improved environmental quality.

To determine the trade pattern we again need to construct relative supply and demand schedules. Relative demand is independent of income and pollution policy and so is the same as in the previous sections. The RD curve is the same as in figure 5.1.

The construction of relative supply is only slightly more complicated than previously. Because North is just a scaled-up version of South, we conclude from (5.7) that relative supplies will differ only if e and e^* differ (the K/L ratios are the same across countries by assumption). But since e and e^* are determined by pollution taxes and common world prices, our focus must then be on comparing Northern and Southern pollution taxes. To proceed, note that the equilibrium condition determining pollution in the North can be written as

$$\tau^D = G_z\,(p,\,\lambda K^*,\,\lambda L^*,\,z),$$
$$\tau^S = MD\,(p,\,G\,(p,\,\lambda K^*,\,\lambda L^*,\,z)\,/\,\beta\,(p),\,z),\tag{5.16}$$
$$\tau^D = \tau^S,$$

where τ^D and τ^S denote the pollution demand and supply curves. In the South a similar expression (with $\lambda = 1$) determines τ^* and z^*.

The key result we need is that pollution taxes are higher in the North than the South whenever they face a common goods price p. To demonstrate that $\tau > \tau^*$ whenever $\lambda > 1$, it suffices to show pollution taxes always rise with λ. Rather than differentiating (5.16), and then solving for the change in τ, we simply note that if both pollution demand and supply shift upwards with λ, then pollution taxes must rise. Holding z constant, the vertical shift in pollution demand as λ rises is given by

$$d\tau^D = (G_{zk}\,K + G_{zL}\,L)\,d\lambda > 0,$$

where the inequality follows because pollution demand is homogenous of degree zero in $\{K,\,L,\,Z\}$ and concave in factor endowments. That is,

$$G_{zk} K + G_{zl} L = - G_{zz} z > 0.$$

Hence the pollution demand curve in the North is higher than in the South. North's larger productive capacity gives it a higher demand for pollution.

The vertical shift in pollution supply is simply

$$d\tau^S = \frac{MD_R}{\beta(p)} (G_K K + G_L L) \, d\lambda \geq 0, \tag{5.18}$$

which is also positive because marginal damage is nondecreasing in real income. That is, North's higher income increases the willingness to pay for environmental quality, and with efficient policy, the pollution supply curve shifts up (reflecting a fall in the willingness to allow pollution).

Consequently, because higher incomes shift the pollution supply and demand curves vertically upward, pollution taxes must be higher in North than South for any given goods price p. This then implies that for any given goods price p, we have $e < e^*$. Referring to (5.7), we conclude that North's relative supply must be to the left of South's as before. More formally we have shown

$$\frac{dRS}{d\lambda} = \frac{\partial RS}{\partial e} \frac{\partial e}{\partial \tau} \frac{\partial \tau}{\partial \lambda} < 0. \tag{5.19}$$

With this result in hand, our analysis proceeds much as before: the equilibrium again looks much like figure 5.1. North's relative supply curve is above South's and therefore the autarky price of X is higher in the North than in the South. North's high income gives it a comparative advantage in the clean good. When trade is opened, North will export the clean good (Y) and import the dirty good (X). The polluting industry will contract in the North and expand in the South.

To determine the impact of trade on national pollution levels, we start by recalling our results linking trade liberalization with pollution levels in chapter 4. We found that trade liberalization must reduce pollution in a country that imports the pollution-intensive good. For a dirty good importer, the sum of scale, composition, and technique effects is always negative. This conclusion does not rest on the marginal analysis we employed in chapter 4 to derive our results. A discrete change in prices—arising from a movement from autarky to free trade—would shift pollution demand and supply in a similar way, ensuring a fall in pollution. Therefore, we can conclude pollution in the North must fall with free trade.

In the South, the results are less clear-cut. In chapter 4 we found that a marginal trade liberalization increases pollution in a dirty good exporter unless the income elasticity of marginal damage was quite large. A discrete change in prices is difficult to examine since each marginal step is itself ambiguous. However, if the income elasticity of marginal damage is less than 1 everywhere along the path of liberalization from autarky to free trade, then pollution must rise in the South.

Welfare-Improving Pollution Havens?

We have already shown that with exogenous differences in pollution policy, a country that becomes a pollution haven can lose from trade. Losses occur as trade alters the composition of output, and thereby raises pollution—which was incorrectly priced to begin with. With optimal policy, Southern production again shifts toward dirty good production and pollution again rises. But the resulting change in pollution cannot cause welfare losses. Recall that the welfare effects of trade liberalization are given by

$$\frac{dV}{V_I} = -\, mdp + [\tau - MD\,(p,\,R,\,z)]\,dz. \tag{5.20}$$

The first term is the standard gains-from-trade effect, which is always positive in both countries. The second term is the welfare effect of trade on pollution. With *optimal* policy, $\tau = MD$, and the second term disappears. Despite the increase in pollution in the South, trade liberalization in the presence of optimal pollution policy must always be welfare increasing for both countries.

The result that both countries always gain from trade despite the concentration of polluting activities in the South is critically dependent on the assumption that externalities are fully internalized. In practice, this may be difficult to achieve, because of reasons of political economy sketched in chapter 4, or because of the complexity of information or the regulatory costs required to implement efficient policy. Full internalization means that the pollution tax must reflect all adverse costs of environmental damage, including effects that are notoriously hard to measure, such as the effects on future generations, long-run effects on the ecosystem, and effects on biodiversity and wilderness conservation.[23] The South could lose from trade if any of these damage costs are not internalized.

This result, however, does not depend on whether governments use pollution taxes or quotas. All that matters is that policy be implemented efficiently. We saw earlier that with exogenous policy, trade increased pollution in the South under a tax regime but not in a permit regime, and that the welfare effects of trade liberalization varied across regimes. With endogenous policy, however, an efficient policymaker will optimally adjust either the pollution tax or the supply of pollution permits to reflect the trade-off between environmental quality and consumption goods. Any equilibrium that can be supported with a tax system can also be supported with a permit system.[24] This means that if the policy regime is efficient, then the choice between a permit regime and a tax regime can be driven by criteria other than the possible effects of trade liberalization. However, if policy is expected to be rigid or respond to trade liberalization with a lag, then the two regimes are not equivalent, and the prospect of trade liberalization will become an important factor in policy choice.

The Basis for Trade

Our model predicts trade flows based on policy differences, and policy differences based on income differences. Despite these features, it is in many ways a model where factor endowments determine trade patterns. Although capital/labor ratios are the same across countries, there is a third factor hidden in the background—the carrying capacity of the environment—that is implicitly fixed and equal in size across both North and South. This is because a unit of pollution emitted in either North or South creates the same disutility for its citizens. Since carrying capacity soaks up, dissipates, and lessens the impact of industrial pollution, our symmetric specification of pollution damages assumes equal carrying capacity across countries.

Therefore, when we increase the productive ability of North, we are essentially making environmental services a relatively scarce factor in the North. Its relative price rises. If environmental services could be

---

23. Uncertainty and lack of information about pollution's effects does not imply policy is too lax. We need to go further and argue that in the face of imperfect information there is a status quo bias leading to suboptimally low regulation.
24. This equivalence result requires that there be no uncertainty, complete information, and no strategic behavior.

directly traded, North would try to import them from the South. But environmental services are a nontradable good, as are the services of immobile capital and labor. Instead, environmental services are embodied in goods trade. When North buys goods from the South, South is exporting environmental services embodied in its goods to the North in exchange for the imports of services of capital and labor embodied in Northern goods. North imports goods that use environmental services intensively—dirty goods; while South does just the opposite by importing goods that use North's abundant productive capacity intensively—clean goods. As long as optimal policy ensures factor services are used efficiently in both countries, both countries gain from this exchange.

A similar motive for trade arises when countries have similar productive capacities but their environments have different abilities to deal with pollution. We discuss this possibility in section 5.5.

5.4 Global Pollution and the World Composition Effect

Thus far we have shown how trade creates asymmetries between North and South in their environmental outcomes. But since pollution rises in one country and falls in the other, the question of how trade affects total pollution generated in the world naturally arises.[25] Indeed, part of the pollution haven rhetoric is that Northern consumers are escaping their environmental responsibilities by importing dirty goods from the South *and* by driving world pollution upwards.

The impact of free trade on global pollution levels relies on three factors: the existing income distribution, the strength of policy responses, and the extent of specialization in dirty goods. In our framework only the first two can be altered exogenously, while the third, the extent of specialization, is determined endogenously as a function of the first two. Consequently in this section we focus on how the strength of policy responses and the world income distribution affects the environmental effects of trade.

---

25. We are considering only local pollution in our model. The issue we are focusing on here is whether the sum of emissions in the North and South rise or fall with trade. This allows us to get at the issue of whether trade simply shifts environmental damage from rich to poor countries, or whether the reduction in environmental damage in rich countries is more than offset (in physical terms) by increased environmental damage elsewhere. Copeland and Taylor (1995) consider a model with global pollution, and in that case the issue of whether trade raises or lowers global pollution has welfare significance for both North and South.

Let $\varphi_x^* \equiv x^*/(x + x^*)$; that is, φ_x^* is the fraction of global X output produced in the South. Similarly, $\varphi_x = 1 - \varphi_x^*$ is the fraction of X produced in the North. Then we can write global pollution as

$$z^w = [e\varphi_x + e^*\varphi_x^*] \, x^W,$$

where x^w is global output of x. Global pollution depends on the average emissions intensity and the scale of the polluting industry.

Taking logs and totally differentiating, we obtain

$$\hat{z}^W = \frac{e^* - e}{e\varphi_x + e^*\varphi_x^*} \, d\varphi_x^* + \frac{\varphi_x de + \varphi_x^* de^*}{e\varphi_x + e^*\varphi_x^*} + \hat{x}^W. \tag{5.21}$$

Trade affects pollution via composition, scale, and technique effects. Because trade shifts the polluting industry to the country with weaker pollution policy ($e^* > e$), the composition effect tends to increase world pollution. In addition, we have a technique effect, given by the second term in (5.21). Emission intensities fall in the North and rise in the South. If trade reduces average emission intensities, then this technique effect would tend to lower pollution. And finally, trade will alter the scale of X production. If trade increases world output of X, then this scale effect would tend to increase pollution. The net effect of trade on global pollution depends on the interaction between these three effects.

The Constant Elasticity Case

To gain more insight into how trade affects global pollution, we make three simplifications to clarify the factors determining the relative strength of scale, technique, and composition effects.

First, we assume preferences over consumption are Cobb-Douglas. This assumption ensures that the share of world income spent on the dirty good is a constant in both autarky and trade. Therefore it allows us to focus on the pollution consequences of trade created by altering the composition of production *across* countries.[26]

---

26. Interested readers can investigate the role played by the elasticity of substitution between goods, but we suspect little is to be gained by doing so. While trade will surely affect the share of dirty goods in consumption by altering relative prices, relative prices move in different directions for both North and South. Therefore, the results would depend not only on the elasticity of substitution between clean and dirty goods but also the relative size of North and South, and the extent to which free trade prices differ from autarky prices.

Second, we assume constant marginal disutility of pollution. This assumption appears to be innocuous.[27] Its purpose is to give us closed form solutions for pollution in autarky and trade that we can readily compare.

Finally, in order for us to vary the strength of the policy response parametrically, we adopt the CRRA utility function for goods consumption. Combining these assumptions yields a utility function of the form

$$V = \frac{R^{1-\eta}}{1 - \eta} - \gamma z, \tag{5.22}$$

where $\eta > 0$, $R = I / \beta\,(p)$ is real income as before, and $\beta\,(p) = p^b b^{-b}\,(1 - b)^{-(1-b)}$ is the exact price index for Cobb-Douglas preferences, with b being the fraction of income spent on the dirty good.

Following our standard derivation, the optimal pollution tax in this case becomes

$$\tau = MD = \frac{\gamma I}{R^{1-\eta}} = \gamma \beta^{1-\eta} I^\eta. \tag{5.23}$$

Since we are interested in the difference between pollution in autarky and trade, we proceed by using (2.16) and (5.23) to note that pollution in the North can be written as

$$z = \frac{apx}{\tau} = \frac{as_x R^{1-\eta}}{\gamma}, \tag{5.24}$$

where $s_x = px / G$ is the value share of X production in national income.

In autarky, the share of X in production and consumption must be the same; hence $s_x = b$. Using (5.24), pollution in autarky in the North, the South, and the world is therefore

$$z^A = \frac{ab}{\gamma} R^{1-\eta}, \quad z^{*A} = \frac{ab}{\gamma} R^{*\,1-\eta} \tag{5.25}$$

$$z^{WA} = \frac{ab}{\gamma} [R^{1-\eta} + R^{*\,1-\eta}]$$

Note how pollution in autarky rises, falls, or stays constant with real income depending on whether η is less than, equal to, or greater than 1. In the absence of trade, an increase in real income corresponds to

---

economic growth, and as we saw in chapter 3, the effects of growth on pollution are critically dependent on the income elasticity of marginal damage, η.[28]

We want to compare autarky pollution with free trade pollution. World pollution in free trade is obtained by adding up (5.24) across North and South, with each evaluated at their free trade levels. This yields

$$z^{WT} = \frac{\alpha}{\gamma} (s_x R_T^{1-\eta} + s_x^* R_T^{*1-\eta}). \tag{5.26}$$

where s_x and s_x^* are the free trade shares of X in national income in North and South, respectively, in free trade. The difference between pollution in trade and autarky is then obtained by subtracting (5.25) from (5.26):

$$z^{WT} - z^{WA} = \frac{\alpha}{\gamma} [(s_x R_T^{1-\eta} + s_x^* R_T^{*1-\eta}) - b (R^{1-\eta} + R^{*1-\eta})]. \tag{5.27}$$

To interpret (5.27), we need to exploit the relation between production and consumption shares of X. Market clearing requires that world production of X must equal world consumption, and world consumption of X must be a fraction b of world income. Using superscript c to denote consumption levels, we have

$$px + px^* = px^c + px^{c*} = b (I + I^*). \tag{5.28}$$

Rearranging, we have

$$b = \frac{px + px^*}{I + I^*} = \varphi s_x + (1 - \varphi) s_x^*, \tag{5.29}$$

where $\varphi = I/(I + I^*)$ is North's share of world income.

Using (5.29) to substitute for b in (5.27) and rearranging yields

$$z^{WT} - z^{WA} = \frac{\alpha [b [R_T^{1-\eta} - R^{1-\eta}]]}{\gamma} + \frac{\alpha [b [R_T^{*1-\eta} - R^{*1-\eta}]]}{\gamma} \tag{5.30}$$
$$+ \frac{\alpha [s_x^* - s_x] [\varphi R_T^{*1-\eta} - (1 - \varphi) R_T^{1-\eta}]]}{\gamma}.$$

The difference between autarky and world pollution levels is composed of three distinct terms. The first term in (5.30) represents the sum

---

28. In chapter 3, we obtained these results for neutral growth and a constant goods price. Here, we need not have neutral growth, but the goods price is endogenous in

of scale and technique effects in the North, the second term represents the sum of scale and technique effects in the South, and the final term represents the world composition effect.

To interpret (5.30), first consider the limiting case where η approaches 1 (we discuss $\eta \neq 1$ below).[29] In this case, the first two terms in (5.30) disappear, leaving only the global composition effect:

$$z^{WT} - z^{WA} = 2 \frac{\alpha}{\gamma} (s_x^* - s_x) (\varphi - \frac{1}{2}) > 0. \tag{5.31}$$

The sign follows since $\varphi > 1/2$ (North is richer than South), and $s_x^* > s_x$ (because South exports dirty goods).[30] Consequently, when the income elasticity of marginal damage is equal to 1, world pollution rises with trade.

To understand why pollution rises from trade in this example, note from (5.25) that autarky pollution levels are independent of scale and income when $\eta = 1$ (and so are the same in North and South):

$$z^{*A} = z^A = \frac{ab}{\gamma}. \tag{5.32}$$

This follows because in autarky the share of dirty good production in national income is a constant—ruling out a composition effect—and with the income elasticity of marginal damage equal to one, the scale and technique effects exactly offset each other.

Now consider the effects of trade. Because the scale and technique effects exactly offset each other, any increase in the scale of production generated by freer trade is exactly counterbalanced by a tightening of pollution policy. Pollution is therefore affected only via the global composition effect that appears in (5.31). The global composition effect reflects the reallocation of output across countries. In a pollution haven model, international trade shifts the dirtiest industries to the country with weakest environmental policy, and shifts the cleanest industries to country with the strictest environmental policy. This world composition effect therefore raises worldwide pollution. Consequently, when $\eta = 1$, free trade raises world pollution.

This example is instructive because it illustrates very clearly that trade liberalization and economic growth have very different effects

---

autarky. Cobb-Douglas preferences are causing goods prices to adjust so that any growth has a neutral-like effect.

29. In this case, the utility function is $V = \ln (R) - \gamma z$.

30. Since South exports dirty goods, we have $s_x^* > b$. Using (5.29), this implies $s_x^* > s_x$.

on pollution. In this example, growth in autarky has no effect on pollution. But trade creates a pollution haven (even with fully efficient pollution policy), and this pollution haven leads to an increase in world pollution because of the composition effect. The key insight here is that composition effects are critically important in understanding the effects of trade on the environment.

Now consider the more general case where $\eta \neq 1$. It is useful to rewrite (5.30) as

$$z^{WT} - z^{WA} = abR^{1-\eta} \left[\left(\frac{R_T}{R} \right)^{1-\eta} - 1 \right] / \gamma + abR^{*1-\eta} \left[\left(\frac{R_T^*}{R^*} \right)^{1-\eta} - 1 \right] / \gamma \qquad (5.33)$$

$$+ \alpha \, [s_x^* - s_x] \left[\frac{I_T}{I_T^*} - \left(\frac{I_T}{I_T^*} \right)^{1-\eta} \right] R_T^{*1-\eta} (1 - \varphi) \, / \, \gamma.$$

First consider the scale and technique effects (the first two terms in (5.33)). Since real income in trade is greater than in autarky, we know that $R_T > R$ and $R_T^* > R^*$. Therefore, the sign of the first two terms in (5.33) depends only on the strength of the income elasticity of marginal damage, η. If the income elasticity of marginal damage is below 1 ($\eta < 1$), the first two terms in (5.33) are positive. This is the case where the policy response is relatively weak (scale effects dominate technique effects), and so the income-generating aspects of trade liberalization tend to raise pollution. On the other hand, if the income elasticity of marginal damage exceeds 1 ($\eta > 1$), the policy response is relatively strong, and the sum of the scale and technique effects alone tends to reduce global pollution.

Next consider the global composition effect (the final term in (5.33)). This is positive in all cases because Northern income exceeds Southern income ($I_T > I_T^*$); and because $s_x^* > s_x$ since South exports the dirty good. As noted above, the composition effect tends to raise world pollution because it shifts dirty good production to countries with weaker environmental policy.

The net effect of trade on world pollution depends on how the scale and technique effects interact with the global composition effect. If the income elasticity of marginal damage is less than 1, global pollution must rise from trade liberalization. Pollution rises both because of the reallocation of dirty industries to the pollution haven, and because of the weak policy response.

On the other hand, if $\eta > 1$, the policy response is stronger, and this tends to work against the composition effect of trade. However, because the composition effect of trade always tends to raise world pollution, the condition $\eta > 1$ is not sufficient to conclude that world pollution falls as trade is liberalized. Moreover, note that stronger policy responses also magnify differences in income across countries into larger differences in pollution policy. That is, they make the world composition effect stronger. Therefore, trade can increase world pollution even when the income elasticity of marginal damage is greater than one.

5.5 Environmentally Friendly Pollution Havens

In the previous two sections, we considered the implications of trade driven by income-induced pollution policy differences across countries. In this section, we consider another source of policy-induced trade—exogenous differences in the assimilative capacity of the environment. In this case we find that trade may well be good for the environment.

Consider two regions where governments fully internalize pollution externalities. The regions have identical preferences, technology, and endowments, but North's environment is more fragile than South's. Specifically, let the harm caused by pollution be $h(z; \xi)$, where ξ is a shift parameter reflecting the assimilative capacity of the environment, and assume $\partial h / \partial \xi > 0$. That is, a given flow of pollution z does more harm when ξ is higher. We can think of a country with higher ξ having a less "productive" environment.

To see the effect of differences in environmental assimilative capacity on the pattern of trade, note that since countries are otherwise identical, the derived demand for pollution will be the same in each country. However, the marginal damage from pollution is higher in the North because North's environment is less productive. Formally, we have

$$\tau = MD(p, R, z; \xi), \tag{5.34}$$

with $\partial MD / \partial \xi > 0$. For any p, R, and z, the North will have stricter pollution policy than the South in order to protect its more fragile environment.

Referring now to a relative demand and supply curve, such as figure 5.1, we see that North's relative supply will again be above South's, since North's stricter pollution regulations make X relatively more expensive there. Once again, North will have a comparative advantage in the clean good, and South in the dirty good. Trade liberalization will cause some shifting of the polluting industry to the South, leading to a fall in pollution in the North and an increase in pollution in the South. South becomes a "haven" for polluting industries, this time because it has the least fragile environment.

Because we are assuming that both countries fully internalize externalities, trade must benefit both countries. Moreover, notice that trade is shifting the pattern of pollution in an environmentally friendly direction: trade causes pollution to fall in the country with the more fragile environment (North) and rise in the country with the more resilient environment (South).

This is another example of a case where trade driven by differences in pollution policy increases global efficiency and raises global welfare. Moreover, this type of trade also relieves pressure on the most fragile environments. We should hasten to add, however, that once we introduce other motivations for trade, these results can become far less environmentally friendly.[31]

5.6 Northern and Southern Institutional Differences

We conclude this chapter by exploring the implications of pollution havens that arise because of differences across countries in institutional capacity. Suppose, for example, that North and South are identical except that North actively regulates pollution and South does not. This case was considered by Chichilnisky (1994),[32] and in this section, we examine the positive and normative implications of trade under these conditions.

The failure of South to regulate pollution presumably reflects a lack of institutional mechanisms, government willpower, or administrative capacity. This explanation for the absence of regulation, however, is strained, given that we are assuming North and South are otherwise identical. However, one way to justify this approach would be to apply

---

31. For example, if low income and environmental fragility are both found in one region (sub-Saharan Africa comes to mind), then dirty good production may migrate to the country with the less resilient environment. This of course has very different implications.

32. Chichilnisky (1994) considered trade in renewable resources when countries differ only in their regulatory capacity. Here we apply her idea to trade in goods with different pollution intensities.

the policy threshold model of chapter 3—if the fixed cost of regulating
pollution is higher in the South than in the North, then we could have
an equilibrium where North regulates and South does not. For simplicity, however, we do not explicitly model the reason for the asymmetry
in this section.

We undertake this analysis in two parts. First, we start with a trading
equilibrium where neither North nor South initially regulates pollution, and consider a marginal Northern policy reform. Second, we consider the positive and normative effects of a discrete movement from
autarky to trade when North and South differ only in regulation.

Marginal Northern Policy Reform

Suppose North and South are initially identical, there is free trade in
goods, and pollution is initially unregulated in both countries. That is,
we start from an initial situation where $\tau = \tau^* = 0$ and $e = e^* = 1$. The
lack of regulation is assumed to be due to policy failure, so both countries would be better off with positive pollution taxes. Since the countries are identical, their relative demand and supply curves coincide,
and there is no trade. The equilibrium free trade price p is equal to the
autarky price.

Both countries are polluting excessively. Suppose North decides to
reform environmental policy and introduces a small pollution tax τ.
The imposition of a pollution tax reduces the relative supply of X in the
North and creates trade as North's pollution tax gives it a comparative
advantage in the clean good (Y).[33] This shifts North's relative supply
curve inward. The equilibrium world relative price of X rises ($dp/d\tau >
0$) because North's reduction in the relative supply of X implies that
the world relative supply of X must also fall. Some of the polluting
industry is relocated to the South, which now imports Y from the
North. The pollution tax reduces pollution in the North as intended,
but it also causes an increase in pollution in the South.

Welfare in the North clearly rises, as there is a drop in pollution to
accompany the standard gains from trade. But this increase in welfare
comes about in part at the expense of the South, which must lose from

33. A small pollution tax will not lead firms to abate unless the marginal product of
abatement approaches infinity as low levels of activity. In our framework this is not the
case; but note the producer price for X output falls nevertheless and the economy moves
along its given gross frontier to produce less X and more Y.

a small Northern pollution tax. To see this, note that the change in Southern welfare is

$$\frac{dV^*}{dV_I} = -m^* dp + [\tau^* - MD\,(p,\,R^*,\,z^*)]\,dz^*. \tag{5.35}$$

There is no pollution policy in the South, so $\tau^* = 0$. In addition, since we are starting from the point of no trade, Southern imports are zero: $m^* = 0$. We therefore have

$$\left.\frac{dV^*}{d\tau}\right|_{\tau = \tau^* = 0} = -V_I^*\,[MD\,(p,\,R^*,\,z^*)]\,\frac{dz^*}{d\tau} < 0, \tag{5.36}$$

since Southern pollution rises. South must therefore lose from a small policy reform in the North.

By similar methods, we have in the North

$$\left.\frac{dV}{d\tau}\right|_{\tau = \tau^* = 0} = -V_I\,[MD\,(p,\,R,\,z)]\,\frac{dz}{d\tau} > 0, \tag{5.37}$$

since Northern pollution falls with the introduction of its tax. It is apparent from (5.36)–(5.37) that North's gain comes about as a result of South's loss.

The opportunity to trade with the South lets Northerners maintain relatively high levels of X consumption and at the same time reduce pollution by purchasing imports from the South. Starting from a position of no trade, South bears the cost of this increased pollution with no first-order consumption gains.

Notice that South can avoid being sideswiped by North's pollution policy reform by simultaneously reforming its own pollution policy. If both countries simultaneously introduce identical pollution taxes $\tau = \tau^*$, then there would no international trade, but the world supply of X would fall, leading to an increase in the price of X, and a fall in the output of X and pollution in both countries. That is, we would have $dz < 0$ and $dz^* < 0$. Both countries would gain from a simultaneous introduction of matching pollution taxes because with $m = m^* = 0$, the only effect on welfare is simply the benefit of reduced pollution. In practice, however, such a simultaneous policy reform may not be feasible. If North's political structure allows it to implement regulatory reforms that South cannot, then South can lose from policy reform in the North.

One might be tempted to conclude from this example that trade between two regions differing greatly in their institutional capacity must lead to losses for countries that do not regulate pollution. That is, the example we employed had a decidedly zero-sum flavor to it. This view may be enhanced by the observation that in the first-best setting, these two countries would not trade at all.

This point has caused much confusion in the literature. In general, however, it is not true that Northern gains from trade always come at the expense of Southern losses when North and South differ only in institutional capacity. Our example was deliberately constructed to eliminate any potential gains from trade between North and South. We did this by considering a marginal change in pollution policy starting from an existing (trading) equilibrium with no trade. More generally, when the two countries differ more than marginally in policy, there will be consumption gains from trade and the $-m^*dp$ term in (5.35) will not be zero. In the South, these must be weighed against the costs of increased pollution. In fact, as we show in the next section, it is entirely possible for South to gain from a discrete increase in trade.

Second, one should not read too much into the statement that North and South would not trade in a first-best world. While true, it is largely irrelevant to whether South gains from trade. We are examining the impact of free trade in a second-best world, and the welfare gains from the South do not depend on some hypothetical first-best outcome. As a general matter, it is unclear whether the South will gain or lose from trade. In fact, we have already given one example where two countries gain from trade, even though they would not trade if environmental policy were first best. Recall our results in section 5.2, where two identical countries with different fixed supplies of emission permits both gained from trade. Trade in that case occurred because of an unwarranted difference in environmental regulation, yet both countries gained from trade. In fact, trade helped to offset the distortion in environmental policy.

As we show below, when North and South differ discretely in their institutional capacity to regulate pollution, the welfare implications of trade are ambiguous. The combination of tight Northern policy and no Southern policy may well lead to welfare gains for both parties in trade. This is true despite the fact that North and South would not trade in the first-best world.

Institutional Differences and Trade: An Extended Example

We now amend our earlier analysis to allow our countries to have discrete differences in their regulation. To illustrate the possibility that South may gain from trade even when it has no pollution regulation at all, we work through an extended example. As well as demonstrating the contrast between discrete and marginal differences in policy, this example allows us to calculate solutions explicitly, and may help to provide readers with additional insight into how to work with simple trade and environment models.

As in Chichilnisky 1994, we assume that North has optimal regulation and South has no regulation; but otherwise the countries are identical. We assume that countries are rich enough to ensure that abatement would occur in equilibrium if they regulated efficiently. As we will see later, a sufficient condition for this is

$$L > \frac{\alpha}{\gamma}. \tag{5.38}$$

We will assume that (5.38) holds, and hence we will have abatement in the North ($e < 1$). Since we are assuming South does not regulate pollution at all, we have $e^* = 1$.

We use the same utility function as in section 5.4:

$$V = \ln \left[I / \beta (p) \right] - \gamma z,$$

where $\beta (p) = p^b b^{-b} (1 - b)^{-(1-b)}$ and b is the fraction of income spent on X. To simplify further, we assume that labor is the only primary factor of production, so that the production functions for X and Y are simply

$$x = z^\alpha L_X^{1-\alpha} \tag{5.39}$$
$$y = L_Y.$$

Noting that $e = z/x$ by definition, we can rewrite the production function for X as

$$x = e^{\alpha/(1-\alpha)} L_X. \tag{5.40}$$

where e is emissions per unit output.

Labor must be fully employed, which implies

$$L_x + L_y = L. \tag{5.41}$$

The analogous condition applies to the South.

Our strategy in analyzing this model is as follows. We first find pollution and welfare in autarky, then solve for the free trade equilibrium, and then finally compare welfare in autarky with welfare in free trade.

We start by determining the autarky equilibrium. In the South, $e = 1$, and this together with (5.40) and (5.39) implies that South's production possibility frontier is linear with a slope of -1. Because both X and Y are always consumed, market clearing in the absence of trade requires that $p = 1$ to ensure that both goods are produced. Hence South's autarky goods price is

$$p^{*A} = 1. \tag{5.42}$$

Southern income is simply $I^* = wL$, but since one unit of labor produces one unit of the numeraire, we must have $w = 1$. Hence income is just $I^* = L$. Given the assumptions on tastes, the demand functions are $x = bI^*/p = bL$ and $y = (1 - b)L$.

To solve for the pollution level, recall that since $e = 1$, we have $z^* = x^*$ and hence in autarky equilibrium $z^* = bL$. Autarky utility in the South is therefore

$$V^{*A} = \ln [L / b^{-b} (1 - b)^{-(1 - b)}] - \gamma bL. \tag{5.43}$$

The Northern equilibrium is more complex because policy is set optimally. From (5.23) the optimal pollution tax is $\tau = \gamma I$. Pollution demand is $z = ex$, where $e = ap/\tau$. Equating supply and demand for pollution yields $z = apx/\gamma I$. In autarky, consumers spend a fraction b of their income on consumption of X, and therefore, $b = px/I$. Hence equilibrium pollution in autarky is simply

$$z = \frac{ab}{\gamma}. \tag{5.44}$$

Recall that Southern pollution is $z^* = bL$. Referring to (5.44), note that our assumption (5.38) implies that Northern pollution is less than Southern pollution in autarky. Pollution is harmful in both countries; but only North is able to regulate pollution.

To solve for autarky prices in the North, we solve for X and Y supply functions, and then equate relative demand to relative supply. The simplest way to determine goods supplies is to determine the allocation of labor across sectors. The value of the marginal product of labor must be equal across sectors, and using (5.39), this implies

$$(1 - a) pz^a L_x^{-a} = w = 1. \tag{5.45}$$

Using (5.44) in (5.45) and solving for L_x yields the allocation of labor to X:

$$L_x = \frac{ab}{\gamma} [p (1 - \alpha)]^{1/a}. \tag{5.46}$$

Substituting (5.46) into (5.39) and using (5.41), we obtain the supply functions for both X and Y:

$$X = \frac{ab}{\gamma} [p (1 - \alpha)]^{(1-a)/a}. \tag{5.47}$$

$$Y = L - \frac{ab}{\gamma} [p (1 - \alpha)]^{1/a}.$$

The supply of X relative to Y is increasing in p, decreasing in γ, and decreasing in L. A higher disutility of pollution increases the pollution tax and favors sector Y. A higher L raises the demand for environmental quality, and also reduces the relative supply of the dirty good (X).

The relative demand curve is given by

$$p = \frac{b}{1 - b} \frac{Y}{X}. \tag{5.48}$$

Substituting (5.47) into (5.48) yields the Northern relative autarky price:

$$p^A = \left[\frac{\gamma L}{\alpha (1 - ab)(1 - a)^{(1-a)/a}} \right]^a > 1. \tag{5.49}$$

The autarky relative price of the dirty good (X) in the North is increasing in income as proxied by L, increasing in the disutility of pollution, γ, and increasing in the share of income allocated to purchasing the dirty good, b. In addition, North's autarky relative price is greater than 1. This follows from our assumption (5.38).[34] To understand this result, recall that in the absence of pollution regulation, the relative price of X is 1. Because North regulates pollution and is sufficiently rich that firms abate in response to a pollution tax, the relative supply of X is reduced, and this pushes its price up.

The autarky equilibrium for the North is shown in figure 5.3. In the figure we have shown both the gross production frontier, which is the same in North and South, and the net frontier, reflecting the policy

---

34. Note that our restriction on L is sufficient, but not necessary for the result that North's autarky price exceeds 1.

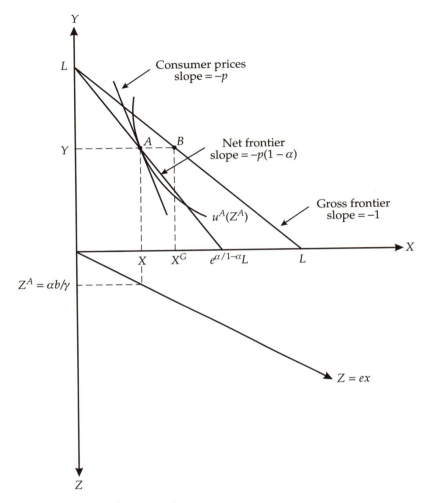

Fig. 5.3. The North in Autarky

choice of the North. In addition, we have indicated equilibrium pollution levels in the quadrant below the production frontiers. Our assumption on parameters in (5.38) ensures $e < 1$ in equilibrium and hence the net frontier lies inside the gross frontier.

The slope of the net frontier is equal to $1/e^{a/(1-a)} > 1$, but this is just $q = p(1 - a)$ or the net price producers get after paying pollution taxes equal to pa per unit of output. Therefore, as in chapter 2, production occurs along the net frontier where the producer price is tangent to the production possibility frontier. The exact point of production, A, is pinned down by the solution we obtained in (5.44) for pollution and the requirement that $z = ex$. At A, the economy as a whole allocates $x^G - x$ units of labor to abatement.

Since we are in autarky, consumption occurs at point A as well, but consumers face the price p for the dirty good. Note that since p is greater than 1, North consumes relatively less X and more Y than South.

Now introduce free international trade between North and South. Since $p^A > 1$ in North in autarky, and $p^{*A} = 1$ in South in autarky, North has a comparative advantage in the clean good. The equilibrium free trade price must lie somewhere between the two autarky prices.

Three types of equilibria can emerge in this model depending on parameter values. If the world demand for the clean good is very strong, then North will specialize in the clean good while South will diversify. In this case, South will have no conventional gains from trade and will pollute more in free trade. South must lose in this case. For an intermediate taste for the dirty good, South and North will both specialize: South in dirty and North in clean. Finally, if the taste for the dirty good is sufficiently strong, both countries will produce some of the dirty good in free trade. Since this third equilibrium has both North and South active in the production of dirty goods, we will focus on it here.

South's move from autarky to trade is illustrated in figure 5.4. As shown earlier, South's production possibility frontier is linear with a slope of −1, and relative prices in autarky are equal to 1. Consumption in autarky occurs at point A^* as shown. Utility is given by u^{*A}, which we have written as a function of pollution to remind the reader of its significance for welfare. Pollution itself is shown in the lower panel where, since $e^* = 1$, X output maps directly into pollution levels as shown.

When the world demand for the dirty good is sufficiently strong, the equilibrium free trade price must be strictly greater than 1. With $p^T > 1$, South must specialize in production at B^* with $x^* = L$. Since South has no pollution regulation, we must also have $Z^{*T} = L$ as shown.[35] As a consequence of trade, South's pollution is higher than it was in autarky. Pollution in autarky was bL; pollution in trade is L.

---

35. This type of equilibrium will obtain if the demand for the dirty good is strong enough. We will verify $p > 1$ in equilibrium.

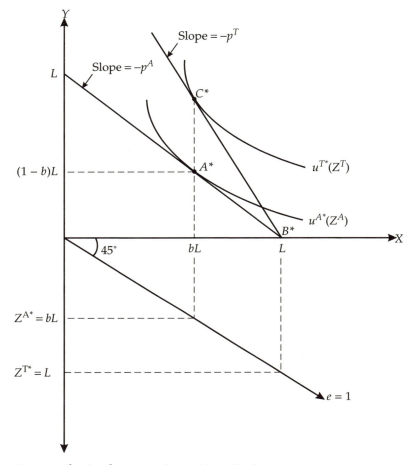

Fig. 5.4. The South in Autarky and Free Trade

South's consumption moves to point C^*, which reflects consumption gains from trade. Since South specializes in the dirty good, Southern income is $I^{*T} = p^T X^{*T}$. Given Cobb-Douglas tastes, the value of its exports is $(1 - b) p^T X^{*T} = (1 - b) pL$, and the volume of exports is $(1 - b) L$. Therefore, consumption must occur at point C^*, as shown.

To evaluate the welfare consequences of trade, refer again to (5.35), which we obtained from our marginal analysis. The consumption gains from trade have to be weighed against the costs of increased pollution. In our marginal analysis, there were no consumption gains from trade because we assumed $m = 0$ initially and considered only a marginal change. Here we are considering a discrete change, and there are consumption gains to potentially offset the costs of increased pollution.

Routine calculation shows that South gains from a discrete movement from autarky to free trade if and only if the following condition holds:

$$u^T - u^A > 0 \Leftrightarrow \ln p^T - \gamma L > 0. \tag{5.50}$$

The first term reflects consumption gains, and the second measures the cost of increased pollution. South gains if the former is greater than the latter.

To determine whether the South can gain despite the increase in pollution, we need to determine p^T. Market clearing in the Y industry requires

$$\begin{aligned}
&(1 - b)(I + I^*) = Y, \\
&I = pX + Y, \\
&I^* = pX^*.
\end{aligned} \tag{5.51}$$

Solving for I yields

$$I = \frac{pX + (1 - b)\,pL}{b}, \tag{5.52}$$

where we have used the result that in the South $X^* = L$. Now employ (5.52) in the demand for pollution to obtain a useful intermediate result:

$$z^T = \frac{ab}{\gamma}\left[\frac{pX}{pX + (1 - b)\,pL}\right] < z^A. \tag{5.53}$$

Pollution in the North has necessarily fallen because trade shifts some of North's dirty good production to the South. Note that the fall in North's pollution reflects the existence of Southern exports of X (given by $(1 - b)\,pL$), which in turn lowers world demand for Northern dirty good production and hence its derived demand for pollution services.

The last step is to solve for relative prices. Solving for the supply of X relative to Y, and equating to relative demand, yields[36]

---

36. Use (5.45) in the production function for X to find

$X = z\,[p\,(1 - a)]^{(1 - a)/a}$.

Combing this with (5.52) we obtain

$$\left[\frac{p^T}{p^A}\right]^{1/a} + \alpha\,(1-b)\,p^T = 1, \tag{5.54}$$

where p^A is North's autarky relative price. While we cannot solve (5.54) analytically, we can characterize the solution. To do so, note that the left-hand side of the equation is monotonically rising in p^T; second, at $p^T = p^A > 1$, the left-hand side exceeds the right; third, at $p^T = 0$ the left-hand side is less than the right. These, together with continuity, imply that a positive solution for the free trade price exists and is unique. In addition, $p^T < p^A$, as claimed.

To gain from trade, p^T must be relatively high. To see when this will occur, rearrange (5.54), using (5.49), to obtain

$$\left[\frac{p^T}{\Omega}\right]^{1/a} (1 - ab) + \alpha\,(1-b)\,p^T = 1, \tag{5.55}$$

where Ω is independent of b. Notice that p^T rises as b increases.

Let us now reconsider South's gains from trade. Since $p = 1$ in the South in autarky and p^T is rising in b, if we assume the taste for the dirty good is strong enough, then gains can occur. As an example, the interested reader can check that for the parameter values $\{\,\gamma L = .15,\ a = .12,\ b = .9\,\}$, the South necessarily gains from trade. The South gains from trade because the additional damage trade does to the environment in this case is quite limited: the South was already allocating 90% of its labor force to X in autarky and hence the added damage caused by allocating 100% in trade is relatively small. Consequently, the consumption gains from trade more than offset the increased environmental damage.[37]

$$z = \frac{\alpha\beta}{\gamma} - \left[\frac{(1-b)\,L}{(p\,(1-\alpha))^{(1-a)/a}}\right].$$

Noting that $Y = L - L_X$, recalling $X^* = L$, using (5.45), and equating relative demand to relative supply, we have

$$p = \frac{b}{1-b} \frac{[L - p^{1/a}\,(1-\alpha)^{1/a}z]}{[z\,(p\,(1-\alpha))^{(1-a)/a} + L]}.$$

Rearranging and using the expression for z above yields (5.54) in the text.

37. While $b = .9$ may seem extreme, so too is the full specialization created in our Ricardian setup. The interested reader should be able to construct similar examples using the model of chapter 2 to replicate this result for much smaller values of b.

Of course, losses from trade are also possible with different parameters. For example, if we let b fall in the above example, then one can generate losses from trade. When b falls, free trade prices are lower and the pollution consequences of specialization in trade are greater.

Our objective in this exercise has been to illustrate that trade between two countries that differ only in their ability to regulate the environment can be Pareto-improving. In this example, trade does not occur in the first-best world, and the only motive for trade is the absence of environmental regulations in the South. Nevertheless, this is not sufficient to conclude that South must lose from trade. Trade generates both consumption gains and environmental losses. If the former dominates the latter, then trade can be a second-best device to raise welfare in both countries. Therefore, even if pollution havens emerge because South lacks the institutional capacity to regulate pollution, North-South trade is not inherently exploitive nor zero sum. The South may in fact gain from such trade.

5.7 Conclusion

We started this chapter by asking whether trade driven by differences in pollution policy is bad for the environment, and whether such trade benefits rich countries at the expense of poor countries. In most cases, we found that we need to ask why regulations differ before we proceed to answer our questions. We showed how pollution havens could emerge when regulatory differences were exogenous, or when they arose endogenously from asymmetries in income levels, institutional capacity, or the resilience of the environment. The observation of a North-South pollution haven trade pattern resulting from differences in regulations is consistent with any or all of these motivations. Any analysis of the effects of such trade has to start with an understanding of the motivation for differences in regulation.

While we found that trade driven by differences in environmental policy tends to increase the concentration of polluting industries in the country with weaker policy, the effect of such trade on the environment depends on the policy instruments in place. For example, if both countries use aggregate pollution quotas, then differences in quota levels across countries will induce trade, and the polluting industry will expand in the country with the more liberal quota. However, if the pollution quota is binding, then pollution will be unaffected by trade.

Instead, increased dirty goods production will be met with declining emission intensities.

In some cases, trade driven by policy differences can actually lead to an improvement in the global environment. This can happen if trade is driven by differences across countries in the fragility of their environments. If this is the only difference between countries and if policy is efficient, the country with the more sensitive environment will implement stricter policy. Trade will cause the polluting industry to shift to the country where pollution causes less damage. Such trade relieves pressure on the most sensitive parts of the global environment.

We also found several instances where trade driven by policy differences was not environmentally friendly. For example, when trade is motivated by exogenous differences in emission intensities, the country with weak environmental policy will suffer increased environmental damage from trade. In addition, when income differences are present, trade-induced pollution havens raise pollution in the South in all but the most optimistic situations. And finally, we found that in many cases global pollution rises when trade is driven by income-induced differences in environmental policy.

Overall, while it would be foolish to assert that pollution-haven-driven trade is always good for the environment, we should be equally wary of drawing quick conclusions on the basis of trade patterns alone.

A second general lesson is that while policy failure is a necessary condition for there to be welfare losses from trade, policy failures are far from sufficient to guarantee losses. From our analysis of exogenous differences in emission intensities it is clear that a country with lax environmental standards will suffer increased environmental damages if pollution rises with trade. But because these losses must be weighed against the conventional gains from trade, no clear-cut welfare result emerges.

Even if policy failures *are the only motivation* for pollution haven trade, such trade can sometimes be welfare improving. For example, we showed how identical countries with different pollution quotas must gain from trade. In this case the role of trade was especially clear. Free trade moved marginal damage closer together and acted as a second-best substitute for environmental policy. In addition, when we considered pollution havens created by institutional differences, we showed how the unregulated South need not necessarily lose from trade. In this case, trade did not substitute for the lack of environmental policy; in fact it exploited it by driving the South to specialize in dirty goods production. Nevertheless, if the gains from selling its dirty goods at world prices far in excess of autarky prices, the South can gain from trade.

We also considered the welfare implications of trade when there was no policy failure. If two countries differ only with respect to per capita income, the rich country will implement stricter pollution policy because the demand for environmental quality rises with income. The poor country will become a pollution haven when trade opens up. However, as long as externalities are fully internalized, both countries gain from trade. Trade simply exploits differences between countries in the marginal rate of substitution between consumption and environmental quality.

Therefore, one important implication of our analysis is that trade induced by policy differences need not be undesirable. Nor is the concentration of polluting activity in one area as a consequence of trading opportunities necessarily undesirable. On a regional basis, such trade is commonplace. Local zoning regulations that keep dirty industry out of urban and suburban neighborhoods are simply mechanisms that induce regional trade by imposing tighter pollution regulations in some areas than others. Trade between countries that leads to a greater concentration of polluting activity in one country than another is in principle no different.

Overall, the welfare effects of pollution-haven-driven trade depend on the policy regime. If prices everywhere fully internalize environmental externalities, then such trade can be beneficial to both the rich and the poor. But if pollution policy does not fully reflect all externalities or if pollution regulations are not enforced, then such trade can be harmful to both individuals and the environment. And because poorer countries tend to have less effective environmental policy than richer countries, the models in this chapter suggest trade that shifts polluting industries to poor countries may indeed be harmful.

But before we condemn trade because it creates harmful pollution havens, we must remember that differences in pollution policy are only one of many factors that cause trade. At the beginning of this chapter, we identified two key assumptions behind most pollution haven models: inequality in the world distribution of income, and relative production costs determined by pollution regulations alone. We cited evidence showing large inequalities in the world distribution of income, but offered no evidence that pollution regulations were an important determinant of costs. If other factors dominate the effects of pollution policy on comparative advantage, then trade may not concentrate polluting industries in countries with weak environmental regulation.

The next step in our analysis, then, is to examine how including additional motives for trade changes these results.

6

Factor Endowments, Policy Differences, and Pollution

The United States and Europe have some of the most stringent emission standards in the world, and yet both export some highly pollution-intensive manufactured goods. A narrow interpretation of this observation is that it directly contradicts the pollution haven hypothesis—after all, the pollution haven hypothesis predicts that the dirtiest industries should locate in countries with weak environmental regulations.[1] A more forgiving interpretation, and one we favor, is that the pollution haven hypothesis identifies one of many forces influencing the location of dirty industry around the world. The real question is whether pollution haven effects are strong relative to other factors that determine the pattern of trade in pollution-intensive goods.

In chapter 5, we explored the logic behind the pollution haven hypothesis by studying models where differences in pollution policy were the *only* motive for trade. This chapter allows countries to differ along another dimension and investigates how differences across countries in factor abundance interact with regulatory differences to determine the pattern of trade. While there are many other potential motives for trade arising from differences in endowments, technologies, preferences, and scale economies, we focus on just one of these: factor endowments. We do so because many of the most pollution-intensive industries are also capital intensive,[2] and because the *factor en-*

---

1. Chapter 5 developed various versions of the pollution haven hypothesis using two-good models. The multigood version of the pollution hypothesis is developed in Copeland and Taylor 1994 and predicts that if industries are ranked by pollution intensity, the most pollution-intensive industries locate in the countries with the weakest environmental policy. With endogenous policy, weak environmental policy is associated with low income, so we expect rich countries to export clean goods and poor countries to export dirty goods.
2. We will present evidence of this in chapter 7.

dowments hypothesis is the preeminent theory linking cross-country differences in national characteristics to trade patterns.

Throughout we focus on two key questions. How do differences in factor abundance interact with policy differences to determine the pattern of trade in dirty goods? What predictions from the pollution haven model need modification in a world where factor endowments are a significant determinant of trade patterns? We start in section 6.1 by assuming North and South have identical and exogenous emission intensities to demonstrate how factor endowment differences create a basis for trade.[3] In section 6.2 we then examine how exogenous differences in both emission intensities and factor endowments together determine trade patterns.

Although these exogenous policy models are very simple, they demonstrate two surprising results. First, they show that the lax-regulation country may end up importing the dirty good in free trade with the stringent-regulation country exporting dirty goods. This result, in effect, reverses the trade pattern prediction from the pollution haven models of chapter 5. Second, under these same conditions we demonstrate that the lax-regulation country must now necessarily gain from trade. This reverses our earlier finding in chapter 5 that the lax-regulation country could lose if the conventional gains from trade were small in relation to trade's environmental consequences.

In section 6.2 we illustrate that the composition of factor endowments together with endogenous policy differences determines comparative advantage and trade.[4] We examine each motive for trade separately, but then combine them in section 6.3 on correlated characteristics. Section 6.4 develops a specific example.

The results we obtain in this chapter are, in many cases, diametrically opposed to those presented in chapter 5. Most of these differences stem from the possibility that the North, rather than the South, may have a comparative advantage in dirty goods. This will occur when factor endowment motives for trade overwhelm pollution haven motives. This trade pattern result has several consequences—both positive and normative. For example, it implies that pollution falls in the

---

3. That is, we demonstrate how our model reduces to the standard Heckscher-Ohlin model of international trade when emission intensities are exogenous and identical across countries. See any textbook on international trade for an exposition of this model, such as Krugman and Obstfeld 2000 for an undergraduate treatment, or Dixit and Norman 1980 for a graduate-level treatment.

4. The interaction between income-induced policy differences and differences in relative factor endowments is studied in Copeland and Taylor 1997; Richelle 1996; and Antweiler, Copeland, and Taylor 2001.

South with trade, that a lax-regulation South must gain from trade, and that free trade relocates dirty good production from a high-emission country (the South) to a low-emission country (the North). This implies that world pollution may well fall with trade.

These results need not always hold, as they depend on the overall strength of factor endowment versus pollution haven motives. In cases where pollution haven motives are dominant our results revert to those of chapter 5. Consequently the results in this chapter underscore the necessity in any empirical investigation to allow for both pollution haven effects and factor endowment effects in determining the trade pattern.

6.1 Exogenous Policy: The Role of Factor Endowments

To introduce differences in factor endowments across countries, we start by assuming countries have identical emission intensities. This allows us to isolate the role of factor endowments. Specifically, we assume countries choose pollution taxes to ensure emission intensities stay constant and equal; therefore, $e = e^*$. From (2.16), North's emission intensity is

$$e = \frac{ap}{\tau} \tag{6.1}$$

Therefore, when North and South trade freely, our assumption of $e = e^*$ implies $\tau = \tau^*$, and this renders moot the role policy differences can have in determining comparative advantage.

Apart from our assumptions on emission intensities and factor abundance, we use the same framework as in chapter 5. To recap, we aggregate countries into two regions, North and South, and denote with an asterisk (*) Southern variables. Countries within each region are identical. Two goods (X and Y) are produced with a constant returns to scale technology using two primary factors, capital (K) and labor (L). Important to our results here is the fact that X is both capital and pollution intensive, whereas Y is labor intensive and does not pollute.

Comparative Advantage and the Pattern of Trade

As in chapter 5, we use a relative supply and demand diagram for the goods market to determine autarky prices and the trade pattern. The demand for X relative to Y is independent of income and pollution and therefore is the same across countries. That is, reproducing (5.4), we have

$$RD\,(p) = \frac{b_x\,(p)}{b_y\,(p)},\tag{6.2}$$

where $RD'\,(p) < 0$.

The relative supply curve was also derived in chapter 5. It depends on pollution policy and relative factor endowments, and is given by (5.7), which we reproduce here:

$$RS\,(p,\,e,\,K/L) = \frac{x\,(p,\,e,\,K/L,\,1)}{y\,(p,\,e,\,K/L,\,1)}.\tag{6.3}$$

Recall that $RS_p > 0$, since an increase in p stimulates the X industry at the expense of Y. Hence the relative supply curve slopes upward as in figure 5.1. South's relative supply is determined in similar fashion:

$$RS^*\,(p,\,e^*,\,K^*/L^*) = \frac{x\,(p,\,e^*,\,K^*/L^*,\,1)}{y\,(p,\,e^*,\,K^*/L^*,\,1)}.\tag{6.4}$$

Given $e = e^*$, the relative supplies differ only if the composition of North and South's factor endowments differ. We assume North is relatively capital abundant; that is,

$$\frac{K}{L} > \frac{K^*}{L^*}.\tag{6.5}$$

Since X is capital intensive and we are holding pollution policy constant, we can now employ the Rybczinski theorem from international trade to determine relative outputs.[5] Given (6.5), North's capital abundance ensures its relative supply curve is to the right of South's, as illustrated in figure 6.1.

World relative supply is again a convex combination of North's and South's relative supplies as illustrated. Moreover, given a common relative demand we can conclude the autarky relative price of X is lower in the North than in the South:

$$p^{A^*} > p^A,\tag{6.6}$$

where A denotes autarky.

---

5. This theorem is discussed in chapter 2. The relevant result is that (with emission intensities held fixed), an increase in the endowment of capital will increase the supply of the capital-intensive good (X) and reduce the supply of the labor-intensive good (Y).

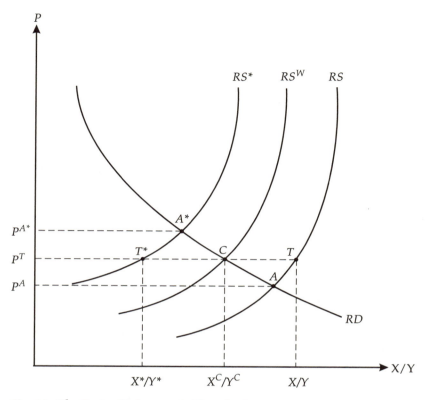

Fig. 6.1. The Factor Endowments Hypothesis

With identical pollution emission intensities across countries, our model reduces to the standard Heckscher-Ohlin model: trade patterns are determined by relative factor abundance. When trade is opened between North and South, world prices are determined at C with Northern and Southern production given by points T and T^* respectively. Since consumption ratios are equal at C, the capital-abundant country must export the capital-intensive good. And in our application, this means that all else equal, the capital-abundant North exports the dirty good in free trade.

Effects of Trade on Pollution and Welfare

The effect of trade on a country's environmental quality follows directly from the trade pattern established in figure 6.1. Trade leads to an expansion of the polluting, capital-intensive industry in the capital-abundant North. Since emission intensities are constant, pollution must rise in the North with trade. In the labor-abundant South, trade leads to a contraction of the polluting industry and a fall in pollution. In the absence of any differences in pollution policy across countries, the effect of trade on the environment is determined by a country's relative factor abundance.

The welfare results also follow quite readily if we recall our decomposition in (5.12). North may either gain or lose from trade in this scenario—its purchasing power of consumption goods will rise via the standard gains from trade effect, but its environmental quality worsens. If the environmental damage is sufficiently severe, and regulation is lax in the North, then North could lose from trade. Alternatively, South must almost surely gain from trade, both because its consumption possibilities increase and because its environmental quality improves. Unless South's regulation is excessively stringent (such that τ exceeds MD), Southern gains are assured.

We have illustrated the factor endowments hypothesis with a very simple example based on capital abundance to focus on a key insight: countries relatively abundant in factors that are used intensively in polluting industries will on average get dirtier as trade liberalizes, while countries that are relatively abundant in factors used intensively in clean industries will get cleaner.

The predictions of this theory therefore contrast sharply with those of the pollution haven hypothesis. If the factor endowments hypothesis is correct, there need not be any link between a country's income and how trade affects its environment. If a poor country is abundant in factors used intensively in clean industries, then the poor country's pollution will fall as trade is liberalized. Of course, it is likely that both regulation and factor endowments differ across countries, and hence the next step is to examine this possibility.

Exogenous Policy: Factor Endowments and Fixed Emission Intensities

When emission intensities are not identical across countries, trade patterns depend on both the relative stringency of pollution policy and relative factor endowments. Since stringent pollution policy lowers dirty good output while capital abundance raises it, these two motivations for trade work in opposite directions.

To demonstrate this tension between pollution policy and relative factor endowments, refer to figure 6.2. South's relative supply curve is

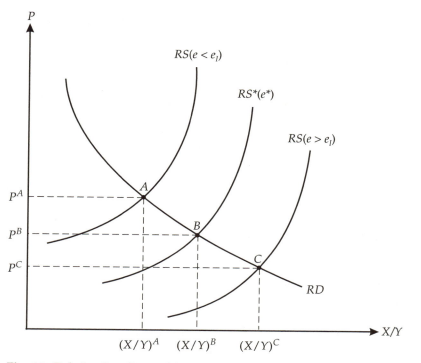

Fig. 6.2. Relative Supplies and Emission Intensities

illustrated as $RS^*(p, e^*, K^*/L^*)$, where e^* is South's (fixed) emission intensity. This intersects relative demand at point B, yielding an autarky price P^B for the South. North is capital abundant relative to South ($K/L > K^*/L^*$). If North's emission intensity e were the same as South's, then North's relative supply would be to the right of South's. However, if North's emission intensity is lower than South's ($e < e^*$), then North's relative supply shifts inward and may possibly lie to the left of South's.[6]

To be more precise about the interaction between these two sources of comparative advantage, define a critical emission intensity

$$e_I = e_I(K/L, K^*/L^*, e^*)$$

for which North's and South's relative supplies both yield the same autarky price p^B. In terms of figure 6.2, for $e = e_I$, North's relative sup-

---

6. If North's emission intensity is greater than South's ($e > e^*$), then its relative supply curve shifts out further to the right, as lax emission standards reinforce a comparative advantage in the dirty good.

ply curve intersects the RD curve at point B, which is the same point where South's relative supply curve intersects RD. That is, e_I is defined implicitly as the solution to

$$RS (p^B, e_I, K/L) = RS^* (p^B, e^*, K^*/L^*),$$ (6.7)

where RS and RS^* are the relative supplies defined in (6.3) and (6.4) respectively.[7]

We can now characterize the trade pattern. Since RS is monotonic in e, we have (at South's autarky price p^B)

if $e > e_I$, then $RS > RS^*$,   (6.8)
if $e < e_I$, then $RS < RS^*$.

This is illustrated in figure 6.2. Given that North is capital abundant, North exports the dirty good if its emission intensity is sufficiently high (as illustrated by the case where its relative supply is $RS (e > e_I)$), and exports the clean good if its emission intensity is sufficiently low (as illustrated by the case where its relative supply is $RS (e < e_I)$).

Moreover, recall that because North is capital abundant, $e_I < e^*$. This together with (6.8) implies that there exists an interval of emission intensities where North has tighter policy than South, but North retains a comparative advantage in dirty goods. That is, for $e \in (e_I, e^*)$, North exports the dirty good, despite having more stringent policy than South.

The possibility that the country with relatively strong pollution policy may end up with a comparative advantage in the dirty good has a number of important implications, which contrast sharply with those obtained from a pure pollution haven model.

First, note that if North's capital abundance results in its exporting the polluting good, then (assuming policy is not excessively stringent) South must gain from trade, while North may lose. Both countries reap standard gains from trade, but pollution will rise in the North and fall in the South. Trade takes pressure off South's environment as pollution-intensive production shifts to the North at the margin. This reinforces the consumption gains from trade in the South. North, however, may lose if the increased pressure on its environment offsets the consumption gains from trade.

---

7. To see that this critical emission intensity exists, note that for $e = e^*$, $RS \geq RS^*$; and for $e = 0$, $RS = 0 \leq RS^*$. (This is because with our assumptions on technology, production of the dirty good is unprofitable for $e = 0$, and so North specializes in the clean good at some point as e is tightened.) Continuity then implies the existence of e_I.

In addition, it is also possible that world pollution may fall in this case. This is because trade reallocates dirty good production to the more stringently regulated country. The world composition effect therefore tends to reduce world pollution, in contrast to the results we obtained in the pollution haven model. A fall in world pollution is only a possibility, and not a necessity, because the share of dirty good output in consumption may be different in trade than autarky as a result of the relative price and income changes brought about by trade. We will consider the issue of world pollution in more depth later in the chapter.

Implications for Empirical Work

This example also has some important implications for empirical work. The literature on the pollution haven hypothesis has often blurred together two separate questions. One issue is whether a tightening of pollution policy in one country will lead to a shift of polluting production (at the margin) to other countries. That is, holding all else constant, is the location of production (in a trading equilibrium) affected by differences in pollution policy across countries? A second question is whether liberalizing trade will lead to a shift in production of polluting industries from countries with tighter pollution regulation to countries with weaker regulation.

It is quite consistent with our theory for the answer to the first question to be "yes," while the answer to the second is "no." Suppose North's pollution policy is tighter than South's, but satisfies $e \in (e_1, e^*)$, so that North's autarky equilibrium is at point C. As we discussed above, if we liberalize trade, then North exports the dirty good, and South exports the clean good. Trade liberalization shifts dirty good production to the country with stricter pollution regulation

But now start from the trading equilibrium and suppose that North tightens its pollution policy. Given the initial world price, this will shift North's relative supply curve inward, create an incipient increase in the world price of the dirty good, and encourage South to increase its dirty good production. That is, a tightening of North's pollution policy causes some dirty good production to shift to the South. Moreover, this occurs regardless of whether North is importing or exporting the dirty good.

One way to think about these results is to note that our second question is asking whether a strong version of the pollution haven hypothesis holds—that is, are differences in pollution regulations the most important motive for trade in dirty goods? The first question is asking instead whether pollution regulations matter at all, or if there exists what we might call a *pollution haven effect*. That is, regardless of the pattern of trade, does a tightening of pollution policy in one country lead to a marginal shift in dirty good production to other countries? Our model suggests that there should always be a pollution haven effect, but that the strong form of the pollution haven hypothesis need not hold if other factors (such as relative capital abundance) more than offset the pollution haven effect.

This distinction is important. It means that if we find evidence that differences in pollution policy affect the location of production, that does not necessarily mean that liberalizing trade will lead to a shifting of pollution-intensive production to countries with weaker policy. In addition, if we fail to find evidence that countries with weaker pollution policy are exporting dirty goods, this does not necessarily imply that differences across countries in regulation have a negligible effect on the location of dirty good production.

6.2. Endogenous Policy: Factor Endowments and Comparative Advantage

We now consider the possibility that countries differ in both income and relative factor endowments to examine the interaction between endogenous policy and factor endowment differences. As before, each country's regulator chooses the level of pollution that maximizes the utility of their representative agent, and the regulator is assumed to act as a price taker in world goods markets when choosing policy. From (2.81), the optimal pollution tax is

$$\tau = MD\,(p,\,R,\,z), \tag{6.9}$$

where recall that $R = I/\beta\,(p)$ is real income and we have normalized the population to $N = 1$. This leads to an upward sloping supply curve for pollution. The demand for pollution is given by (2.69) and depends on the supply of X and the endogenous emissions intensity:

$$z = e\,(p/\tau)\,x\,(p,\,\tau,\,K,\,L) = Le\,(p/\tau)\,x\,(p,\,\tau,\,K\,/\,L,\,1). \tag{6.10}$$

Combining pollution demand and supply and noting that $I = G\,(p,\,K,\,L,\,z)$ yields the equilibrium pollution tax τ and the equilibrium level of pollution, z.

To determine the trade pattern, we have to determine how endogenous changes in pollution policy interact with factor endowment differences to determine the relative supply curve. We start by examining the determinants of the equilibrium pollution tax more closely. Totally differentiating (6.9) and (6.10), holding p constant, and combining yields

$$\hat{\tau} = \frac{\varepsilon_{MD,R}\hat{R} + \varepsilon_{MD,z}\varepsilon_{x,K}\hat{K} + \varepsilon_{MD,z}\varepsilon_{x,L}\hat{L}}{1 - \varepsilon_{MD,z}\varepsilon_{z,\tau}}, \tag{6.11}$$

where $\varepsilon_{MD,R}$ is the elasticity of marginal damage with respect to real income, $\varepsilon_{MD,z} \geq 0$ is the elasticity of marginal damage with respect to pollution, $\varepsilon_{z,\tau} < 0$ is the elasticity of pollution demand with respect to the pollution tax, $\varepsilon_{x,K} > 0$ is the elasticity of X supply with respect to an increase in capital, and $\varepsilon_{x,L} < 0$ is the elasticity of X supply with respect to an increase in the supply of labor. Note that the denominator in (6.11) is positive.

The pollution tax in (6.11) is increasing in real income, increasing in capital, and declining in labor. Higher real income leads to higher pollution taxes because of increased demand for environmental quality. Increases in K (holding R constant) raise the pollution tax because pollution demand shifts out as the dirty good industry is stimulated by capital accumulation. If marginal damage is increasing in pollution, the regulator responds to higher pollution demand by raising the pollution tax. That is, the increase in the pollution tax is caused by an upward shift in demand along a rising supply curve. On the other hand, an increase in L stimulates the clean industry and relieves pressure on the environment, allowing the regulator to reduce the pollution tax.

The Constant Marginal Disutility of Pollution Case

To illustrate the different impacts of change in real income and changes in factor abundance on relative supply, we start with the very clean special case where the marginal disutility of pollution is constant. We then have $\varepsilon_{MD,z} = 0$, and (6.11) reduces to

$$\hat{\tau} = \varepsilon_{MD,R}\hat{R}, \tag{6.12}$$

which simply says that the pollution tax is higher in countries with higher real income. In this case, the pollution supply curve is horizontal for given levels of p and real income R.[8] Increases in the K/L ratio shift pollution demand rightwards. This raises pollution but leaves taxes—and hence emissions per unit output—unaffected. Increases in real income shift up the supply curve and trace out points along the pollution demand curve.

To examine the effects of endogenous policy on the pattern of trade, note that, as before, relative demands are the same across countries. Relative supply curves, however, differ across countries because of differences in policy and in factor endowment ratios. To start, assume North and South have the same K/L ratio, but that North is richer (i.e., has a larger endowment of both K and L). Referring to (6.12), the pollution tax τ is higher in the North than South because $R > R^*$. If we refer to (6.3) and (6.4), this implies that North's relative supply of X is less than South's for any p, and hence North has a comparative advantage in the clean good. This is just a special case of the pollution haven model of the previous chapter. North exports the clean good and South exports the dirty good.

Now suppose real incomes are the same in North and South, but North is capital abundant. Specifically, consider increasing K and reducing L in the North, while holding real income constant. From (6.12), pollution taxes are unaffected, and hence so too are emission intensities. But referring to (6.3), increased capital abundance increases the relative supply of X, since X is capital intensive. This shifts out North's relative supply curve and gives it a comparative advantage in the dirty good. If North is relatively capital abundant but has the same real income as the South, then North exports the dirty good and imports the clean good. This is simply the factor endowments hypothesis.[9]

---

8. The pollution supply curve when drawn as a function of z slopes upward as usual. However, if we artificially hold real income R fixed as we vary z, K and L, then the pollution supply curve is flat. That is, for given R, changes in pollution z do not lead to an increase in the willingness to pay to abate pollution.

9. To confirm that relative supply shifts out as K/L rises in the presence of endogenous policy, note from the national income function G that if we consider varying K/L, while holding R and p constant, we must be considering variations in K, L, and z satisfying

$$\hat{I} = s_k \hat{K} + s_L \hat{L} + s_z \hat{z} = 0,$$

where s_i is the share of factor i in national income. Differentiating pollution demand, and noting that emissions per unit of output are constant because R is held fixed, yields

$$\hat{z} = \hat{L} + \varepsilon_{x,\,k} (\hat{K/L}).$$

We can use the above two expressions to solve for the $\hat{L}$ needed to hold income constant. Substituting this into the equation for output yields

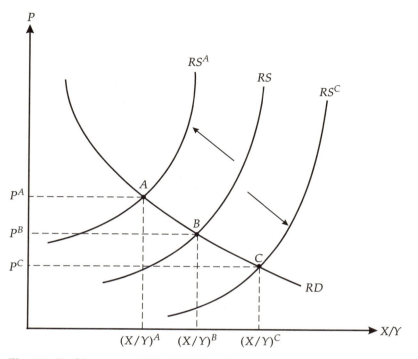

Fig. 6.3. Real Income and Capital Abundance

The interaction between relative factor abundance and relative income levels is illustrated in figure 6.3. An increase in income—holding relative factor endowments fixed—shifts relative supply upwards to RS^A, changing the autarky equilibria from B to A. In contrast, an increase in relative capital abundance—holding real income constant—shifts relative supply outwards to RS^C, changing the autarky equilibria from B to C.

The General Case: Increasing Marginal Disutility of Pollution

In the above discussion, we assumed that the marginal disutility of pollution was constant, so that the pollution tax did not vary with the K/L ratio for given levels of real income. More generally (if the mar-

---

$$\hat{x} = [\varepsilon_{x,K} \, s_L + (\varepsilon_{x,K} - 1) \, s_K] \, (\hat{K}/L) > 0.$$

Moreover, because L falls and K/L rises, we also conclude that Y must decrease. Consequently, relative supply shifts outward as argued above.

ginal disutility of pollution is increasing), an increase in relative capital
abundance stimulates the polluting industry, and with an upward
sloping pollution supply curve, this puts increased pressure on the environment and leads to more stringent policy, even for given levels of
real income. This change in the pollution tax however creates only a
dampening effect. As we increase K/L, holding real income constant,
the endogenous increase in the pollution tax dampens, but cannot reverse, the expansion of X.[10] Consequently, the same qualitative results
we found above when marginal damage was independent of emissions
hold in the more general case. Holding K/L constant, an increase in
real income tends to generate a comparative advantage in the clean
good; while if real income is held constant, an increase in capital abundance tends to generate a comparative advantage in the dirty good.

6.3 Correlated Characteristics: Being Rich and Capital Abundant

Rich Northern countries are likely to be both capital abundant and
have stricter pollution policy than poorer Southern countries. North's
strict pollution policy will tend to make it a dirty good importer, but
its capital abundance tends to make it a dirty good exporter. The pattern of trade depends on which of these effects is stronger.

To study the pattern of trade, we assume that North is capital abundant relative to the South, and for clarity, we present only the case
where the marginal disutility of pollution does not vary with the level
of pollution. We also make one additional assumption. Assume that
there exists an $\varepsilon > 0$ such that for all $p > 0$ and $R > 0$, we have

$$\frac{\partial MD}{\partial R} \geq \varepsilon. \qquad (6.13)$$

This means that as income rises, marginal damage always rises, no
matter how high income is. This ensures that sufficiently rich countries
have a comparative advantage in the clean good.

---

10. Following the same procedure as in the previous footnote, the effect of an increase
in K/L on X, holding real income constant, is

$$\hat{x} = \frac{[\varepsilon_{x,K}\, s_L + (\varepsilon_{x,K} - 1)\, s_K]\,(\hat{K/L})}{s_Z + (1 + \varepsilon_{c,p/\tau}\varepsilon_{MD,Z})\,(s_L + s_K)} > 0.$$

This differs from our previous result only via the dampening effect in the denominator.

Since we have assumed that marginal damage does not vary with pollution, we can write the emission intensity as a function of R and p alone: $e = e(p, R)$. Denote the Southern autarky equilibrium by (p^{*A}, R^{*A}). Taking factor endowment ratios in both North and South as given, define R_I as the real income in the North that renders North's relative supply equal to South's at price p^{*A}; that is, define R_I implicitly as the solution to

$$RS\,[p^{*A}, e(p^{*A}, R_I), K/L] = RS^*\,[p^{*A}, e(p^{*A}, R^*), K^*/L^*], \qquad (6.14)$$

where RS and RS^* are the relative supplies defined in (6.3) and (6.4) respectively, and we have made use of (6.12) and (6.1). Our assumption (6.13) ensures that R_I exists.[11]

The critical income level R_I is the point where pollution policy in the North is strict enough to exactly offset the effects of North's capital abundance. Hence for $R = R_I$ there is no trade despite differences between North and South in both pollution policy and factor abundance.

We can now consider the trade pattern. Since RS is decreasing in R, North's relative supply is to the right of South's for all real income levels below R_I. For all real income levels above R_I, the opposite is true. That is, North exports the clean good for $R > R_I$, and exports the dirty good for $R < R_I$.

Moreover, there must exist an interval of real income levels in the North such that[12]

$$R_I > R > R^* \text{ and } RS > RS^*. \qquad (6.15)$$

This implies, employing (6.14), that there exists an interval of Northern real income levels where North has tighter policy than South but retains its comparative advantage in dirty goods.

Note also that R_I is increasing in K/L and falling in K^*/L^*. Therefore, as we hold R^* constant but make the countries more dissimilar in relative factor endowments, the range of Northern real income levels satisfying (6.15) grows. That is, the greater are relative factor endowment differences across countries; the larger is the range of income levels that are consistent with North's exporting dirty goods.

---

11. To see this, note that for $R = R^*$, $RS \geq RS^*$, because North is capital abundant. Using (6.13), we know that e falls to zero as R gets very large; hence there will be some $R > R^*$ at which North specializes in Y. At this point $RS = 0 \leq RS^*$. By continuity, there must therefore be a critical value of $R = R_I$ that satisfies (6.14).

12. Note from (6.14) that $R_I > R^*$ since $K/L > K^*/L^*$.

The interaction of factor endowment and income differences can therefore lead to two quite different trade patterns. If North is capital abundant and relative factor endowment differences are large relative to real income differences, then North exports dirty goods. On the other hand, if income differences are large relative to factor endowment differences, then a pollution haven emerges in the South.

Effects of Trade on Pollution When North Exports the Dirty Good

The implications of a Southern pollution haven are similar to those discussed in chapter 5, so here we focus on the case where North exports the dirty good.[13] When North is sufficiently capital abundant, trade will lead to an expansion of the dirty industry in the North, despite North's stricter pollution regulation and higher income. Although North's stricter environmental regulations do raise Northern production costs in X, this is more than offset by the relative abundance of factors used intensively in X. Trade need not induce migration of dirty industry from rich to poor countries.

Trade reduces the demand for emissions in the South, but raises income (which shifts pollution supply back). Both effects will reduce pollution in the South. In the North, the demand for emissions rises, while the supply shifts back. As shown in chapter 3, if the income elasticity of marginal damage is not too high, then the demand effect dominates and pollution rises in the North. But if the income elasticity of marginal damage with respect to income is sufficiently high in the North, then it is possible that trade may reduce pollution in both North and South. This will occur if North's pollution supply shifts back far enough to offset the increased pollution demand.

Effects of Trade on World Pollution

If North exports the dirty good, world pollution is now much more likely to fall than in the pure pollution haven model of chapter 5. When the rich North exports the dirty good, trade shifts some dirty good production from the country with weak pollution standards (South) to the country where pollution regulations are more stringent (North). The global composition effect of trade therefore tends to reduce pollu-

---

13. Note that our focus in this section is on the effects of trade on pollution, not welfare. Because we are assuming that all countries have efficient pollution policy, trade is wel-

tion: each unit of dirty good production that shifts to North from South as a result of trade is produced with a lower emission intensity than previously. In contrast, in the pollution haven model of chapter 5, the composition effect tended to increase world pollution by shifting dirty industries to the South.

To make this discussion more concrete, adopt the assumptions used in chapter 5 when we discussed global pollution. Suppose utility is Cobb-Douglas and the income elasticity of marginal damage is constant. Under these assumptions the difference between global pollution levels in autarky versus trade was given by

$$z^{WT} - z^{WA} = \frac{ab\,[R_T^{1-\eta} - R^{1-\eta}]}{\gamma} + \frac{ab\,[R_T^{*1-\eta} - R^{*1-\eta}]}{\gamma}$$
$$+ \frac{\alpha\,[s_x^* - s_x]\,[\varphi R_T^{*1-\eta} - (1-\varphi)\,R^{1-\eta}]}{\gamma}, \tag{6.16}$$

where recall that s_x and s_x^* are the free trade income shares of dirty good production in North and South, and φ is North's free trade share of world income.

Recall that the difference between autarky and world pollution levels is composed of three distinct terms. The first two terms in (6.16) represent the sum of scale and technique effects in the North and South. Since real income in trade is greater than in autarky, the sign of the sum of these two effects depends only on the strength of the elasticity of marginal damage, η.

The last term is the world composition effect, which we rewrite as

$$\frac{\alpha}{\gamma}\,[s_x^* - s_x]\,(1-\varphi)\,R_T^{*1-\eta}\left[\frac{I_T}{I_T^*} - \left(\frac{I_T}{I_T^*}\right)^{1-\eta}\right] \le 0. \tag{6.17}$$

When North, which is both rich and capital abundant, exports the dirty good in trade, the world composition effect is negative because $s_x > s_x^*$.[14] Consequently, the first bracketed term is negative, while the second is positive whenever $I > I^*$ (which is true by construction).

To put these three effects together, it is useful to start with the case where the income elasticity of marginal damage is equal to 1; that is, $\eta = 1$. In this case, the first two terms in (6.16) drop out because scale

---

fare improving. If policy is not efficient, then welfare effects may be ambiguous in countries where pollution rises or falls.

14. This obtains because if South imports dirty goods, then $s_x^* < b$, and so for North we must have $s_x > b$.

and technique effects just offset each other. This leaves only the global composition effect, which is negative. That is, free trade leads to a fall in global pollution when North has a comparative advantage in the dirty good, and the income elasticity of marginal damage is equal to 1. This is opposite to the result that we obtained in chapter 5, where trade created a pollution haven in the South.

More generally, world pollution must fall with trade liberalization if $\eta \geq 1$, and the North exports dirty goods. This is because in these cases scale effects are being dominated by technique effects, and the world composition effect is lowering world pollution. If instead $\eta \leq 1$, then policy responses are weaker and scale effects dominate technique effects, which tends to raise global pollution. However, the world composition effect remains negative and so the net effect of freer trade on global pollution is ambiguous.

Implications for Empirical Work

One important implication of endogenous policy in models with more than one determinant of comparative advantage is that interpreting simple correlations between the stringency of pollution regulations and trade patterns is fraught with peril.

Suppose three countries have similar real incomes but differ in relative factor abundance and are engaged in free trade with each other, so that all face the same goods prices. Then each country will have similar marginal damage curves, and for clarity we assume that real income differences are such that the *MD* curves are the same across countries,[15] as shown by the common pollution supply curve drawn in figure 6.4.

Suppose, though, that the three countries differ in factor abundance. Specifically, suppose that country 2 is more capital abundant than country 1, which in turn is more capital abundant than country 0. Country 2's pollution demand will therefore be farther out to the right than country 1's, which is turn is farther out than country 0's. Consequently, pollution taxes are highest in country 2. That is, we have $\tau_2 > \tau_1 > \tau_0$.

From our earlier analysis, we know that the most capital abundant country has a comparative advantage in the dirty good (the higher pollution taxes dampen, but do not reverse, the effect), and the least capi-

---

15. This can always be implemented with judicious choices of K and L across countries.

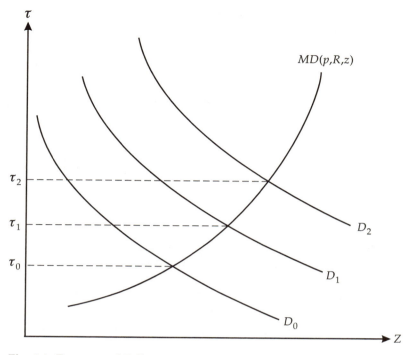

Fig. 6.4. Exports and Pollution Taxes

tal abundant county has a comparative advantage in the clean good. Suppose we now decide to test the pollution haven hypothesis, but neglect to control for the country-specific effects, such as factor abundance. A simple regression of dirty good exports on the stringency of pollution regulation would find that countries with more stringent pollution regulation are more likely to export the dirty good! That is, not only would the pollution haven hypothesis be refuted, but we would find, paradoxically, that stringent pollution regulation does not appear to deter exports of dirty goods, and in fact seems to encourage it.

This should not, however, be interpreted as evidence against the hypothesis that high pollution taxes tend to deter exports of dirty goods. Even though higher pollution taxes are correlated with higher exports of dirty goods, it is still nevertheless true that high pollution taxes reduce dirty good exports as they act to dampen the effects of capital abundance on the trade pattern. Put another way, if we control for capital abundance, then increases in pollution taxes will reduce dirty good exports.

While the potential misinterpretation of the evidence highlighted here can be rectified by controlling for capital abundance, this exercise serves to point out a more general problem that arises in testing for the effects of pollution regulation on trade patterns. If there are unobserved variables (such as technology differences, etc.) that are positively correlated with pollution demand, then there is the possibility of obtaining a positive correlation between pollution regulation and exports of dirty goods. But this should not be interpreted as evidence against the hypothesis that high pollution taxes tend to erode a country's comparative advantage in dirty goods. Rather, the analyst must take care to control for the endogeneity of pollution policy.[16]

6.4 An Illustrative Example

We conclude this chapter by providing an extended illustrative example that demonstrates the offsetting influences of income and factor abundance very clearly. The example contains two major simplifications. First, we employ our log utility framework with a Cobb-Douglas sub-utility function as in the example of chapter 5. Second, to solve for relative supply transparently, we eliminate any competition between industries for mobile factors.

Assume the clean industry Y uses only labor, so that

$$Y = L. \tag{6.18}$$

And assume that the dirty industry uses only capital,[17] so that

$$X = K^{1-\alpha} Z^{\alpha}. \tag{6.19}$$

We assume Cobb-Douglas preferences over consumption goods and adopt the following simple indirect utility function

$$V = \ln (I/\beta (p)) - \gamma Z. \tag{6.20}$$

With these preferences, the optimal pollution tax is proportional to income:

---

16. See Levinson 1999 for an empirical application that illustrates the potential importance of endogeneity when studying the effects of differences in pollution policy. Levinson uses U.S. data to study the effects of state-level differences in hazardous waste disposal taxes on trade in waste between states. Using an OLS regression, higher taxes are associated with higher imports of waste, contrary to what one would expect. After controlling for endogeneity, he finds that, all else equal, higher taxes deter waste imports.
17. That is, in (2.2) we let $F = K$, and in (2.1) we let $H = L$.

$$\tau = \gamma I. \tag{6.21}$$

To solve for the relative supply curve, use the production functions to obtain

$$RS = \frac{X}{Y} = \frac{K^{1-a}\,Z^a}{L}. \tag{6.22}$$

But pollution Z is given by $Z = ex$, where $e = ap/\tau$. Substituting for Z in (6.22) and rearranging, we obtain relative supply as[18]

$$RS = \frac{X}{Y} = e^{a/(1-a)}\frac{K}{L} = \left[\frac{ap}{\tau}\right]^{a/(1-a)}\frac{K}{L}. \tag{6.23}$$

Exogenous Policy and Factor Endowments

In section 6.1 we compared relative supplies by defining a hypothetical indifference emission level denoted by e_I. Using (6.23) this is simply defined by

$$e_I^{a/(1-a)}\frac{K}{L} = e^{*a/(1-a)}\frac{K^*}{L^*} \tag{6.24}$$

$$\Rightarrow e_I = e^*\left[\frac{K^*/L^*}{K/L}\right]^{(1-a)/a}.$$

For $e > e_I$, relative supply of the North exceeds that of the South; conversely for $e < e_I$, the opposite is true. We also noted earlier that $e^* > e_I$ whenever $K/L > K^*/L^*$; the reader can confirm this in our example using (6.24). Note also from (6.22) that as emission intensities in the North fall, its relative supply of X to Y goes to zero. Hence we can be assured that an indifference level of e_I exists.

In section 6.1 we also noted that for any Northern emission intensity, e, such that $e^* > e > e_I$, the North has a comparative advantage in dirty goods despite its tighter emission regulation. With slight rearrangement and using (6.24), we can find

$$\frac{e^* - e_I}{e_I} = \Lambda^{(1-a)/a} - 1, \tag{6.25}$$

where $\Lambda = (K/L)/(K^*/L^*) > 1$ is the ratio of North's capital-to-labor ratio to South's. Therefore, the range of emission intensities in the

---

18. We note that relative supply is a function only of e, and not e and p because in the absence of abatement both X and Y are fixed by endowments.

North consistent with North exporting the dirty good get larger as the gap between Northern and Southern factor endowments grows. This is as it should be, since a greater difference in factor endowments means the comparative advantage of North in dirty good is stronger; hence tighter Northern emission intensities will remain consistent with North exporting dirty good over a wider range.

Finally, note from (6.23) that relative supplies of North and South revert to their pure factor endowment analogs as α goes to zero. Recall that α is the share of pollution taxes in the value of production of the dirty good. Therefore, our example bears out the common claim that differences in pollution charges will have little effect on comparative advantage when they represent a small portion of costs. That is, as α falls, the cost differential created by regulations becomes less and less important in affecting trade patterns.[19] In contrast, as α increases in magnitude (reflecting increased importance of pollution charges), differences in emission intensities become a relatively more important determinant of the trade pattern.

Endogenous Policy and Factor Endowments

Now consider endogenous policy. Substituting in (6.23) for the pollution tax via (6.21), we obtain

$$RS = \left[\frac{\alpha p}{\gamma} \right]^{\alpha/(\alpha - 1)} I^{\alpha/(\alpha - 1)} \left[\frac{K}{L} \right]. \tag{6.26}$$

Relative supply is increasing in p and K/L, but decreasing in income levels.

To determine autarky prices, we solve for autarky pollution. Recalling $Z = ex$, using (6.21), and noting that $pX = bI$ in autarky, we find $z = \alpha b / \gamma$, as we did in our example in chapter 5. Substitute this into the production function for X, and equate X/Y with relative demand (which recall is $x/y = b/(1 - b)p$) to solve for the autarky relative price of X:

$$p^A = \left[\frac{b}{1 - b} \right]^{1 - \alpha} \left[\frac{K}{L} \right]^{\alpha - 1} \left[\frac{\gamma L}{\alpha (1 - b)} \right]^{\alpha}. \tag{6.27}$$

The autarky relative price of X is increasing in consumer's taste for X, as given by b; increasing in L, which proxies for the economy's income

---

19. Note that when e is endogenous, the emission intensity itself would be changing with α, and so the argument above would have to be altered.

level; increasing in the disutility of pollution, γ; and decreasing in the economy's capital-to-labor ratio.

With the solution for p in hand, we now check to ensure that $e < 1$, as implicitly assumed in our analysis. Substituting for τ from (6.21), we require

$$e = \frac{\alpha p}{\gamma I} < 1. \tag{6.28}$$

We will assume this holds in both autarky and free trade, but will here just solve for the conditions required in autarky. In autarky, note that $I = L/(1-b)$. Employing (6.27) and rearranging, we obtain the condition that

$$\frac{\alpha b}{\gamma} < (1-b)\, I \left[\frac{K}{L} \right] = K. \tag{6.29}$$

Abatement will occur if either income is relatively high (since this drives up pollution taxes), or the relative price of abatement inputs, X, is low, which is the case when the economy is very capital abundant. Assuming (6.29) is met, we now proceed to compare relative supply curves across countries.[20]

Factor Endowments and Income Differences

To determine the trade pattern, we compare relative supplies for a given world price p. Substitute for taxes using (6.21) and divide to find

$$\frac{RS}{RS^*} = \left[\frac{I^*}{I} \right]^{\alpha/(1-\alpha)} \left[\frac{K/L}{K^*/L^*} \right]. \tag{6.30}$$

Consider two countries that differ only in the scale of the consumer's wealth. To eliminate factor composition differences, suppose North's endowment vector is a scaled-up version of South's, so that $(K, L) = \lambda\,(K^*, L^*)$, where $\lambda > 1$. This yields the pollution haven model of the previous chapter. From (6.30) we have

$$\frac{RS}{RS^*} = \left[\frac{I^*}{I} \right]^{\alpha/(1-\alpha)}.$$

With $\lambda > 1$, we have $I > I^*$.[21] Hence the relative supply of X is smaller in the high-income country (North) than in the low-income country

---

20. A similar condition must be met in any trading equilibrium.
21. Note here that the incomes I and I^* in this expression are the equilibrium free trade incomes for the given level of p under consideration.

(South), as illustrated previously in figure 5.2. Because of North's higher productive capacity, the environment is a relatively scarce factor there, and hence pollution permit prices are higher than in South. Consequently, North has a comparative advantage in the clean good, and South in the dirty good. This is apparent from (6.27), which we can use to solve for autarky relative prices to compare them and find:[22]

$$\frac{p^A}{p^{A*}} = \left[\frac{I_A}{I_A^*}\right]^\alpha > 1.$$

When we open up these countries to trade, the relative price of X will rise in South and fall in North. This has consequent effects on the level of pollution. In South this implies $s_x^* > b$: pollution will rise in South with trade. On the other hand, the relative price of X will fall in North, and hence in North we have $s_x < b$ and pollution will fall. Trade thus leads to a change in the global incidence of pollution, shifting some polluting activity from the rich country to the poor country.

To compare world pollution in free trade and autarky, we again employ a result from chapter 5:

$$z^w - (z^a + z^{a*}) = \frac{2\alpha}{\gamma}(s_x^* - s_x)\left(\varphi - \frac{1}{2}\right), \tag{6.31}$$

where $\varphi = I/(I + I^*)$ is North's share of world income. Since $s_x^* > b > s_x$, and North is richer than South, the above expression is positive and world pollution rises with free trade.

Alternatively, consider two countries that have the same income at the free trade price p,[23] but different relative capital abundance. Referring to (6.30), we now have

$$\frac{RS}{RS^*} = \left[\frac{K/L}{K^*/L^*}\right]. \tag{6.32}$$

If North is capital abundant relative to South, then $K/L > K^*/L^*$, and North has a larger relative supply of X, given p. Hence North (the capital-abundant country) exports the dirty good. Moreover, pollution will

---

22. Note that the incomes in this expression are autarky incomes (each country's autarky income is evaluated at its autarky price). Moreover, note that in autarky, incomes are $(1 - b) L$ and $(1 - b) L^*$.

23. Note that in autarky, we have $I = L/ (1 - b)$, and $I^* = L^*/(1 - b)$—incomes in autarky are determined by labor endowments. However, this is not true in free trade. In free trade, world income depends on labor endowments, (we have $I + I^* = (L + L^*)/(1 - b)$), but each country's income will also depend on its supply of capital. Since we are considering a case where $I = I^*$, and since $K/L > K^*/L^*$, then we must have $L < L^*$. Note that

rise in the capital-abundant North and fall in the capital-scarce South upon the opening of trade.

To compare world pollution in free trade and autarky, we make use of (6.31) to conclude, since $I = I^*$, that

$$z^w - (z^a + z^{a^*}) = \frac{2\alpha}{\gamma} (s_x^* - s_x) \left(\varphi - \frac{1}{2} \right) = 0.$$

World pollution is unaffected by trade. Recall that under our log utility assumption scale effects offset technique, leaving only the world composition effect to determine the change in pollution levels. But if $I = I^*$, then $\tau = \tau^*$ and $e = e^*$; therefore, although dirty good production is concentrated in the capital-abundant country, this has no effect on world pollution levels.

Correlated Attributes: Capital Abundance and Income

Suppose North is both rich and capital abundant. Then North exports the dirty good if for any given p, North's relative supply of X is greater than South's. To investigate the offsetting forces of income and factor endowment differences, we earlier defined an indifference real income level R_I such that the two effects just offset each other. Using (6.26) and recalling $R = I/\beta(p)$ we have

$$R_I = R^* \left[\frac{K/L}{K^*/L^*} \right]^{(1-a)/a}. \tag{6.33}$$

which is just a special case of (6.14). We then note that if $R > R_I$, then North imports the dirty good; if $R < R_I$, then it exports the dirty good. Since North is capital abundant relative to South, we must have $R_I > R^*$. Therefore, North is both richer than South and an exporter of the dirty good when $R_I > R > R^*$.

In our specific context, North will export the dirty good whenever

$$\frac{K/L}{K^*/L^*} > \left[\frac{R}{R^*} \right]^{a/(1-a)}. \tag{6.34}$$

That is, for any given relative income level, North exports the dirty good if it is sufficiently capital abundant relative to South. Equivalently, given any level of relative factor abundance, North exports the dirty good if it is not too rich. That is, North exports the dirty good if

---

this implies that even though incomes may differ in autarky, they may be equalized by free trade.

$$\frac{R}{R^*} < \left[\frac{K/L}{K^*/L^*} \right]^{(1-a)/a}.$$ (6.35)

Again, notice that while R is endogenous, we can always vary R/R^* independently by varying K and K^*, holding K/L and K^*/L^* (and p) constant.

Alternatively, if $R > R_l > R^*$, then North exports the clean good. Therefore the gap between R_l and R^* is important, as it tells us the admissible range of Northern real income for which North will retain a comparative advantage in the dirty good. Again, to measure this gap we have

$$\frac{R_l - R^*}{R^*} = \Lambda^{(1-a)/a} - 1 > 0,$$ (6.36)

where Λ is the ratio of North's capital abundance to South's. The range of possible Northern incomes consistent with it remaining a dirty good exporter are increasing in the gap in Northern and Southern factor endowments. To get a feel for just how big a gap (6.36) represents, suppose pollution charges are 10% of the value of output. Our data from chapter 7 shows that the ratio of U.S. to Chinese K/L ratios is approximately 9.0. Hence the right-hand side of (6.36) becomes $9^9 - 1$ when $a = .10$. Therefore the range of U.S. income consistent with it remaining a dirty good exporter to China is huge!

Finally, note that when (6.35) holds, we have that $s_x > b$ for the North and $s_x^* < b$ for the South. Consequently, we can conclude that pollution rises in the North with trade and falls in the South. Moreover, again employing (6.31), we now have that

$$z^w - (z^a + z^{a^*}) = \frac{2\alpha}{\gamma}\,(s_x^* - s_x)\left(\varphi - \frac{1}{2}\right) < 0,$$ (6.37)

and world pollution falls with trade. Alternatively, when equation (6.35) fails, we have world pollution rising with trade.

Global composition effects drive these results. The income elasticity of marginal damage is equal to 1 in this example, and so scale and technique effects exactly offset each other, leaving the global composition effect to determine the consequences of trade on world pollution. If North is rich and exports the dirty good, then trade liberalization leads to a shifting of some dirty good production to the North, which has more stringent pollution policy because of its higher income. Consequently, trade leads to a reduction in average global pollution intensity of production, and world pollution falls. On the other hand, if North is not sufficiently capital abundant to offset the pollution haven effect, then South exports the dirty good, and we are back to the results of chapter 5.

6.5 Conclusion

We began this chapter with a puzzle: why are some of the most pollution-intensive goods produced in developed countries with stringent regulation? This observation seems to contradict the pollution haven hypothesis. To investigate, we introduced one additional motivation for trade in our model. Since dirty industries are often capital intensive, we allowed countries to differ in relative factor endowments. That is, we investigated the implications of the *factor endowments hypothesis* as a competing theory of trade in dirty goods.

The chapter then proceeded to work through the implications of countries differing in both pollution policy and factor endowments. The overall message is simple: the effects of trade on both the local and global environment depend quite critically on the distribution of factor endowments across countries. Since comparative advantage is determined jointly by differences in pollution policy and differences in factor endowments, most of the predictions of the pollution haven model can be reversed in a world where factor endowments matter, and hence our simple model with two sources of trade can provide a potential resolution to the puzzle we began with. Dirty good production can remain in high-income countries despite much tighter regulation if these cost disadvantages are offset by other factors.

For example, we found that Southern pollution havens need not emerge in trade if rich Northern countries tend to be relatively abundant in factors used intensively in pollution-intensive industries. And if this is the case, then trade may lead to both a cleaner environment in poor countries and a reduction in global pollution. Poorly regulated Southern countries will necessarily gain from trade, while more stringently regulated Northern countries will gain as well. Our results also point out that differences in pollution policy alone need not imply that trade liberalization will force dirty industries to migrate to less regulated countries. Therefore, concerns that the North may end up with "regulatory chill" because of dirty industry migration may be misplaced.

However, it is also possible that factor endowment differences may not be sufficient to offset the cost differential created by different regulations. When this is the case, we obtain results much like the pollution haven model of chapter 5, albeit in a world where countries differ along more than one dimension.

Our results also suggest that for some industries, factor endowment effects can reinforce pollution policy effects. Polluting industries that are intensive in unskilled labor or in natural resources that are abundant in low-income countries will be attracted to those low-income countries by both factor abundance and less stringent policy. We would therefore expect to see heterogeneity across industries as well as countries in how policy differences and factor endowments interact to determine trade patterns.

Finally, even if rich countries do turn out to have a comparative advantage in dirty industries because of factor endowment effects, this does not mean that pollution policy is irrelevant for trade patterns. As our analysis indicates, for given levels of capital abundance, increases in the stringency of pollution policy erode a country's comparative advantage in dirty goods and tend to reduce dirty good exports.

7

Is Free Trade Good for the Environment? An Empirical Assessment

The previous five chapters set out a theoretical framework to examine the links between free trade, growth in income, and environmental outcomes. We asked how free trade affected pollution levels, and we asked whether different sources of income growth produced different environmental impacts. In many cases the answers we obtained were conditional. The impact of free trade on the environment depended quite importantly on the strength of policy responses. And even in a world where policy was flexible and responsive to trade-created income gains, the impact of free trade still depended on a country's comparative advantage. Accordingly, we set out the factor endowments and pollution haven hypotheses as two theories linking national attributes to comparative advantage. Both theories provided logically consistent and compelling explanations linking national attributes to comparative advantage in dirty goods. But these two theories predicted very different environmental consequences from trade. It became apparent that the answer to almost any policy question would require us to weigh their relative merits.

This chapter provides empirical evidence useful in this weighing. We ask two key questions of the data. What are the magnitudes of scale, composition, and technique effects? What is the relative strength of pollution haven versus factor abundance motives in determining comparative advantage in dirty goods? In asking these questions we provide a tentative answer to the question of how openness to international goods markets affects pollution concentrations, and we provide estimates linking different sources of income growth to their pollution consequences.[1]

This chapter uses the models and analysis developed in previous chapters to divide the impact of trade liberalization into scale, technique, and composition effects and then estimate their magnitude using data on sulfur dioxide concentrations from the Global Environment Monitoring Project. The data set we employ contains observations of pollution concentrations measured at 290 sites in 108 cities located in 43 developed and developing countries over the period 1971 to 1996. Our analysis focuses on just one pollutant—sulfur dioxide— but sulfur dioxide emissions are closely tied to other noxious pollutants such as nitrogen oxides and particulates. Therefore our results may well generalize, and in the final chapter we discuss how the methods we develop could be employed in other circumstances. Since sulfur dioxide is a major pollutant, our empirical results should be of direct interest to many in the policy community.

Our empirical results are surely provocative. We find that the composition effect created by international trade is statistically significant, but relatively small. Our estimates of the associated technique and scale effects created by trade imply a net reduction in pollution from these sources. Combining our estimates of scale, composition, and technique effects yields a surprising conclusion: freer trade appears to be good for the environment—at least for the average country in our sample, and for the pollutant we study.

We also find that changes in pollution concentrations caused by international trade vary across countries, as one would expect from either the pollution haven or the factor endowments hypothesis. But our estimates of the composition effect of trade weigh in favor of factor endowments being the dominant motive for trade in dirty products. This empirical result together with our theory of chapter 6 implies that dirty good production should migrate Northward and not Southward with liberalized trade; world pollution may well fall as dirty good production is shifted to more tightly regulated economies; and, finally, if the rich developed world's environmental policy is quite income elastic, pollution levels will fall in both the developed and developing world with liberalized trade.

---

1. The empirical work presented in this chapter draws heavily on joint work (Antweiler, Copeland, and Taylor 2001) with Werner Antweiler of the University of British Columbia. Portions of this chapter were reproduced with permission from the *American Economic Review*.

In addition to our empirical results, this chapter provides five methodological contributions to research in this area. First, we demonstrate how to derive a simple reduced form equation from our general equilibrium pollution-and-trade model. This reduced form is useful for estimation here and we suspect elsewhere.

Second, we illustrate how one can separately identify both scale and technique effects from the data. Previous work had been unable to estimate these effects, although having separate estimates would be quite useful.[2] For example, income transfers across countries raise national income but not output: creating a technique effect but no scale effect. Foreign direct investment raises output more than national income: creating a scale effect but a smaller technique effect. An initial step toward evaluating the environmental consequences of either requires separate estimates of technique and scale effects.

Separate estimates have been unavailable because any increase in income is likely to shift both pollution supply and demand, making identification of their separate impacts on pollution difficult. We address this problem in several ways. Our primary method is to exploit the within-country variation in our data set. Under the assumption that pollution policy is set at the national level, pollution supply is common for all cities within a given country. But cities differ in the scale of their output. Therefore, differences within countries but across cities in scale can be used to distinguish between scale and technique effects.[3] Our estimates indicate that a 1% increase in the scale of economic activity raises concentrations by 0.25 to 0.5%, but the accompanying increase in income drives concentrations down by 1.25–1.5% via a technique effect.

Third, we show that our approach provides a method for determining how trade-induced changes in the composition of output affects pollution concentrations. Many empirical studies include some measure of openness to capture the impact of trade, but there is very little reason to believe that openness per se affects all countries similarly. Both the pollution haven hypothesis and the factor endowments hypothesis predict that openness to trade will alter the composition of

---

2. For example, Grossman and Krueger (1993, 1995) do not attempt to measure these effects separately. Hilton and Levinson 1998 comes quite close to estimating the scale and technique effects separately.

3. This is not the only means we employ for separating these effects. We also exploit variation across time, and cross-country variation in the relationship between GDP and GNP.

national output in a manner that depends on a nation's comparative advantage.[4]

Therefore, it does not make sense to ask how openness per se affects pollution levels. The answer has to be conditional on a country's comparative advantage. To do so, we capture trade's composition effect by interacting a measure of openness with country characteristics determining comparative advantage.

This approach receives some support in the data. For example, after accounting for variables capturing scale and technique effects, simple measures of openness per se, measured in a variety of ways, have very little impact on pollution concentrations.[5] In contrast, when we condition openness on country characteristics, we find a highly significant, but relatively small, impact on pollution concentrations.

Fourth, we provide a method for evaluating the environmental consequences of growth that is more theoretically based than that of the current environmental Kuznets curve literature. Our approach allows us to distinguish between the pollution consequences of income growth brought about by increased openness from those created by capital accumulation or technological progress.[6] We find that income gains brought about by increased trade or neutral technological progress tend to lower pollution, while income gains brought about by capital accumulation raise pollution. The key difference is that capital accumulation favors the production of pollution-intensive goods, whereas neutral technological progress and increased trade do not. One implication of this finding is that the pollution consequences of economic growth depend on the underlying source of growth. This provides some evidence in support of our analysis of growth and pollution in chapter 3. Another more speculative implication is that pollution concentrations should at first rise and then fall with increases in income per capita, if capital accumulation becomes a less important source of growth as development proceeds.

---

4. Recall from chapter 5 that the composition effect of trade for poor countries makes them dirtier, while the composition effect for rich countries makes them cleaner. The full effect of trade may be positive even for poor countries, depending on the strength of the technique and scale effects.
5. See table 2, p. 30 from Antweiler, Copeland, and Taylor 1998.
6. Gale and Mendez (1998) in their environmental Kuznets curve study investigate the role that capital abundance may play in predicting cross-country differences in pollution levels. They use only one year of data and cannot separate scale from technique effects, but their work is important in suggesting a strong link between factor endowments and pollution levels, after controlling for income differences.

And finally, we provide a method for adding up the "full implications of international trade" on the environment while challenging researchers to expand on these methods to allow capital flows and technological progress to respond to trade liberalization. Once we have
estimated scale, composition, and technique effects, we use our theory
to combine these estimates to arrive at an assessment of the environmental impact of freer trade. Grossman and Krueger's (1993) influential study of NAFTA presented an argument based on the relative
strength of these same three effects, but here we go further by estimating scale, technique, and composition effects jointly on a data set that
includes over 40 developed and developing countries.

The model we develop and estimate combines elements from several
chapters. We assume the world is populated with small open economies, as we did in chapters 2–4. We adopt a political economy structure
with Greens and Browns as two groups in society, similar to that developed in chapter 4. And we allow for both pollution haven and factor
endowment motives to determine comparative advantage, as discussed in chapters 5 and 6. Considering these two possible motivations
for trade is especially important in an empirical exercise because many
of the most polluting industries are also highly capital intensive.[7]

One noteworthy feature of our work is simply that estimation and
inference is guided by theory to a much greater extent than previous
work. The overall impression one gets from the empirical literature in
this area is that while there are some interesting findings, a consensus
view does not exist.[8] For example, many researchers have documented
a rising share of dirty good production and exports in developing
countries and a falling share of these same industries in the developed
world.[9] To some, this is prima facie evidence of the pollution haven
hypothesis. But at the same time other researchers have had difficulty
finding a strong link between the level of pollution abatement costs
and import penetration.[10] This suggests that the costs imposed by

---

7. See appendix B, section B.2 of Antweiler, Copeland, and Taylor 1998 for evidence linking capital intensity and pollution intensity.

8. For a survey of the empirical literature, see Copeland and Taylor 2001.

9. For early work along these lines see Low and Yeats 1992 or Lucas, Wheeler, and Hettige 1992. More recent analysis is contained in Mani and Wheeler 1997.

10. A much-cited early study is Tobey 1990, which found no evidence that abatement
costs affect trade patterns. Jaffe et al. (1995) provide a review of the literature. A recent
paper by Levinson (1999), however, points out that the endogeneity of environmental
policy may be confounding estimates in this literature. He studies the effects of taxes on
hazardous waste on interstate trade in waste in the United States. After correcting for

tighter pollution regulation may not be a major determinant of trade patterns. Unless we develop a theoretical framework to guide empirical work, it will remain difficult to disentangle the many conflicting forces that shape both trade patterns and environmental outcomes. And as we discussed in chapter 6, it will be impossible to reconcile finding support for a pollution haven effect, with an overall rejection of the pollution haven hypothesis.

While this chapter is a useful first step toward determining the effect of trade on the environment, it is clearly not the last. We view the attempt to integrate theory with empirical work as our major contribution to research in this area. The benefit of presenting an explicit pollution demand and supply model is that researchers should now be drawn to deeper questions concerning endogeneity, omitted variables, and sample selection. In our final chapter we set out an agenda for research addressing some of these deficiencies.

The rest of the chapter is organized as follows. In section 7.1 we consider three basic questions about our analysis. Following this in section 7.2 we discuss the pollution data employed in our work. In section 7.3 we develop the reduced form for pollution concentrations and discuss how to use the reduced form to determine the effects of trade on the environment. Measurement issues and our strategy for dealing with econometric difficulties are covered in section 7.4. Section 7.5 contains our empirical results, and section 7.6 considers robustness. The final section concludes.

7.1 Three Questions That Deserve an Answer

Any study claiming to find a link between pollution levels and liberalized trade has to address three basic questions. How does the method identify variation in the pollution data arising from liberalized trade? What is trade liberalization? And why should we believe the results? We start by addressing these questions.

---

endogeneity, he finds evidence that policy differences do indeed affect trade flows. See also Ederington and Minier (2003), who also find evidence that endogeneity issues have affected previous work in the area.

There is also a literature on the effects of environmental regulations on plant location. Until recently, the consensus view in this literature was that there was no evidence that differences in environmental regulations affect plant locations. Levinson (1996) provides a good review of the early work. More recently, Becker and Henderson (2000) and Greenstone (1998) have found evidence that the Clean Air Act has affected plant location in the United States.

Looking for the Effects of Trade Liberalization

We identify the variation in pollution created by trade by employing theory to tell us what other determinants to hold constant, and where to look for trade's effect. Our model yields a reduced form relating a parsimonious number of country characteristics to pollution concentrations. These characteristics for the most part describe a nation's production possibilities frontier, which is determined by the composition of its factor endowments and its income level. Other determinants of pollution such as production and abatement technology or the world price for dirty versus clean goods are assumed to be common across countries.[11]

For any given country in our sample we isolate the impact of trade by exploiting a theoretical result first demonstrated in chapter 4 on trade liberalization: a reduction in trade frictions shifts pollution demand to the right or left depending on a country's comparative advantage. This response to trade liberalization must differ across countries if they differ in their comparative advantage. Therefore, after accounting for differences across countries in a set of what theory indicates are relevant characteristics, there is additional variation in pollution levels explained by a country's depth of exposure to international markets and its comparative advantage. It is this variation that we hope to capture in the trade-induced composition effect.

What Is Trade Liberalization?

We define trade liberalization as the gradual reduction in trade frictions that moves domestic prices closer to world prices. We include in trade frictions explicit trade barriers limiting imports or restricting exports, the sum of communication and logistical costs endemic to any real world trading relationship, and, of course, the costs of international shipment. These costs have been trending downward as globalization and the GATT/WTO process has continued.

Falling trade frictions increase exposure to world markets and therefore affect domestic prices, incomes, and production patterns. Operationally, the role of trade frictions in our analysis is the same as it was in chapter 4: they drive a wedge between domestic and world prices,

---

11. Countries need not have identical technologies. For example, factor-augmenting technological differences across countries are consistent with our methods.

raising the relative price of imported goods. Since countries differ in their location, proximity to suppliers, and existing trade barriers, domestic prices will not be identical to world prices. Recall from chapter 4 that ρ denoted our measure of trade frictions. Let $\delta \equiv 1 + \rho$ denote the wedge between domestic and world prices induced by trade frictions. Accordingly we write,

$$p^d = \delta p, \tag{7.1}$$

where p is the common world relative price of X. Note $\delta > 1$ if a country imports X and $\delta < 1$ if a country exports X.

For example consider transport costs. Let v be the level of iceberg transport costs (that is, $v < 1$ is the fraction of the good that arrives at the destination when a unit is exported). Then if the good is exported from Home, we have $p^d = vp$, and if the good is imported, we have $p^d = p/v$. A reduction in transport costs (an increase in v) raises p^d if X is exported and lowers p^d if X is imported. Similarly, if we replace v with $1/(1 + t)$, then we can interpret t as either an ad valorem tariff or an export tax. In this case, a trade liberalization lowering t again moves domestic prices closer to world prices.

Our definition of trade liberalization is problematic when trade liberalization is coupled with other significant domestic reforms, as was the case, for example, in the opening up of Chile and in the reintroduction of former Eastern bloc countries into the global trading system. If environmental policy, trade policy, access to capital markets, and other domestic regulations are all being reformed simultaneously, these other changes will make it difficult to isolate the role of trade. Comprehensive policy reforms alter country type in our framework, but we assume this is constant in our empirical analysis.

Are the Results Credible?

Any empirical investigation has to pass what applied people often call the sniff test. We refer to these as reality checks and present several as we proceed. In the end, whether the analysis and results are credible is a matter of judgment. Our own belief in the research arises in part from the investigation of alternative functional forms and sensitivity analysis, but also from its congruency with both basic theory, and in a broad sense, the history of empirical results in this area.

One of our major results is that trade in dirty goods appears to be driven more by factor endowment considerations than pollution haven motives. The richest countries in our sample are dirty good exporters. This conclusion may seem radical if you are steeped in the pollution haven tradition, but it was foreshadowed by earlier work.[12]

Another important result is the finding of a surprisingly strong technique effect. This result has been anticipated by Hilton and Levinson (1998), Pargal and Wheeler (1996), and in a more general sense, the work of Grossman and Krueger (1993, 1995). While no one estimated the strength of technique effects before, there was ample evidence suggesting their strength.

7.2 The Pollution Data

To analyze the interaction between the pollution haven and factor endowments hypotheses, our data set must have a reasonably broad cross-country coverage. A time-series dimension is also important since we would like to employ panel data methods to account for unobserved determinants of pollution. Sulfur dioxide is ideal for our purposes because (1) it is a by-product of goods production; (2) it is emitted in greater quantities per unit of output in some industries than others; (3) it has strong local effects; (4) it is subject to regulations because of its noxious effect on the population; (5) well-known abatement technologies are available for implementation; and (6) sulfur dioxide concentration data is available from a mix of developed and developing as well as "open" and "closed" economies.[13]

Sulfur dioxide is a noxious gas produced by the burning of fossil fuels. Natural sources include volcanoes, decaying organic matter, and sea spray. Anthropogenic sources are thought to be responsible for somewhere between one-third and one-half of all emissions (United Nations Environment Programme 1991; Kraushaar and Ristinen 1988). Sulfur dioxide is primarily emitted as either a direct or indirect product

---

12. For example, Low and Yeats (1992, 95) find that over 90% of dirty good exports come from OECD countries, which are not desperately poor unregulated economies. Even when he corrects for country size and examines which countries exports are heavily reliant on dirty goods, Low finds these are natural resource exporters like Canada, Finland, Venezuela, Brazil, and Norway. Therefore the composition of factors within these countries seems key to their specialization and trade patterns.

13. In some cases sulfur dioxide emissions cross national borders and fall as acid rain particles rather than remain in the locality and raise concentration levels. Long-range transport may make it more difficult for us to link local economic activity to local sulfur concentrations. It has, of course, also led to numerous agreements over acid rain. We control for the most important of these treaties in our empirical work.

of goods production and is not strongly linked to automobile use. Because energy-intensive industries are also typically capital intensive, a reasonable proxy for dirty SO_2-creating activities may be physical capital-intensive production processes. Readily available, although costly, methods for the control of emissions exist, and their efficacy is well established.

The Global Environment Monitoring System (GEMS) has been recording sulfur dioxide concentrations in major urban areas in developed and developing countries since the early 1970s. Our data set consists of 2,555 observations from 290 observation sites located in 108 cities representing 43 countries spanning the years 1971–1996. The GEMS network was set up to monitor the concentrations of several pollutants in a cross-section of countries using comparable measuring devices.[14] The panel included primarily developed countries in the early years, but from 1976 to the early 1990s the United Nations Environment Programme provided funds to expand and maintain the network. The coverage of developing economies grew over time until the late 1980s. In the 1990s coverage fell with data only from the United States for 1996. The World Health Organization (1984) reports that until the late 1970s data comparability may be limited as monitoring capabilities were being assessed, many new countries were added, and procedures were being developed to ensure validated samples. Accordingly, we will investigate the sensitivity of our findings to the time period we employ in our analysis.

The GEMS data comprises summary statistics for the yearly distribution of concentrations at each site. In table 7.1 we list the top 25 dirtiest cities in our sample ordered by their highest annual (median) sulfur dioxide concentrations. (See table 7A.1 at the end of the chapter for a list of countries with their ISO-3166 codes).

The table shows, perhaps surprisingly, that 7 of the top 12 dirtiest cities in the sample—Rome, Milan, Madrid, Vienna, Brussels, London and Tokyo—are located in developed countries. A similar pattern emerges in the top 25. The most common attribute among these cities is their large and dense metropolitan characteristic. Anyone visiting these cities recognizes them as cities where a large scale of economic activity occurs within their boundaries.

---

14. The range of sophistication of monitoring techniques used in the network varies quite widely, but the various techniques have been subject to comparability tests over the years. Some stations offer continuous monitoring, while others only measure at discrete intervals.

TABLE 7.1

Top 25 Cities (ordered by descending maximum of annual median SO_2, concentration)

City	Country Code	Number of Observation Stations	Minimum	Maximum
Seoul	KOR	6	25	115
Rome	ITA	3	2	103
Milan	ITA	2	17	100
Tehran	IRN	3	7	93
Shenyang	CHN	4	1	89
Vienna	AUT	3	40	80
Madrid	ESP	5	2	73
Prague	CSK	3	13	65
Brussels	BEL	4	9	64
Cairo	EGY	4	1	61
London	GBR	3	11	58
Tokyo	JPN	3	5	58
Osaka	JPN	4	5	56
Guangzhou	CHN	4	2	55
São Paulo	BRA	5	8	51
Manila	PHL	3	2	50
Santiago	CHL	3	11	49
Rio de Janeiro	BRA	2	20	46
Beijing	CHN	5	1	44
Xian	CHN	4	3	41
Shanghai	CHN	4	1	40
Boston	USA	2	3	40
Frankfurt	DEU	3	5	38
Toulouse	FRA	4	19	38
Amsterdam	NLD	3	6	37

Note: The column n is the number of observation stations in each city. The minimum and maximum columns show the lowest and highest measured level of the annual median SO_2 concentration in each city, measured in parts per billion. Note that a maximum or minimum concentration of 1 is equivalent to the measurement threshold of the measurement device.

A second feature of note is the country composition. The city and country coverage, although quite large in our sample, still reflects developed countries to a large extent. Although developing countries are represented in our sample, the coverage is not ideal. Large shares of observations are from the United States due to this country's extensive network of air quality measurement stations. Other large contributor countries were China, Canada, and Japan. Many of the other observa-

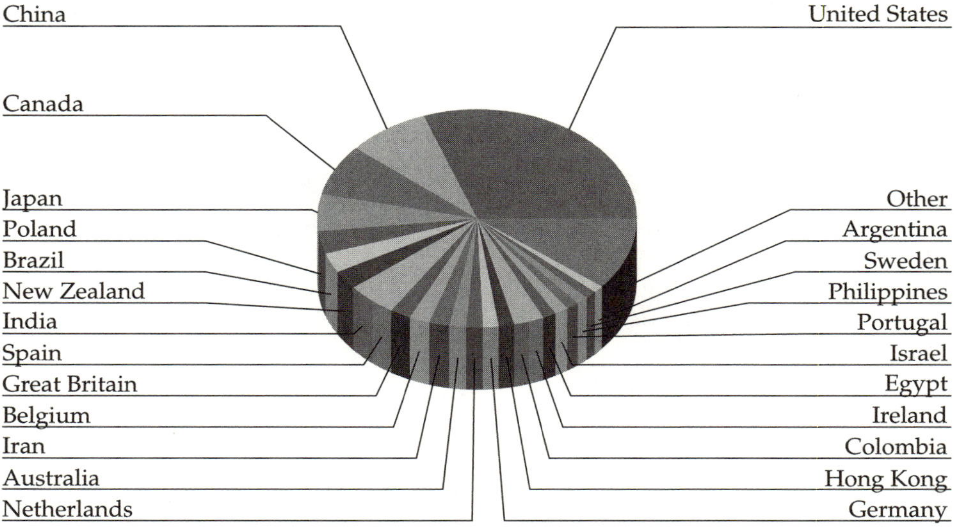

Fig. 7.1. Composition of GEMS Data Set Observations per Country

tion stations provided short or discontinuous streams of data while participating in the GEMS/AIR project. We present the distribution of observations in figure 7.1.

The last feature to note from table 7.1 is the very large variance between maximum and minimum values for any given city. Recall that the table lists annual median concentrations and therefore both the time-averaging and median characteristic of this summary statistic should lessen the variance in measured concentrations. Some of the variance may reflect the placement of measuring stations within the cities themselves, but even for cities with only two sites there exists large variation in pollution levels. This large variance is unlikely to reflect changes in economic fundamentals, but instead reflect weather influences. Therefore, our ability to predict or explain sulfur dioxide concentrations via economic factors alone is likely to be limited. Weather-related variables seem to be a key determinant.

We employ the log of median sulfur dioxide concentrations at a given site, for each year, as our dependent variable. We use a log transform because the distribution of yearly summary statistics for sulfur dioxide appears to be log normal (World Health Organization 1984). Previous work in this area by the WHO and others has argued that a log normal distribution is appropriate because temperature inversions or other special pollution episodes often lead to large values for some observations. In contrast, even weather very helpful to dissipation cannot drive the level of the pollutant below zero.

To see this characteristic of the data clearly, we present the distribution of all observations on a linear scale in figure 7.2 and on a logarithmic scale in figure 7.3. The extreme right tail of figure 7.2 is likely due to idiosyncratic weather factors. Hence the log scale is quite appealing for empirical work.

7.3 Deriving the Reduced Form

Greens, Browns, and Pollution Supply

The countries in our data set differ in many dimensions, several of them unmeasured. To account for some of these differences, we extend the analysis presented in earlier chapters to reflect heterogeneity across countries in two dimensions. First, we allow citizens to differ in preferences over pollution, again naming our two citizen groups Greens and Browns. In chapter 4 we assumed Greens and Browns differed in factor ownership, but here we assume they differ in their preferences over pollution. Second, as in chapter 4, we assume governments may differ in their weighing of Greens' and Browns' wishes.

Specifically, we assume two groups in society: N^g Green consumers who care greatly about the environment (Greens), and $N^b = N - N^g$ Brown consumers (Browns) who care less about the environment. We allow for individuals to differ in tastes and write the indirect utility function of a consumer in the ith group as

$$V^i (p^d, I, z) = u [I / \beta (p^d)] - \gamma^i z, \qquad i = g, b, \tag{7.2}$$

where $\gamma^g > \gamma^b \geq 0$, $I = G/N$ is per capita income, $\beta (p^d)$ is a price index, and u is increasing and concave. As shown, pollution is a pure public bad, but Greens suffer a greater disutility than Browns. We again define real per capita income as $R = [G/N]/\beta (p^d)$ and rewrite indirect utility as simply $u (R) - \gamma^i z$.

We allow for the realistic possibility that government behavior varies across countries (perhaps across Communist and non-Communist countries), while still allowing for an endogenous link between pollution policy and economic conditions. We assume governments choose a pollution tax to maximize a weighted sum of each group's preferences. Each government solves

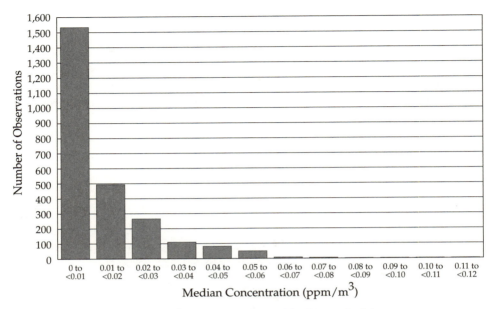

Fig. 7.2. Distribution of the Dependent Variable (Linear Scale)

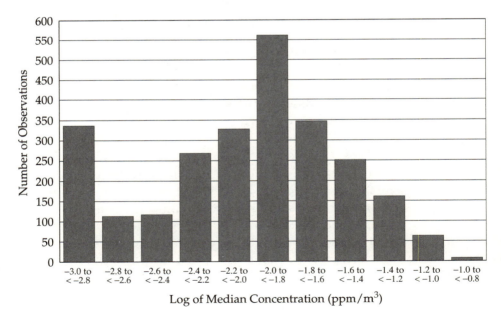

Fig. 7.3. Distribution of the Dependent Variable (Logarithmic Scale)

$$\text{Max } N\left[\lambda V^g + (1 - \lambda) V^b\right], \tag{7.3}$$
$$\tau$$

where λ is the weight put on Greens. λ may vary across governments. For example, if the government is utilitarian, then $\lambda = N^g/N$; if the government is controlled by the Greens $\lambda = 1$, and if controlled by Browns, $\lambda = 0$.

The government's preferred pollution tax maximizes the weighted sum of utilities in (7.3) subject to private sector behavior, production possibilities, fixed world prices, and fixed trade frictions. Private sector behavior is again represented by a standard GNP function giving maximized private sector (net of tax) revenue. Using (2.58) and suppressing our numeraire, this becomes $\tilde{G}(p^d, \tau, K, L)$. Overall income is private sector revenue plus rebated taxes, or $G = \tilde{G}(p^d, \tau, K, L) + \tau z$.[15] The first-order condition for the maximization in (7.3) yields, after slight rearrangement,[16]

$$\tau = N\left[\lambda MD^g(p^d, R) + (1 - \lambda) MD^b(p^d, R)\right]; \tag{7.4}$$

where $MD^i(p^d, R) = \gamma^i \beta(p^d)/u'(R)$ is marginal damage per person, and $MD^i_R > 0$ given the concavity of the utility function.[17] We rewrite (7.4) as

$$\tau = T\varphi(p^d, R) \tag{7.5}$$

and refer to $T = \lambda N\gamma^g + (1 - \lambda) N\gamma^b$ as country type and $\varphi(p^d, R) = \beta(p^d)/u'(R)$ as marginal damage.

Equation (7.5) is a pollution supply curve relating country type, domestic prices, and real income to pollution policy. Note that since marginal damage is independent of pollution, pollution supply is horizontal in $\{\tau, z\}$ space. This simplification allows us to easily derive our reduced form.

Pollution supply sets the price for polluting. Using (7.1) and (7.5), we can obtain a decomposition of pollution supply:

$$\hat{\tau} = \hat{T} + \varepsilon_{MD, p}\hat{\delta} + \varepsilon_{MD, p}\hat{p} + \varepsilon_{MD, R}\hat{R}. \tag{7.6}$$

This pollution supply curve is very similar to that developed in chapter 6 when we considered the constant marginal damage case. It differs

---

15. In chapter 2, we showed $G(p^d, K, L, z) = \tilde{G}(p^d, \tau, K, L) + \tau z$ for $\tau = G_z$.

16. To derive this, note that $R_\tau = \tau z_\tau/(N\beta)$ and that $V^g_I = V^b_I$ because all consumers have the same per capita income and because of the separability of V in emissions. Hence the first-order condition is $N\{\lambda[V^g_I \tau/N - \gamma^g] + (1 - \lambda)[V^b_I \tau/N - \gamma^b]\} z_\tau = 0$, which simplifies to (7.4).

17. Note that marginal damage does not depend directly on pollution z because we have assumed the marginal disutility of pollution is constant.

from that earlier formulation because of the addition of country type considerations. Country type now matters because if Greens are given a greater weight in social welfare, or become a larger fraction of the population over time, then policy becomes more stringent and pollution supply shifts upwards.

Pollution Demand

In order to provide measures of scale, technique, and composition effects, we write our direct pollution demand in a form convenient for empirical work. Recall from (2.46) and (2.47) that we have defined an economy's scale, S, as the value of national output at base-year world prices:

$$S = p_x^0 x + p_y^0 y. \tag{7.7}$$

Choosing units so that base-year prices are unity, we now write pollution emissions as

$$z = ex = e\varphi S, \tag{7.8}$$

where φ is the share of X in total output. Equation (7.8) provides our decomposition: pollution demand depends on the pollution intensity of the dirty industry, $e(\theta)$, the relative importance of the dirty industry in the economy, φ, and the overall scale of the economy, S. In differential form it becomes

$$\hat{z} = \hat{S} + \hat{\varphi} + \hat{e}, \tag{7.9}$$

where "$\wedge$" denotes percent change. We will use a quantity index of output to measure the scale effect. But because a change in prices creates opposing composition and technique effects, it is necessary to divide each into its more primitive determinants.

We can solve for the share of X in total output, φ, as a function of the capital/labor ratio $\kappa = K/L$, relative prices p^d, pollution taxes, τ, and base-year world prices (suppressed here). To do so, recall that output supplies depend on pollution taxes only through their impact on emission intensities. That is, we can write

$$x = x\,(p^d,\, e\,(p^d/\tau),\, K,\, L), \tag{7.10}$$
$$y = y\,(p^d,\, e\,(p^d/\tau),\, K,\, L).$$

Given base-year world prices (normalized to 1) and the linear homogeneity of supplies in K and L, the composition of output, φ, can be written as

$$\varphi = \frac{x}{x + y} = \frac{x/y}{x/y + 1} = \varphi\,(p^d,\,e,\,\kappa). \qquad (7.11)$$

Therefore, differentiating the composition effect yields

$$\hat{\varphi} = \varepsilon_{\varphi p}\hat{p}^d + \varepsilon_{\varphi e}\hat{e} + \varepsilon_{\varphi \kappa}\hat{\kappa}, \qquad (7.12)$$

where again all elasticities are positive. Next differentiate (7.1) to find

$$\hat{p}^d = \hat{\delta} + \hat{p}. \qquad (7.13)$$

Similarly, using (2.16) and (7.13) we find

$$\hat{e} = \hat{\delta} + \hat{p} - \hat{\tau}\,. \qquad (7.14)$$

Combining (7.9) and (7.12)–(7.14), we obtain a decomposition of the private sector's demand for pollution:

$$\hat{z} = \hat{S} + \varepsilon_{\varphi,\kappa}\hat{\kappa} + [\varepsilon_{\varphi,\,p} + (1 + \varepsilon_{\varphi,\,e})]\,\hat{\delta} + [\varepsilon_{\varphi,\,p} + (1 + \varepsilon_{\varphi,\,e})]\,\hat{p} - [1 + \varepsilon_{\varphi,e}]\,\hat{\tau}\,. \qquad (7.15)$$

All elasticities in (7.15) are positive. An increase in scale, S, raises the output of both goods and hence raises the demand for pollution. An increase in a nation's capital-to-labor ratio raises the output of the dirty good and hence raises the demand for pollution. And an increase in the relative price of dirty goods stimulates their output and raises pollution demand as well. Finally, a fall in trade frictions shifts pollution demand in a direction determined by a country's comparative advantage.

The Reduced Form

Combining pollution supply (7.6) and demand (7.15) yields a simple reduced form linking pollution emissions to a small set of economic factors.

$$\hat{z} = \pi_1\hat{S} + \pi_2\hat{\kappa} - \pi_3\hat{R} + \pi_4\hat{\delta} + \pi_5\hat{p} - \pi_6\hat{T}$$

where

$$\pi_1 = 1 > 0 \qquad (7.16)$$
$$\pi_2 = \varepsilon_{\varphi,\,\kappa} > 0$$
$$\pi_3 = [1 + \varepsilon_{\varphi,\,p}]\,\varepsilon_{MD,\,R} > 0$$
$$\pi_4 = [\varepsilon_{\varphi,\,p} + (1 + \varepsilon_{\varphi,\,e})\,(1 - \varepsilon_{MD,\,p})] > 0$$
$$\pi_5 = [\varepsilon_{\varphi,\,p} + (1 + \varepsilon_{\varphi,\,e})\,(1 - \varepsilon_{MD,\,p})] > 0$$
$$\pi_6 = [1 + \varepsilon_{\varphi,\,e}] > 0$$

Three features of (7.16) warrant further comment.

First, since a change in relative prices shifts pollution supply and demand in opposing directions, we need to clarify why π_4 and π_5 are positive. The sign hinges on the magnitude of the elasticity of marginal damage with respect to prices. But as we showed in chapter 4, $\varepsilon_{MD,\,p} < 1$, and hence both π_4 and π_5 are positive.

Second, we claim that a reduced form links emissions to our economic factors despite the fact that emissions, real income, and the scale of economic activity are all endogenous variables in our framework. The key to this result is the recursive structure of our model. There are three endogenous variables we need to be concerned with: emissions, the pollution tax, and national income (which enters both R and S in (7.16)). Real income is just national income deflated by a price index, and national income is given by

$$\tilde{G}\,(p^d \tau,\, K,\, L) + \tau z = p^d\,(1 - \theta)\,x + y.$$

The pollution tax is determined by the equation $\tau = T\varphi(p^d,\, R)$. Writing out the arguments for real income and the tax rate more completely gives us

$$R = [p^d\,(1 - \theta\,(\tau/p^d))\,x\,(p^d,\, \tau,\, K,\, L) + y\,(p^d,\, \tau,\, K,\, L)]/\beta\,(p^d), \qquad (7.17)$$
$$\tau = T\varphi\,(p^d,\, R).$$

Equation (7.17) is a two-equation simultaneous system solving for the pollution tax τ and real income R, as functions of (what we have assumed are) exogenous factors: factor endowments, trade frictions, and world prices. Therefore, the pollution tax and real income are solved for independently of z. We then find z by substituting these solutions into (7.8) to find pollution emissions recursively. That is, pollution emissions are given by

$$z = e\,(p^d/\tau)\,x\,(p^d,\, e\,(p^d/\tau),\, K,\, L),$$

where all variables are exogenous, except for τ, but as noted above, τ is completely determined by exogenous variables. This is in fact what (7.16) represents. Given the recursive nature of the system, the equilibrium level of emissions is affected by shocks to either factor endowments in pollution demand, or preference parameters in the pollution supply function but only through their impact on either emissions per unit of output or the output of the dirty good. Moreover, the resulting change in emissions has no effect on real income or the pollution tax.

Consequently, estimation of our reduced form by OLS yields unbiased and consistent estimates.[18]

This result follows for two reasons. First, a society may decide to spend some of its potential income on improving environmental quality and the remainder on consumption goods—but higher pollution does not *cause* higher real income. This should be apparent from our consideration of the net and potential production possibility frontiers in chapter 2. The location of the potential frontier is determined independently of the level of pollution, and its location (together with world prices) determines a country's potential income. Countries choose their net frontier by trading off a cleaner environment for less goods consumption.

Second, in order to deal with country type and consumer heterogeneity in a tractable manner, we have assumed marginal damage is independent of z. This renders the pollution supply horizontal for given levels of income as shown in (7.17). Consequently, a change in emissions does not create second-order changes in the composition of output, measures of scale, or income.[19]

---

18. The recursive nature of the system is necessary but not sufficient for OLS to be appropriate. We also need to assume that shocks to factor endowments, technologies, or preferences are independent of measurement error. To see this, note that before we enter any economic determinants into equation (7.8), it is virtually a definition: emissions equal emissions per unit of output (e) times output (x). The only difference between what (7.8) predicts and our actual concentration data must be due to measurement error. Examples of measurement error would be transcription error (we didn't record x or e right), or error created because sulfur dioxide (SO_2) is generated by unaccounted for economic activity such as automobile exhaust or from a natural source of SO_2 such as volcanic eruptions (so x is not the only determinant). A shock to factor endowments, preferences, and so on would alter both real income and the pollution tax, but as long as these shocks are independent of this measurement error, OLS is appropriate. This may or may not be true. For example, suppose a technology shock both raised real income and drove down measurement error. In this case, our regressor using real income would be correlated with the error term in our reduced form, making OLS inappropriate (recall however that GEMS data was collected by comparable methods and funded by the UN to minimize exactly this issue). Alternatively suppose there was a shock to preferences raising the value of the environment. This would surely raise the pollution tax since it alters country type, but as long as this preference shock had no relationship to any of our sources of measurement error, then estimating our reduced form via OLS is appropriate.

19. This feature of the model relies on assumptions that future researchers may want to relax. For example, if marginal damage is a function of emissions, then contemporaneous real income and emissions will be correlated. And if trade and environmental policy are jointly determined, then trade frictions may not be independent of pollution emissions. We have dealt with these complications in a variety of ways. In our empirical work we lag our real income measure to lessen the potential contemporaneous correlation with pollution emissions. We have also investigated elsewhere a 2SLS system where

Using the Reduced Form: The Trade-Induced Composition Effect

To see how we isolate the composition effect of trade on pollution, consider two economies that differ only in their trade frictions. That is, they have the same country characteristics such as income, factor endowments, and so on. Then from our reduced form it follows that if both countries export the polluting good, pollution is higher in the country with lower trade frictions. Use (7.16) and hold T, S, R, κ and p constant to find

$$\hat{z} = [\varepsilon_{\varphi, p} + (1 + \varepsilon_{\varphi, e})(1 - \varepsilon_{MD, p})]\,\hat{\delta}. \tag{7.18}$$

For a dirty good exporter, a reduction in trade frictions increases δ, and this implies an increase in pollution. For a dirty good importer, a reduction in trade frictions lowers δ, and this implies a fall in pollution. This comparative static isolates the trade-induced *composition effect*. The sign of this composition effect differs across countries. We illustrate this in the pollution supply and demand figure 7.4.

Suppose we start at point A, where equilibrium taxes and pollution are given by τ_0 and Z_0. Now consider a fall in trade frictions. If the country shown is an exporter of the polluting good, then δ rises, and this raises the relative price of the dirty good X. This shifts a dirty good exporter's pollution demand curve to the right and shifts its pollution supply curve up. The direct demand side effects swamp the substitution effect in supply, and pollution rises to Z_1 at the new equilibrium point B. Consequently, holding all other determinants of pollution supply and demand constant, emissions must rise to z_1 despite the tax increase to τ_1. This increase in emissions represents the trade-induced composition effect for a dirty good exporter.

In contrast, δ falls with freer trade for an importer of the polluting good. This raises the relative price of the clean good Y, and again shifts both pollution demand and supply. Demand side determinants dominate, and emissions fall. This reduction in emissions is shown by the movement from A to C. The fall in pollution to Z_2 represents the trade-induced composition effect for a clean good exporter.

The result developed here has a simple message: if we look across all countries and hold other determinants of emissions constant, we

---

real income and pollution are estimated jointly (see the appendix in Antweiler, Copeland, and Taylor 2001). The potential endogeneity of trade policy is more difficult to deal with, and we discuss its impact on our results in the concluding chapter.

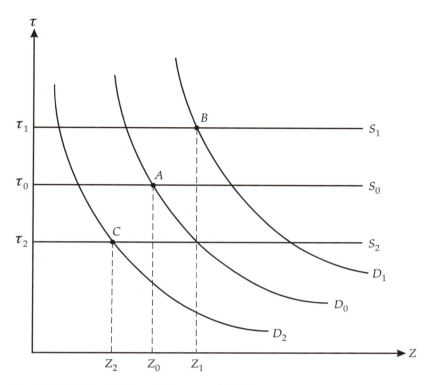

Fig. 7.4. The Trade-Induced Composition Effect

should not expect to find openness per se related in any systematic way to emissions.

The Full Effect of Liberalized Trade

The composition effect is just one of the channels through which trade affects the environment. To find the full impact of a change in trade frictions, differentiate (7.8) with respect to δ, holding world prices, country type, and factor endowments constant, to find

$$\frac{dz}{d\delta} \frac{\delta}{z} = \pi_1 \frac{dS}{d\delta} \frac{\delta}{S} - \pi_3 \frac{dI}{d\delta} \frac{\delta}{I} + \pi_4 . \tag{7.19}$$

A fall in trade frictions produces a scale effect, a technique effect, as well as the trade-induced composition effect discussed above. To understand how these three effects interact to determine the environmental consequences of trade, we can again employ figure 7.4, albeit with some modifications.

To depict the pollution supply and demand response for a dirty good exporter, we start at point C, where equilibrium taxes and pollution are given by τ_2 and Z_2. Next consider a fall in trade frictions. We have already established that the trade-induced composition effect for a dirty good exporter correspond to a movement like that from C to A. This is represented in (7.19) by the third term and is positive as shown. Pollution rises from Z_2 to Z_0. But we now also need to account for the positive scale effect shifting pollution demand further to the right to D_1 from D_0; and the effect of higher income creating a technique effect and shifting the pollution supply upwards to S_1 from S_0. The full impact of trade liberalization is then captured by the movement from C to B. It reflects scale, composition. and technique effects.

For a dirty good exporter both the trade-induced composition effect and the scale effect are positive. Pollution demand shifts right from these two forces, and if the policy response is sufficiently weak (an elasticity of marginal damage with respect to income less than 1), emissions will rise as shown. That is, the upward shifts in pollution supply are overwhelmed by the demand shifts. As we demonstrated in chapter 4, however, if the elasticity of marginal damage is sufficiently strong, then emissions will fall as the technique effect dominates. Therefore, while the diagram shows trade liberalization for a dirty good exporter leading to greater pollution, this is only a possibility and not a necessity.

A similar analysis for a dirty good importer shows the full effect of a small reduction in trade frictions is to reduce pollution emissions. For dirty good importers the trade-induced composition effect is negative, and since X production falls, the sum of composition and scale effects must also be negative. To this we add the technique effect lowering pollution. Consequently, pollution emissions will fall for a dirty good importer.[20]

---

20. We could use figure 7.5 to depict this case as well with some amendment. If we start at point B before the trade liberalization, then the scale and composition effects of trade would shift pollution demand back to D_0, while the price change would shift pollution supply down to S_0. The demand shift dominates, so pollution falls. To this we now need to add the technique effect. The income increase created by trade would then shift pollution supply up, perhaps to S_2. The final level of pollution would be given at the intersection of S_2 and D_0 (the new equilibrium level is not shown).

Adding Up Scale, Composition, and Technique Effects

The amount of information required to implement an adding-up exercise akin to (7.19) is great. In our empirical work we develop estimates for π_1, π_3, and π_4. But even with these estimates in hand we are faced with estimating the impact of trade liberalization on both the scale of output ($dS/d\delta$) and income per capita ($dI/d\delta$). Since attempts to link trade to growth and income levels are the subject of an already large and controversial literature, we do not attempt to measure trade's effect on GDP or GNP per person. Instead we employ economic theory to add up our estimated scale, composition, and technique effects.[21]

Taking factor endowments as fixed, a reduction in transport costs or trade barriers raises the value of domestic output and real income by approximately the same percentage. This implies that scale and income elasticities in (7.19) will be of approximately the same magnitude. The result is approximate because if GNP differs from GDP due to receipts or payments from abroad, then we would need to correct for the (generally small) share of these payments in GNP. In addition, if significant population growth is ongoing, then the percentage change in GNP needs adjustment to obtain growth in GNP per capita.[22] Neglecting these complications, we simplify (7.19) to obtain an approximation for the change in pollution as

$$\frac{dz}{d\delta} \frac{\delta}{z} \cong [\pi_1 - \pi_3] \frac{dI}{d\delta} \frac{\delta}{I} + \pi_4 . \tag{7.20}$$

In some circumstances we can add up these three effects to come to an overall assessment of trade without knowledge of trade's effect on income or scale.

For example, consider a dirty good exporter. Note that $dI/d\delta$ is positive since an increase in δ represents lower trade frictions. If we find $\pi_1 > \pi_3$ and $\pi_4 > 0$, then we conclude trade liberalization raises pollution for a dirty good exporter: scale effects dominate technique, and the

---

21. Both Dean (2002) and Frankel and Rose (2002) try to include the impact of trade on growth in their calculations.

22. Changes in population have two effects on pollution supply. First, if population growth is significant, it is possible for national income to rise because of trade liberalization but per capita income (which is relevant to pollution supply) to fall. Second, holding incomes per capita constant, population growth shifts pollution supply upwards as more individuals are adversely affected by pollution. With an approximately constant population, gains in national income translate directly into income per capita gains, and there is no additional shift in pollution supply.

trade-induced composition effect is positive. Under these same circumstances, trade liberalization would have an ambiguous effect on emissions for a clean good exporter. Consequently, even to implement our more limited adding-up exercise, it is necessary to ask who exports dirty goods, and why.

Pollution Haven versus Factor Abundance Motives

In chapter 6 we showed that comparative advantage is determined by both relative factor abundance and relative incomes. While limiting cases of our model reflect only pollution haven motives or pure factor endowment motives, in general, from our analysis in chapter 6 we know both determinants of comparative advantage matter. To investigate further, we follow a slightly different tack from chapter 6 and solve for autarky prices. Recall the relative price of good x is determined by the intersection of the relative supply and demand curves

$$RD\,(p) = RS\,(p) = \frac{x\,(p,\,e,\,K/L)}{y\,(p,\,e,\,K/L)}\,. \tag{7.21}$$

Totally differentiating and rearranging gives an expression linking autarky prices to real income and endowments:

$$\hat{p}^A = \frac{-\,[\varepsilon_{RS,\,\kappa}]\,\hat{\kappa} + \varepsilon_{MD,\,R}\,\varepsilon_{RS,\,e}\,\hat{R}}{\Delta}\,, \tag{7.22}$$

$$\Delta = [\varepsilon_{RS,\,p} + \varepsilon_{RD,\,p} + \varepsilon_{RS,\,e}\,(1 - \varepsilon_{MD,\,R})] > 0,$$

where all elasticities are positive. Unless both the dirty and clean sectors use identical factor proportions, then $\varepsilon_{RS,\,K}$ is not zero, and equation (7.22) shows that capital abundance matters to comparative advantage. Similarly, if the environment is a normal good, then $\varepsilon_{MD,\,R}$ is nonzero and real income matters as well.

The Role of Factor Endowments

Standard factor endowment theories predict that capital-abundant countries export capital-intensive goods. In our model this need not be true because pollution policy can reverse this pattern of trade. Nevertheless, capital abundance is still a key determinant of comparative advantage in our model. Because X is relatively capital intensive, an increase in κ, holding all else constant, increases Home's relative supply of X and lowers Home's autarky relative price of X. Using (7.22), we obtain $\hat{p}^A < 0$ since $\varepsilon_{RS,K} > 0$. All else equal, an increase in the abundance of the factor used intensively in the pollution-intensive sector increases the likelihood a country will export pollution-intensive goods. Moreover, as we saw in chapter 6, for any given income level, if a country is *sufficiently* capital abundant, then it must export the capital-intensive good.

The Role of Income Differences

According to the *pollution haven hypothesis*, poor countries have a comparative advantage in dirty goods because they have lax pollution policy, and rich countries have a comparative advantage in clean goods because of their stringent pollution policy. If all countries have the same relative factor endowments, but differ in per capita incomes, then richer countries will have stricter pollution policy. Using (7.22), we note p^A is higher whenever R is higher across countries. When countries differ in factor endowments and income levels, we showed in chapter 6, if a country is *sufficiently* rich, it must export the labor-intensive (clean) good. Hence for sufficiently large R, Home must import X and export Y. The fall in pollution from the trade-induced composition effect follows directly.

7.4 From Theory to Estimation

The theory contains a very simple message concerning the environmental consequences of freer trade: comparative advantage matters. If we compare countries with similar incomes and scale, openness should be associated with higher pollution in dirty good exporters and lower pollution in dirty good importers. Therefore, to isolate the trade-induced composition effect, we must condition on country characteristics. This observation begs several questions. How are we to measure openness? What country characteristics should we use? How should we condition on these characteristics? We deal with these in turn below.

Various measures of "openness" exist. We need a measure with both time-series variation and a wide cross-country coverage. In our theory a reduction of trade frictions brings domestic prices closer to world prices, and it does not matter whether this occurs because of a fall in transport and communication costs or (apart from revenue effects) because of a GATT-inspired reduction in trade restrictions. But since we do not observe movements in δ directly, we must make use of an observable consequence of heightened integration: increases in a country's trade intensity ratio (defined as the ratio of exports plus imports to GDP, valued at world prices). Within our model, a movement of δ toward 1, for either a dirty good importer or exporter, raises its trade intensity ratio holding constant factor endowments, income, and world prices. Lower trade frictions mean greater trade intensity, regardless of a country's comparative advantage.[23] Therefore, in our empirical work we replace unobservable trade frictions with observable trade intensity.

To address our second question, interpret the hat notation in equation (7.22) as describing small differences across countries. With this interpretation, (7.22) links differences in autarky relative prices across countries to differences in their relative factor abundance and real income levels. If we take the rest of the world as our small country's partner in this exercise, we can then write the dependence of any one country's comparative advantage on its country characteristics relative to those in the rest of the world: that is, as $\Psi(\kappa_i, \iota_i)$, where κ_i is capital abundance in country i relative to a world average and ι_i is real income in country i relative to a world average. While other factors play a role in determining comparative advantage, capital abundance and real income are the key country characteristics within our model.

Finally, how are we to condition on these characteristics? Our theory does not give us any strong guidance in this regard. The interaction between these two motives depends quite delicately on elasticities of substitution in production, factor shares, and (unknown) third derivative properties of our more basic functions. This is apparent from (7.22) because the elasticities in this expression are functions of prices, incomes, and trade frictions. Consequently, we adopt a flexible approach to capturing these influences by adopting a second-order Taylor series approximation to Ψ in our empirical work. That is, we employ

$$\Psi_i \cong \Psi_0 + \Psi_1 \kappa_i + \Psi_2 \kappa_i^2 + \Psi_3 \iota_i + \Psi_4 \iota_i^2 + \Psi_5 \iota_i \kappa_i \qquad (7.23)$$

and then interact this measure of country characteristics with trade intensity to capture the trade-induced composition effect.

This method has several advantages. It allows the impact of further openness on emissions to depend on country characteristics. It does

---

23. See Antweiler, Copeland, and Taylor 2001 for a proof of this assertion within a slightly more general model.

not dictate whether one or both motives are present in the data or how they interact. And we can evaluate Ψ using our estimates to provide some simple reality checks. For example, does the pollution demand curve shift right for some countries and not for others (i.e., does Ψ_i vary in sign depending on country characteristics)? For which countries does it shift right? Are these countries poor, as predicted by the pollution haven hypothesis, or are they capital abundant, as predicted by the factor abundance hypothesis? Finally, the formulation is a relatively parsimonious and reasonably flexible method for estimating an unknown nonlinear function.

Summary Statistics and Measurement Issues

In moving from our theoretical model to its empirical counterpart we need to include variables to reflect scale, technique, and composition effects.[24] In addition, we have to include site-specific variables to account for meteorological conditions. Our estimations will require the use of data on real GDP per capita, capital-to-labor ratios, population densities, and various measures of "openness." The majority of the economic data were obtained from the Penn World Tables 5.6. The remainder was obtained from several other sources.[25] Table 7.2 summarizes the means, standard deviations, and units of measurement for the data. Some of the variables warrant further explanation.

First, we measure the scale of economic activity, S, at any site by an intensive measure of economic activity per unit area. This intensive measure is GDP per square kilometer. Lacking detailed data on Gross City Product, we construct GDP per square kilometer for each city and

---

24. Readers can find more detail on our data and methods at pacific.commerce.ubc.ca/download/appendix.pdf.

25. Data sources for our regressors include the Penn World Tables, in Summers and Heston 1991, available in revision 5.6 from the Center for International Comparisons at the University of Pennsylvania at http://www.pwt.econ.upenn.edu (all cited URLS are accessible as of 1 January, 2003). For macroeconomic data, see the World Investment Report from the United Nations Centre on Transnational Corporations, 1992 and 1999 volumes. See the World Resources Database (World Resources Institute et al. 1998) for natural resources and physical endowments, and data from the Global Historical Climatology Network for information on monthly average temperatures, monthly precipitation, and atmospheric pressure. Data and description file are available from the National Climatic Data Center of the U.S. National Oceanic and Atmospheric Administration ftp://ftp.ncdc.noaa.gov/pub/data/ghcn/v1/. Time series were obtained for educational attainment from Robert J. Barro and Jong-Wha Lee's 1994 study, available from the NBER website at http://www.nber.org/pub/barro.lee/ZIP/.

TABLE 7.2
Summary Statistics

Variable	Dimension	Observations	Mean	S.D.	Minimum	Maximum
Log of SO_2	$\log_{10}$ (ppm)	2,555	−2.112	0.481	−3	−0.939
City economic intensity	$m per km^2	2,555	0.79	0.878	0.01	5.934
GDP per capita (current)	$10k	2,555	1.478	0.862	0.109	2.718
Population density	1,000p/km^2	2,555	0.063	0.055	0.001	0.276
Capital abundance (adjusted)	$10k/worker	2,555	5.612	2.497	0.829	17.189
Capital abundance (unadjusted)	$10k/worker	2,555	3.207	1.763	0.13	7.75
Education attainment	0–1 range	2,555	0.54	0.226	0.088	0.799
GNP per capita, 3-year average	$10k	2,555	1.396	0.815	0.111	2.635
Communist country	[—]	2,555	0.125	0.331	0	1
C.C. × income	$10k	319	0.302	0.208	0.127	0.716
Trade intensity $(X + M)/GDP$	[—]	2,555	0.409	0.322	0.088	2.617
Relative (K/L) (adj.)	World = 1.00	2,555	1.357	0.605	0.203	4.174
Relative income	World = 1.00	2,555	2.5	1.392	0.221	4.138
Inward FDI stock/ capital stock	[—]	2,525	0.106	0.25	0.001	2.193
Average temperature	deg C	2,555	14.689	5.6	2.617	28.967
Precipitation coefficient of variable	[—]	2,555	0.011	0.006	0.001	0.054
Hard coal reserves	GJoule/worker	2,555	0.04	0.043	0	0.146
Soft coal reserves	GJoule/worker	2,555	0.038	0.052	0	0.348

Note: All monetary figures are in 1995 U.S. dollars. The interaction term for income with the Communist countries dummy only shows the case where the dummy is equal to 1; thus the mean for this line is the mean for the Communist countries only.

each year by multiplying city population density with country GDP per person. As a result, scale is now measured in intensive form, as is our dependent variable.[26] To explain *concentrations of pollution* we need a measure of scale reflecting the *concentration of economic activity* within the same geographical area. Other possible measures of scale fail this

---

26. This is admittedly a rough measure of economic activity, and the quality of this proxy may vary systematically with a country's development level. To investigate this concern we have allowed the scale effect to vary across countries divided by income category, by allowing for nonlinearities in the response to scale, and by excluding the perhaps most troubling rural observations. Our results are similar to those reported for our simpler specification. For one such sensitivity see tables 7.5–7.7.

test. We refer to our scale measure as City Economic Intensity (GDP per square kilometer).

Extrapolations for per capita GDP were carried out for the years past 1993 based on real growth rates obtained from the International Monetary Fund's International Financial Statistics. Population densities were available only for 1990. The highest scale measure is an observation in 1992 for Tokyo (with London and Osaka close behind); the lowest scale occurs in San Lorenzo, Argentina in 1989.

The capital abundance (K/L) of countries was obtained from the physical capital stock per worker variable in the Penn World Tables. Rather than treat workers in all countries as equivalent in terms of productivity, we adjust each country's labor force for differences across countries in their average level of human capital. To do so we multiply the raw labor force by an index number reflecting the average education level in the country. The index is constructed using the Barro/Lee (1993) data set that distinguishes between primary, secondary, and tertiary education. A country composed of only college graduates (with 10 years of schooling) has an index value of 1. The most highly educated labor force in our sample is the United States, where the index obtains a value of .79. In China, the index takes a value of .23.

Relative capital abundance is obtained by dividing each country's capital abundance by the corresponding world average for the given year, where "world average" is defined relative to all the countries in the Penn World Tables.

Our income variable I_t is the three-year average of lagged GNP per capita. We therefore smooth out some business-cycle variation. For a given year t we compute $I_t = (y_t + y_t + y_t)/3$, where y_t represents income per capita in year t. Relative income is constructed by the same method used for relative capital abundance. GNP figures were obtained by adjusting GDP figures with a GNP/GDP correction factor obtained from the International Monetary Fund's International Financial Statistics. Correction factors were unavailable for the former Czechoslovakia, Egypt, Hong Kong, Iraq, Peru, Poland, and the former Yugoslavia. Unadjusted GDP figures were used in these cases.

The Communist countries dummy is equal to one for China, Czechoslovakia, Poland, and Yugoslavia. In some cases we employ a dummy to denote countries that are signatories to the Helsinki Protocol on acid rain. The country dummy for the Helsinki Protocol identifies Austria, Belgium, Bulgaria, Canada, Czechoslovakia, Denmark, Finland,

France, Germany, Hungary, Italy, Luxembourg, the Netherlands, Norway, and Switzerland, in the years after 1985.

The data on foreign direct investment were obtained as percentages of the stock of inward FDI relative to GDP, and interpolated where necessary. Then these figures were divided by GDP to capital stock ratios obtained from the Penn World Tables in order to obtain the percentage of inward FDI stock relative to a country's entire capital stock. We have also interacted our FDI and City Economic Intensity variables with indicator variables that identify rich and poor countries.

We define as rich those countries that in a given year belonged to the richest 30% of countries listed in the Penn World Tables, as measured by their per capita GDP. Likewise, poor countries are those in the bottom 30%. As countries' positions change over time, our two indicator variables are not fixed over time. Based on the 2,555 observations used in our regressions, 29% are from rich countries, 11% from poor countries, and the remaining 60% are from the middle-income group.

Econometric Issues

In moving from our theoretical model to estimation we face several econometric issues. Here we discuss three: identification, excluded variables, and functional form.

Identification

The private sector's demand for pollution, written in differential form, is given by (7.15). The pollution supply curve is given by (7.5). A problem arises because most measures of the scale of economic activity, S, that shifts pollution demand (for example real GDP or real GDP per person) will be highly or perfectly correlated with real income per capita (real GNP/person), R, which shifts pollution supply. This identification problem is illustrated quite simply in figure 7.5.

In figure 7.5 we depict typical pollution demand and supply curves determining an initial level of pollution that we observe as Z_0 and an initial pollution tax τ_0 that we do not observe. According to our theory, we interpret the observation of Z_0, for given income, output, and factor endowments (all observed), as the intersection of pollution supply S_0 and demand D_0. At some future time, we observe an increase in pollu-

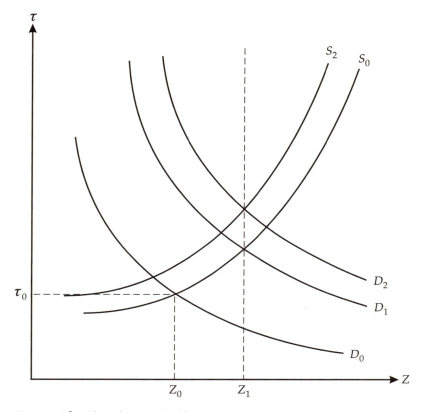

Fig. 7.5. The Identification Problem

tion to Z_1. At the same time, assume income and output measures have risen as well (not shown). Our theory tells us that income gains shift both pollution supply and demand.

The observation of Z_1 with higher income is consistent with a zero technique effect and a positive scale effect. This is represented by supply remaining fixed at S_0 while demand shifts to D_1. Alternatively, observing Z_1 is consistent with a very large scale effect—a shift to D_2— and a significant technique effect—the shift back to S_2. In fact, any combination of demand-and-supply shifts leading to an intersection along the vertical dotted line at Z_1 is consistent with the observation that pollution rose, as did income.

All that we can infer, given a restriction that scale shifts demand out and technique shifts supply back, is that scale effects are dominating technique effects. This observation is of course exactly why Grossman and Krueger (1993) state that their evidence on the EKC reflects the *relative strength* of scale versus technique effects.

In order to provide separate estimates of scale and technique effects we have to address this problem. We do so by exploiting three different sources of variation in our data. First, we assume national averages for income per capita and the number of exposed individuals determine pollution policy. We are, by assumption, fixing the pollution supply curve for all cities within a given country. This "allows" us to employ the within-country variation in scale across cities to separate the influence of scale from that of technique. This method is not costless, as it implicitly assumes all cities within a given country share similar compositions of output. Since the cities where pollution is measured are all typically quite large metropolitan areas, this may be an innocuous assumption. For example, we assume the composition of output is similar in Tokyo and Osaka; similar in Toronto and Hamilton; and similar in Chicago and New York. The composition of output produced in Osaka, Toronto, and New York may differ, however, because of differences in national factor endowments and openness to world markets.

This method of identification is shown in figure 7.6, where we have depicted several city-specific pollution demand curves and a common country supply curve. (The supply curve is horizontal given our constant marginal disutility of pollution assumption.) Note that for all cities within a given country, pollution supply is identical, as we have assumed pollution policy is primarily determined by national characteristics. In contrast, pollution demand can differ across cities depending on their scale. We have depicted three cities in the figure, labeled 1, 2, and 3. If S_0 is the relevant supply curve for each, and if the cities differ only in their scale, then the observations on pollution can be employed to separate the impact of scale from that of technique.

Second, we note that changes in the scale of output must have contemporaneous effects on pollution concentrations, whereas pollution policy is likely to respond slowly to changes in income levels. Consequently, we use as our proxy for the income measure relevant to technique effects a one-period-lagged, three-year moving average of income per capita. In contrast, we link pollution concentrations to a contemporaneous measure of economic activity. For example, we expect that a significant recession would drive down concentrations (a scale effect) but not lead to a rewriting of pollution control laws (i.e., a technique effect). To the extent that there is significant variation over

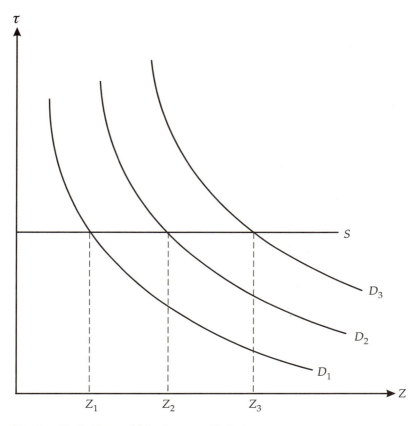

Fig. 7.6. Exploiting within Country Variation

time in income and activity measures, this source of variation will help in our identification.[27]

Finally we note that the scale of economic activity should be measured by economic activity within a country's borders—that is, GDP—whereas the income relevant to the technique effect should reflect the income of residents wherever it is earned—that is, GNP. Therefore, we can exploit the difference between GDP and GNP measures to separate technique from scale effects. While the gap between these two figures is not large for most economies, it is significant for some. This cross-country variation will be useful in separating scale from technique.

---

27. This source of variation in pollution data has been exploited before. See Chay and Greenstone 1999.

Unobservable Variables: Fixed or Random Effects?

Several variables relevant to our theory are unobservable. To account for these exclusions, we estimate an individual effects model for ε_{ijkt} given by

$$\varepsilon_{ijkt} = \xi_t + \theta_{ijk} + \nu_{ijkt}, \tag{7.24}$$

where ξ_t is a time-specific effect, θ_{ijk} is a site-specific effect, and ν_{ijkt} is an idiosyncratic measurement error for observation station i in city j in country k in year t. Our common-to-world, but time-specific effect is included to capture changes in knowledge concerning pollution, changes in the world relative price of dirty goods, and improvements in abatement technologies. While proxies for some of these variables could be constructed, choosing proxies will of course introduce new issues of data quality, coverage, and so on. Instead we note that because each of these variables affects all countries in a similar way, a preferred method may be to treat them as unobservable. For example, a rise in the world price of dirty goods affects all countries in a similar way. Accordingly, we capture these common-to-world excluded variables with a set of unrestricted time dummies.

θ_{ijk} is a site-specific effect representing excluded site (or country-specific) variables such as excluded economic determinants, or excluded meteorological variables. For example, country type T appears in pollution supply but is virtually unobservable since it relies on both knowledge of the weight governments' apply to Greens and Browns in their economy and the share of each in the overall population. Since the panel is relatively short for almost all countries, we take these country type and distribution parameters as fixed over time. In addition, there are unmeasured topographical and meteorological features that undoubtedly affect the dissipation of pollution at each site. Finally we allow for an idiosyncratic measurement error ν_{ijkt}. Two sources of this error would be machine error in reading concentrations and human error in calculation or tabulation.

Throughout we present both fixed and random effects estimates for every model. While random effects estimation is in theory more efficient, it is unclear whether excluded country-specific effects subsumed in our error term are uncorrelated with our regressors. And while fixed-effects estimation is preferable in just these cases, fixed effects limits the cross-sectional variation we can exploit for separating scale from technique effects.

Functional Form

Our model predicts emission levels, but our data is on concentrations. Meteorological models mapping emissions from a (single) stack into measured concentrations at a receptor are functions of emission rates, stack height, the distance to the receptor, wind speed, temperature gradients, and turbulence. Much of this information is not presently available. In view of these limitations we adopt a linear approximation to measured concentrations by writing concentrations at site *ijk*, at time *t* as

$$Z^C_{ijkt} = X_{jkt}{}' \alpha + Y_{ijkt}{}' \zeta + \varepsilon_{ijkt}, \tag{7.25}$$
$$X_{jkt}{}' \alpha = \alpha_0 + \alpha_1 \mathrm{SCALE}_{jkt} + \alpha_2 KL_{kt} + \alpha_3 \mathrm{INC}_{kt} + \alpha_4 \Psi_{kt} \mathrm{TRADEINTENS}_{kt},$$
$$\Psi_{kt} = \Psi_0 + \Psi_1 \mathrm{REL.}KL_{kt} + \Psi_2 \mathrm{REL.}KL^2_{kt} +$$
$$\Psi_3 \mathrm{REL.INC}_{kt} + \Psi_4 \mathrm{REL.INC}^2_{kt} + \Psi_5 \mathrm{REL.INC}_{kt} \mathrm{REL.}KL_{kt},$$

where SCALE is city-specific GDP/km^2, *KL* is the national capital-to-labor ratio, INC is a one-period-lagged three-year moving average of GNP/N, TRADEINTENS is $(X + M)/\mathrm{GDP}$, REL.KL is country *k*'s capital-to-labor ratio measured relative to the world average, and REL.INC is country *k*'s real income measured relative to the world average. Note that world price and country type variables are captured via (7.24), and trade intensity has replaced trade frictions as discussed previously. Y contains site-specific weather variables and site-specific physical characteristics (discussed below), and ε_{ijkt} is a site-specific error reflecting unmeasured economic and physical variables. We refer to equation (7.25) as model A in our estimations.

Model A follows from our reduced form if we assume our π coefficients are in fact constants. This assumption is, however, somewhat at odds with our theory. In theory, the impact of capital accumulation on pollution depends on the techniques of production in place. But when countries differ in income per capita, they will also differ in producer prices and hence their techniques of production. Consequently, the impact of capital accumulation on the composition of output is not a linear function of KL. Similarly, the impact of income gains on pollution depends on the existing composition of output and hence the existing capital-to-labor ratio and income per capita. To account for these possibilities we amend model A by adding the squares of income per capita ($\mathrm{INC}_{kt}{}^2$) and the capital-to-labor ratio ($KL_{kt}{}^2$) as well as their cross-product ($\mathrm{INC}_{kt} KL_{kt}$). We refer to this amended form of (7.25) as model B.

As a consequence, the impact of factor accumulation can now differ across countries and over time in closer accord with our theory. Finally, we consider a further nonlinearity by adding $SCALE_{kt}^2$ to model B. A nonlinearity in the impact of scale could arise from nonhomotheticities in production or consumption. We refer to this slightly amended model as model C.

7.5 Empirical Results

Scale, Composition, and Technique Effects

Table 7.3 presents estimates from models A, B, and C using both random and fixed effects. In addition to the regressors already discussed, we also include a set of interactions between income per capita and our Communist country dummy. This is to allow for the country type—Communist—to affect pollution supply. In addition we include a dummy for a country's signing of the Helsinki Protocol on Acid Rain. All specifications include a full set of time dummies.

Consider first our core variables representing scale, composition, and technique effects. In all columns of table 7.3 we find a positive and significant relationship between the scale of economic activity as measured by GDP/km^2 and concentrations. The coefficient estimates increase in magnitude as we move from model A through to C, but the estimates differ only slightly across random and fixed effects. Next consider the impact of a nation's capital-to-labor ratio. In all columns we find a positive composition effect arising from an increase in capital to labor ratios. The estimates in table 7.3 also predict a strong and significantly negative relationship between per capita income levels and concentrations.

Since the models are nested, we can test the restrictions imposed in model A and B via a likelihood ratio (LR) test. The test statistics are reported in the second to last line of the table. It appears there is little gained in moving to the slightly more general model C from model B; conversely, the restrictions imposed by model A are rejected by the data as shown by the significant LR test statistics in columns 1 and 4. These empirical results together with our knowledge of theory suggest that less emphasis be placed on the estimates from model A.

To get a feel for the magnitudes involved, we report the elasticity of concentrations to an increase in scale (GDP/km^2), composition (KL), technique (I), and trade intensity (TI) in table 7.4. The elasticities are

TABLE 7.3
Alternative Hypotheses Tests

	Estimation Method					
	Random Effects			Fixed Effects		
	Model A (1)	Model B (2)	Model C (3)	Model A (4)	Model B (5)	Model C (6)
Intercept	−2.865***	−3.279***	−3.311***	−2.506***	−4.324***	−4.299***
City economy intensity (GDP/km²)	0.042***	0.058***	0.07***	0.024*	0.058***	0.089*
(City economy intensity)²/ 1,000			−0.244			−0.34
Capital abundance (K/L)	0.102**	0.293**	0.286*	0.165**	0.461**	0.437*
(K/L)²		0.014	0.013		0.006	0.008
Lagged per-capita income	−0.982***	−1.248***	−1.312***	−1.326***	−0.096	−0.228
(Income)²		0.708***	0.669***		0.559***	0.578***
$(K/L) × (I)$		−0.309***	−0.285***		−0.381***	−0.386***
Trade intensity TI = (X + M)/GDP	−0.915	−0.488	−0.51	−3.677***	−3.142**	−3.216**
TI × relative K/L	−0.462	−1.952*	−1.828*	0.159	−2.252*	−2.121
TI × (relative K/L)²	0.018	−0.23	−0.248	−0.168	−0.123	−0.176
TI × relative income	0.47	1.056*	1.011*	2.128**	2.687***	2.614***
TI × (relative income)²	0.118	−0.308*	−0.285*	−0.108	−0.595**	−0.584**
TI × (relative K/L) × (relative income)	−0.165	0.87***	0.822***	−0.28	0.9**	0.924**
Suburban dummy	−0.299	−0.435*	−0.422*			
Rural dummy	−0.623	−0.674	−0.631			
Communist country dummy	0.312	−0.252	−0.257			
Communist country dummy × income	−0.283	4.569*	4.641*	1.17	9.621**	9.639**
Communist country dummy × (income)²		−5.755**	−5.788**		−8.931***	−8.806**
Average temperature	−0.055***	−0.052***	−0.052***	−0.06*	−0.057*	−0.056*
Precipitation variation	3.446	5.86	6.158	8.599	10.81*	10.716*
Helsinki protocol	−0.232*	−0.092	−0.114	−0.179	0.016	0.016
Observations	2,555	2,555	2,555	2,555	2,555	2,555
Groups	290	290	290	290	290	290
R²	0.3395	0.3737	0.374	0.2483	0.131	0.1499
Log likelihood	−2550	−2523	−2522	−3964	−3906	−3905
LR Test / X² (df)	55.596***	1.604		118.42***	2.035	
Hausman test / wald X² (df)	65.761**	15.158		53.789		

Note: To conserve space, no standard errors or *t*-statistics are shown. The dependent variable is the log of the median of SO_2 concentrations at each observation site. Model A follows directly from our empirical implementation, while model B allows for additional interaction between capital abundance and income. In addition to model B, model C allows for nonlinearity in our scale variable. All model specifications use time-fixed effects. Elasticities are evaluated at sample means using the Delta method. Empty cells were not estimated.

*p < .05. **p < .01. ***p < .001.

TABLE 7.4
Estimated Elasticities

	Estimation Method					
	Random Effects			Fixed Effects		
	Model A (1)	Model B (2)	Model C (3)	Model A (4)	Model B (5)	Model C (6)
Scale elasticity	0.192***	0.265***	0.315***	0.112*	0.266***	0.398**
Composition elasticity	0.583*	0.948***	0.993***	0.945**	1.006**	0.975*
Technique elasticity	−0.905***	−1.577***	−1.577***	−1.222***	−1.153***	−1.266**
Trade intensity elasticity	−0.436***	−0.388***	−0.394***	−0.641***	−0.864***	−0.882***

Note: Elasticities are evaluated at sample means using the Delta method.
$*p < .05.$ $**p < .01.$ $***p < .001.$

evaluated at the sample mean and apply to a "statistically average" country in our sample.

As shown by the table, the technique elasticity varies between −0.9 and −1.5; whereas the scale elasticity ranges from only .2 to approximately .4. The estimated gap between the scale and technique effect seems large, and should be investigated further.[28] It is however consistent with the work of Pargal and Wheeler (1996), who study the link between informal pollution regulation and community characteristics in India. Using plant-level data, they find a 1% increase in community income drives pollution down by 2.8–4%; while a 1% increase in output raises pollution by 0.6–0.7%.[29] The strong policy response is also consistent with the results of Hilton and Levinson (1998) on lead. Alternative specifications (discussed below) lead to somewhat different conclusions, but the technique elasticity is almost universally estimated to be greater than −1 in magnitude, suggesting a strong policy response to income gains.

The estimated impact of factor composition is typically quite large. With the exception of column 1, we find a 1% increase in a nation's capital-to-labor ratio, holding scale, income, and other determinants constant, leads to perhaps a one percentage point increase in pollution. Our success in finding a link between factor endowments and pollution may appear surprising given the universal difficulties researchers

---

28. Country-specific estimates of course differ, with some point estimates of the net effect being positive. The hypothesis that scale dominates technique is, however, rejected by every individual country in the sample.
29. See Pargal and Wheeler 1996, table 2, p. 1324.

have had in finding a strong link between endowments and trade flows. We note, however, that the production side of the Heckscher-Ohlin model has received some support (Harrigan 1995, 1997), and our model focuses on a highly aggregative relationship between overall pollution-intensive output and factor endowments.

This result is also consistent with the computable general equilibrium (CGE) results of Brown, Deardorff, and Stern (1992) linking a 10% change in the Mexican capital stock with a 9% increase in electric utility output. The conclusion we draw from this CGE comparative static is simply that electricity generation is highly capital intensive, and this creates a strong link between capital accumulation and sulfur dioxide pollution. This is, in effect, what our estimates bear out.

The Trade-Induced Composition Effect

Next consider the estimates for the trade-induced composition effect. In all columns of table 7.3 we reject the hypothesis that the terms reflecting the trade-induced composition effect are jointly zero.[30] While the sign and significance of some individual coefficients varies across specifications, the results from model B and model C in both random and fixed effects are very similar. As shown by table 7.4, at the sample mean, the overall elasticity of concentrations to an increase in trade intensity is relatively constant ranging from approximately −0.4 to −0.9. Therefore, for an average country in our sample the trade-induced composition effect is negative.

Considering the individual coefficient estimates in our interaction, it is clear that both relative income and capital abundance are important country characteristics determining comparative advantage, but it is difficult to evaluate the relative strength of pollution haven and factor abundance motives. To assess the plausibility of our trade intensity elasticity, we calculated the trade intensity elasticity for all countries in our sample. Recall that country-specific estimates of this elasticity should reflect comparative advantage in dirty goods. That is, a positive value for a country implies that trade liberalization shifts pollution demand to the right; a negative value for a country implies that trade liberalization shifts pollution demand to the left. Therefore it is not

---

30. This is in contrast to the case where trade intensity appears alone or is replaced by other measures of "openness." We investigated this issue more fully in Antweiler, Copeland, and Taylor 1998, table 2, p. 29.

plausible that all countries in the world have negative trade intensity elasticities. Although we have only a sample of countries, it seems reasonable to expect both positive and negative elasticities. The magnitude of the elasticity relates a 1% change in trade intensity $(X + M)/$ GDP to an x% change in sulfur dioxide concentrations.

We plot the elasticity estimates from column (3) and column (5) against income per capita in figures 7.7 and 7.8.

While there are more positive point elasticities in figure 7.7 than in 7.8, in both there is a distribution of elasticities around zero. Our inference is simply that some countries' pollution demand shifts right with a fall in trade frictions and some shifts left—*because countries differ in their comparative advantage.*[31] For example, from figure 7.7 we conclude a small trade liberalization in Canada, all else equal, shifts its pollution demand curve to the right. The inference is that despite Canada's relatively high income, its comparative advantage lies in capital-intensive dirty products. The same is true for the United States. Alternatively, we conclude a small trade liberalization in India shifts its pollution demand curve to the left. The inference is that despite its relatively low income, its comparative advantage lies in labor-intensive and relatively clean goods production. While these two countries estimates may accord well with our intuition, other country-specific elasticities are harder to explain. (For example, why is Malaysia's elasticity so negative and Switzerland's so positive?) Since our country specific estimates do vary across specifications, we caution the reader from drawing too strong an inference from any one of them.

We note that if the pollution haven hypothesis were an accurate description of world trade in dirty goods, then we would expect to see a strong negative relationship in both figures. Rich countries would have a comparative advantage in clean goods; therefore further trade liberalization should shift their pollution demand left, leading to a negative elasticity estimate. The opposite should be true for poor countries. Nothing like this pattern emerges from the figures. In fact, the relationship is positive and significantly so. Moreover, since capital-to-labor ratios are higher in richer economies, the figures suggest further trade liberalization will shift dirty and capital-intensive production to the

---

31. The random effects implementation in figure 7.8 has more positive point elasticities than the fixed effects in figure 7.9, but relatively small changes in specification moves the entire set of fixed-effects estimates upwards.

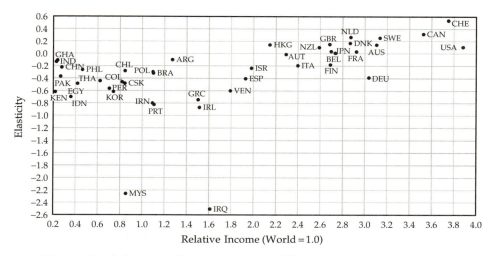

Fig. 7.7. Trade Intensity Elasticity (Random Effects)

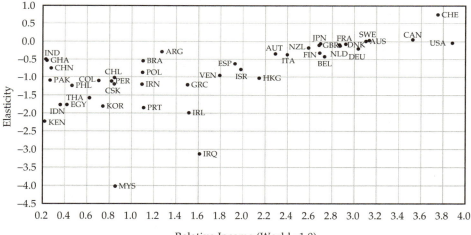

Fig. 7.8. Trade Intensity Elasticity (Fixed Effects)

developed economies. Factor endowment determinants of trade appear to be dominating pollution haven motives.

To some extent this result should not be surprising. Although the methods here are different, the conclusions were foreshadowed in earlier work. For example, Walter (1973) calculates the direct and indirect environmental control costs in both U.S. exports and imports to find that U.S. exports are actually very dirty by this measure, more than 15% more than its imports.[32] And Xu (1999) reports that in 1995, almost 80% of the world's exports of environmentally sensitive goods come from the OECD (Organisation for Economic Cooperation and Development) countries. Finally, the figure is consistent with the CGE evidence of Brown, Deardorff, and Stern (1992) predicting a reallocation of energy-intensive manufactures toward the United States and Canada. To a certain extent the figure merely formalizes what we should have expected *ex ante*.

While changes in trade intensity seem to matter, the magnitude of the induced change in pollution concentrations appears relatively small. In both figures the vast majority of countries have trade intensity elasticities less than 1 in absolute value; and given the relatively slow movement of trade intensity over time, the changes in pollution due to trade influences must be relatively small indeed. For example, over the 26-year period of our sample, the median change in trade intensity was only 7.8 percentage points. On a yearly basis, this is incredibly small.

To get a feel for how a large trade liberalization can affect trade intensity consider the case of Canada and its 1988 free trade agreement with the United States. Over the 20 years prior to the agreement, 1969–88, trade intensity in Canada grew by about 0.5% per year. In the 13 years after the agreement, 1988–2001, trade intensity grew at over triple this rate, rising by almost 1.75% per year. If we attribute the majority of this difference to the advent of the free trade agreement, then Canada's trade intensity has grown by an additional 1% per year because of the policy change. We estimate the trade intensity elasticity for Canada to be 0.30; therefore, the trade-induced composition effect created by the free trade agreement has raised Canadian sulfur dioxide concentrations by about one-third of a percent per year. This seems quite small despite a massive increase in Canadian exports to the United States.

One explanation for the relatively small trade-intensity elasticities is simple: low-income countries typically have both low incomes per capita and low capital-to-labor ratios. The pollution haven hypothesis suggests that a low-income economy should be made dirtier by trade, but

---

32. See Walter 1973, 67. Pollution-related costs amounted to 1.75% of the value of U.S. exports, about 15% higher than the 1.51% estimated for U.S. imports.

if pollution-intensive industries are also capital-intensive, then whatever cost reductions lax pollution regulation brings could be largely undone by the relatively higher price of capital in this capital-scarce country. As a result, further openness to trade will have a very small effect on the pollution intensity of output for low-income countries. Similarly, high-income countries have both high income and high capital-to-labor ratios. The former argues in favor of trade lowering the pollution intensity of output, while the latter argues in favor of trade raising it. It is not that the (ceteris paribus) pollution haven hypothesis is wrong, or that the (ceteris paribus) factor endowment–driven basis for trade is absent. But rather, because these two partial theories work against each other, the net result of the potentially very large composition effects predicted by either theory turns out to be rather small in practice.

Site-Specific and Country Type Considerations

To allow for country type considerations, we created Communist country interactions with income and income squared in models B and C. The results suggest the technique effect is very small or nonexistent in Communist countries. For example, using the fixed-effects results from column 6 of table 7.3, we cannot reject the hypothesis of a zero technique effect in Communist countries! In the random effects case in column 3, the technique elasticity is fully one-third of that for our average, non-Communist, country.[33]

The results also indicate that site-specific land use and weather variables have a bearing on concentrations. The suburban and rural location type dummy variables are always negative, indicating these locations are on average cleaner than the third (default) location, central city. Higher temperatures both dissipate pollution faster and reduce the need for home heating; precipitation highly concentrated in one season reduces the ability of rain to wash out concentrations.

Not shown in the table is the set of time dummies estimated. These dummies trace out a significant downward trend in concentrations. While we cannot identify the exact source of this trend, likely candi-

---

33. The technique elasticity in the random effects case is the much smaller −.50 but is significantly different from zero; the technique elasticity in the fixed-effects case is −.062 with a 95% confidence interval of (−.90, .78).

dates would be a gradual change in the population mix toward Greens, an increased weight placed on the concerns of Green citizens, or perhaps improvements in abatement technology.

An Environmental Assessment of Freer Trade

As shown earlier, we can approximate the full impact of falling trade frictions by adding up the various components. Repeating (7.20), we have

$$\frac{dz}{d\delta}\frac{\delta}{z} = [\pi_1 - \pi_3]\frac{dI}{d\delta}\frac{\delta}{I} + \pi_4 . \tag{7.26}$$

Since we do not have information on the income gains created by trade, $dI/d\delta$, any conclusions we draw have to rest on further assumptions.

One approach is to simply restrict our conclusion to the sample-average country. Using the estimates from either model B or C in table 7.3, the net effect of a 1% change in income created by trade is a 0.8–0.9% fall in emissions: that is, we have $\pi_1 - \pi_3 < 0$. The composition effect of trade for our average country is also negative; that is, we have $\pi_4 < 0$. Therefore, for an average country in our sample, the full impact of further openness to international trade—through scale, technique, and composition effects—will be a reduction in sulfur dioxide concentrations!

Similar results follow from almost all of our specifications: the scale elasticity is almost universally dominated by the technique elasticity, while the trade-induced composition effect of trade is typically small in magnitude.[34] How large a reduction any one country reaps from a fall in trade frictions will of course depend on country characteristics, the impact further trade has on domestic income and output, and how the ongoing process of globalization is affecting country characteristics elsewhere in the world.

Since countries differ in their particular scale, technique, and trade intensity elasticities, some may indeed be made dirtier from a reduction in trade frictions, but we expect that trade's effect—whether positive or negative—will be small. After all, the estimated impact of even

---

34. For some countries in our sample the estimated scale elasticity exceeds the technique elasticity; but no country has a difference between these two that is both positive and statistically significant.

a large trade liberalization on GDP is small, and when this small increase in GDP is then filtered through our estimated scale and technique elasticities, the net effect is likely to be smaller still.[35] While in theory, trade's impact on the pollution intensity of output can be large, in practice our estimates suggest a much more muted response.

Sources of Growth, the EKC, and Other Methods for Free Trade Assessments

Our assessment of international trade's effect on pollution was limited to adding up the conventional implications of a fall in trade frictions. But if freer trade spurs capital accumulation or hastens technological advance, then the full implications we measure may in fact only be partial. While a complete answer to this question requires further empirical work, our results do provide us with some information on this score.

Recall that in order to isolate the role of international trade, we control for other potentially confounding determinants of pollution. As a consequence, our approach forced us to distinguish the pollution consequences of income changes brought about by changes in openness from those created by capital accumulation or technological progress. We can now exploit this fact to provide a back-of-the-envelope calculation of trade's effect when it induces other effects.

Consider the possibility that further trade accelerates technological progress via diffusion of new technologies from abroad. Assume it arrives as neutral technological progress. Neutral technological progress of $x\%$ raises both GDP and GNP per person by $x\%$, and according to our estimates from table 7.4, the positive scale effect from this growth will always be dominated by the negative technique effect. Neutral technological progress by itself lowers pollution while raising income levels. Therefore, a trade liberalization that brings with it technological advance is greener than one that does not.

Conversely, suppose increased openness spurs capital accumulation. Capital accumulation creates not only scale and technique effects, but also changes the composition of output by increasing dirty good production. Differentiating pollution demand with respect to k shows the full impact of capital accumulation is

---

35. Some models with imperfect competition predict large income gains from trade liberalization, although typically CGE studies predict gains on the order of 0.5 to 2% of GNP. See Cox and Harris 1985 for estimates from a model with imperfect competition.

$$\frac{dz}{dk}\frac{k}{z} = \pi_1 \frac{dS}{dk}\frac{k}{S} + \pi_2 - \pi_3 \frac{dI}{dk}\frac{k}{I},\qquad(7.27)$$

where π_2 is the elasticity of pollution with respect to a change in a nation's capital-to-labor ratio. From table 7.4 this direct effect of capital accumulation is approximately 1. We take our estimates of π_1 and π_3 from table 7.4, column 6. To go further we need additional assumptions. Assume capital's share in national income is one-third, and population growth is zero over the time period considered; then (7.27) becomes

$$\frac{dz}{dk}\frac{k}{z} = \pi_2 + \frac{1}{3}[\pi_1 - \pi_3] = 1 + \frac{1}{3}[.39 - 1.26] = .61 > 0.\qquad(7.28)$$

Capital accumulation raises pollution concentrations.

While these last two exercises are not tests of our theory, the conclusions are reassuringly close to what we might have expected *ex ante*. Neutral technological progress lowers pollution concentrations because it raises incomes and does not favor dirty good production; capital accumulation raises pollution because it favors the production of dirty goods.

Despite their back-of-the-envelope flavor, these results give us some pause for thought. Recall that Grossman and Krueger (1993) examined the implication of NAFTA plus an exogenous 10% increase in Mexico's capital stock. Using the model of Brown, Deardorff, and Stern (1992) and the Toxic Release Inventory (TRI) data, they found capital accumulation had very negative consequences for the environment. Electric utility output rose almost lockstep with capital accumulation, and toxic releases increased dramatically.[36] One could rightly conclude from their results that trade liberalization had little effect on Mexico's environment, but trade liberalization plus its induced capital accumulation had a very negative effect. Here we temper this conclusion.

Capital accumulation appears to raise pollution levels, even after accounting for the induced policy response.[37] Therefore, trade liberalization plus capital accumulation is far less environmentally friendly than trade liberalization alone. We would stress, however, that once we de-

---

36. Electric utilities are typically the major source of sulfur dioxide emissions, and hence utility output may be a good proxy for emissions.

37. Note that the Brown et al. result of a 9% change in the output of electric utilities arising from a 10% change in the capital stock corresponds very closely to the elasticity of 1 found for capital accumulation's effect on sulfur dioxide concentrations.

part from the standard analysis of trade liberalization to include its potential effects on capital accumulation, we should also include its potential role in facilitating technology transfer and accelerating technological change. Given the estimates presented earlier for neutral technological progress, these induced effects appear to work in opposing directions.

One final implication of our calculations is that the pollution consequences of economic growth are dependent on the underlying source of growth. While EKC studies often find initially rising pollution levels at low incomes, this result may reflect the type of growth common at the first stages of development (capital accumulation) rather than the relative strength of scale and technique effects. In fact, if capital accumulation becomes a smaller source of growth as development proceeds and technological progress a more important source, then our results suggest pollution should at first rise and then fall with income per capita.

7.6 Alternative Specifications and Theories

It is important to investigate whether our results are robust to reasonable changes in specification, time period, and so on. We have conducted numerous sensitivity tests of our specification and report four alternatives in tables 7.5, 7.6, and 7.7. In all columns we amend our full model C from table 7.3 to include other determinants, investigate other time periods, or adopt more flexible specifications. Table 7.5 contains random effects estimates, table 7.6 fixed-effects estimates, and table 7.7 the implied elasticities for scale, and so on, for both random and fixed effects. The columns in tables 7.5 and 7.6 are numbered consecutively to avoid any ambiguity, and this numbering is carried over to table 7.7.

In column 1 of table 7.5 and column 5 of table 7.6 we have restricted the time period of our analysis to the years 1976–91. Before 1976 only a few countries participated in the GEMS project, and after funding ceased in 1991 country coverage was reduced. To allow for possible problems in data quality and sample selection, we consider this shorter time period. This shortened period has 489 fewer observations, but as shown in table 7.5, column 1, and table 7.6, column 5, the results are similar both in terms of elasticity estimates and significance levels. Our overall conclusions regarding the relative strength of scale versus technique effects remain, as does the muted response to changes in trade intensity.

TABLE 7.5
Sensitivity Tests, by Model Specification, Using Random Effects Estimation Method

Variable	Time (1)	Factors (2)	FDI (3)	Scale (4)
Intercept	−2.545***	−3.141***	−3.65***	−3.635***
City economic intensity (GDP/km²)	0.068***	0.075***	0.07***	0.154***
(City economic intensity)²/1,000	−0.054	−0.275	−0.231	
Capital abundance (K/L)	−0.115	0.289*	0.439***	0.279*
(K/L)²	0.036**	0.012	−0.002	0.01
Lagged per capita income	−1.771***	−1.629***	−1.451***	−0.852*
(Income)²	0.585***	0.717***	0.66***	0.611***
$(K/L) \times (I)$	−0.147*	−0.276***	−0.255***	−0.278***
Trade intensity TI = (X + M)/GDP	−2.466***	−0.671	−0.198	−0.501
TI × relative K/L	0.934	−1.758*	−2.879**	−1.89*
TI × (relative K/L)²	−0.876**	−0.252	0.304	−0.142
TI × relative income	1.344**	1.167*	1.518*	1.212*
TI × (relative income)²	−0.228	−0.309*	−0.308*	−0.354**
TI × (relative K/L) × (relative income)	0.333	0.803***	0.519	0.784**
Suburban dummy	−0.284	−0.424*	−0.445*	−0.49**
Rural dummy	−0.519	−0.62	−0.655	−0.73*
Inward FDI stock / capital stock			0.039	
FDI/K × poor countries			4.736	
FDI/K × rich countries			−0.362	
Communist country dummy	−0.971*	−0.326	−0.11	−0.475
Communist country dummy × income	7.785***	4.602*	4.201	5.668**
Communist country dummy × (income)²	−8.683***	−5.683*	−5.677*	−7.127**
Average temperature	−0.061***	−0.056***	−0.051***	−0.052***
Precipitation variation	8.867*	5.859	7.633	5.882
Hard coal (per worker)		−0.69		
Soft coal (per worker)		2.998*		
Helsinki protocol	−0.242*	−0.157	−0.092	−0.094
Observations	2,066	2,555	2,525	2,555
Groups	274	290	284	290
R²	0.3243	0.3779	0.3684	0.389
Log likelihood	−2030	−2519	−2496	−2512
Hausman test / wald X²(df)	94.211***	55.536	84.269***	59.331*

Note: The dependent variable is the log of the median of SO_2 concentrations at each observation site. All model specifications use time-fixed effects. Elasticities are evaluated at sample means using the Delta method. Model "Time" only includes the years 1976–91 of the primary GEMS phase; model "Factors" introduces factor endowment–related variables; and model "FDI" allows for an inward foreign direct investment stock relative to the overall capital stock, interacted with income. The terms *rich countries* and *poor countries* refer to the top and bottom 30% of countries in the Penn World Tables with respect to per capita GDP. Empty cells were not estimated.

*$p < .05$.   **$p < .01$.   ***$p < .001$.

TABLE 7.6

Sensitivity Tests by Model Specification, Using Fixed Effects Estimation Method

Variable	Time (5)	Factors (6)	FDI (7)	Scale (8)
Intercept	−1.697	−4.679***	−4.679***	−4.345***
City economic intensity GDP/km²	0.091*	0.087*	0.092*	0.029
(City economic intensity)²/1000	−0.254	−0.329	−0.373	
Capital abundance (K/L)	−0.077	0.426*	0.754***	0.489**
(K/L)²	0.032	0.008	−0.024	0.006
Lagged per capita income	−3.109**	−0.428	−0.981	−0.052
(Income)²	0.512*	0.757***	0.563***	0.564***
$(K/L) \times (I)$	−0.041	−0.401***	−0.297***	−0.4***
Trade intensity TI = (X + M)/GDP	−7.161***	−3.333**	−3.747***	−2.964**
TI × relative K/L	1.699	−2.281*	−2.737	−2.541*
TI × (relative K/L)²	−1.043**	−0.131	0.811	−0.112
TI × relative income	4.495***	3.097***	2.72**	2.677***
TI × (relative income)²	−0.742**	−0.723***	−0.36	−0.617**
TI × (relative K/L) × (relative income)	0.164	0.922**	0.092	0.993**
Suburban dummy				
Rural dummy				
Inward FDI stock / capital stock			1.234*	
FDI/K × poor countries			6.314	
FDI/K × rich countries			−0.828	
Communist country dummy				
Communist country dummy × income	16.809***	11.751***	10.271**	9.819**
Communist country dummy × (Income)²	−14.13***	−10.84***	−8.84**	−9.039***
Average temperature	−0.072*	−0.055*	−0.049	−0.062*
Precipitation variation	14.298**	10.893*	13.972**	11.471*
Hard coal (per worker)		4.217		
Soft coal (per worker)		4.12		
Helsinki protocol	−0.173	−0.054	0.036	0.035
Observations	2,066	2,555	2,525	2,555
Groups	274	290	284	290
R²	0.1677	0.0605	0.1577	0.1337
Log likelihood	−2982	−3900	−3858	−3899
Hausman test / wald X²(df)				

Note: The dependent variable is the log of the median of SO_2 concentrations at each observation site. All model specifications use time-fixed effects. Elasticities are evaluated at sample means using the Delta method. Model "Time" only includes the years 1976–91 of the primary GEMS phase; model "Factors" introduces factor endowment–related variables; and model "FDI" allows for an inward foreign direct investment stock relative to the overall capital stock, interacted with income. The terms *rich countries* and *poor countries* refer to the top and bottom 30% of countries in the Penn World Tables with respect to per capita GDP. Empty cells were not estimated.

*$p < .05$. **$p < .01$. ***$p < .001$.

TABLE 7.7
Sensitivity Test Elasticities, by Estimation Method and Model Specification

	Random Effects				Fixed Effects			
Variable	Time (1)	Factors (2)	FDI (3)	Scale (4)	Time (5)	Factors (6)	FDI (7)	Scale (8)
Scale elasticity (all/middle)	0.314***	0.333***	0.318***	0.499***	0.414*	0.388*	0.412**	0.094
Scale elasticity (poor countries)	...	...	...	0.643***	...	...	...	0.355*
Scale elasticity (rich countries)	...	...	...	0.537***	...	...	...	0.598***
Composition elasticity	0.985***	1.008***	1.026***	0.803***	1.442**	0.864*	1.15**	1.056**
Technique elasticity	-1.425***	-1.74***	-1.551***	-1.218***	-2.22**	-1.23*	-1.505***	-1.204**
Trade intensity elasticity	-0.266**	-0.351***	-0.364**	-0.292*	-0.543**	-0.791***	-1.189***	-0.899***
FDI elasticity (poor countries)	...	...	0.091	...	...	...	0.143	...
FDI elasticity (middle)	...	...	0.004	...	...	...	0.121*	...
FDI elasticity (rich countries)	...	...	-0.039	...	...	...	0.049	...

Note: The dependent variable is the log of the median of SO_2 concentrations at each observation site. All model specifications use time-fixed effects. Elasticities are evaluated at sample means using the Delta method. Model "Time" only includes the years 1976–91 of the primary GEMS phase; model "Factors" introduces factor endowment–related variables; and model "FDI" allows for an inward foreign direct investment stock relative to the overall capital stock, interacted with income. The terms *rich countries* and *poor countries* refer to the top and bottom 30% of countries in the Penn World Tables with respect to per-capita GDP. Empty cells were not estimated.

*$p < .05$.   **$p < .01$.   ***$p < .001$.

In columns 2 and 6 we investigate the importance of other factor endowments. In our parsimonious model of pollution demand and supply "factor endowments" enter directly only through the inclusion of the capital-to-labor ratio. Other potential factor endowments were excluded because while they are relevant to income levels, there is little reason to believe that they have an *independent* effect on either the demand for a clean environment or the derived demand for pollution emissions.[38] Local abundance in either clean or dirty fuels may, however, affect emissions. We investigate this possibility by adding in columns 2 and 6 country-specific measures of hard and soft coal deposits per worker. Overall the results support our earlier conclusions.[39]

While a greater endowment of high-sulfur soft coal leads to more concentrations, at least in the random effects implementation in column 2, this effect disappears in the fixed-effects estimation in column 6. These results are not surprising: an abundance of soft coal means that countries like China will have higher concentrations all else equal, but since mineral endowments have very little time-series variation, they will be well captured by country fixed effects. Consequently, while abundance of high-sulfur coal surely adds to emissions, its inclusion has very little effect on our results.

In columns 3 and 7 we investigate the impact foreign direct investment may have on our results. If multinational corporations have common production methods in both developed and developing countries for engineering, quality control, or other reasons, then the pollution intensity of their production may be determined by the income per capita of the source country rather than the host country. As a result, a larger multinational presence in a poor country may mean its capital is cleaner, all else equal. There are, however, forces working in the other direction. If multinationals locate in the poor country because of their lax environmental protection, then we may instead find a positive relationship between FDI and pollution.

To investigate this issue we have calculated for each year and country in our sample the ratio of its inward stock of FDI to its overall capital stock.[40] We refer to this as FDI intensity: it measures the share of the

---

38. That is, we are assuming other factors enter separately and identically across both dirty and clean industries.
39. When trade frictions exist, the local abundance of fuels may mean lower prices and greater intensity of use.
40. In theory we may also want to distinguish between acquisitions and new green-field investments under the assumption that in the case of acquisitions it is less likely foreign-

domestic capital stock that may have cleaner than expected techniques of production. We then interact this measure with a categorical variable representing a country's income per capita to allow the multinational effect to differ across rich and poor countries.

The results from this exercise are mixed. In the fixed-effects estimation, there is a slight positive relationship between FDI and concentrations for poor, middle-income, and rich countries. Only the middle-income relationship is statistically significant. Moreover, the coefficient estimates imply that a 10% point increase in the *ratio* of the FDI stock to K stock would raise concentrations by about 1%. This is a small effect on pollution concentrations arising from a very large change in FDI. In the random effects estimation, none of the coefficients are significantly different from zero. Overall, we find little relationship between the extent of FDI in an economy (even a poor one) and its pollution level. Again our other elasticity estimates are only changed slightly from our earlier specification.

Finally, in columns 4 and 8 we investigate whether our scale effect differs significantly across countries categorized by income per capita levels. If there were important nonhomotheticities in production or consumption, or if our method of constructing scale was more appropriate for some income categories than for others, this may show up when we allow for disaggregation. The results in column 4 indicate that while separate estimation of scale across income categories tends to raise the overall elasticity estimates to approximately .5 or .6, the results are very similar to those presented earlier. In column 8 we find similar results for the poor and rich categories, but the middle-income group has a much lower elasticity, and it is not precisely estimated. The middle-income group results may be a consequence of the exclusive reliance of fixed effects on the (now smaller) within-group variation for estimation. Despite these caveats, the elasticity estimates, although different across categories, are not significantly different from each other.

Alternative Dependent Variables

We have employed the log of median sulfur dioxide concentrations in our estimations, but readers may be concerned that this choice affects our results. The choice for how we measure sulfur dioxide reflects two decisions: one to use the median, and two, to use a log transform. To

---

ers bring their own plant-specific technology to the foreign country. This data is not available on a broad cross-country basis.

investigate the robustness of our findings to the first decision, we present in table 7.8 fixed-effects estimates using alternative dependent variables. The random-effect results are very similar and hence not reported here.

The results shown in the table are very similar to those presented earlier. The elasticity estimates are very close to those given earlier, and the significance levels of the individual coefficients, while naturally different, still support our interpretations of the data. Therefore, our choice of the median as our summary statistic is shown to have very little effect on our results.

To investigate our log assumption, we present in table 7.9 our log specification together with a linear specification and a Box-Cox transform. All of these alternatives are based on our fixed-effects model. We apply a Box-Cox transformation to our dependent variable y_{it} as a generalization to our fixed-effects model. The model can be specified as

$$\hat{y}_{it} \equiv \begin{cases} y_{it} - 1 & \text{for} & \lambda = 1 \\ (y_{it}^{\lambda} - 1)/\lambda & \text{for} & 0 < \lambda < 1 \\ \log(y_{it}) & \text{for} & \lambda = 0 \end{cases},$$

where the transformation parameter λ is determined by the estimation.

The linear specification employs median sulfur dioxide as the dependent variable, whereas the Box-Cox estimation chooses the best λ to maximize the log likelihood.[41] Comparing columns 1 and 2, we see that a simple linear specification has similar properties to the log transform. The elasticities are, however, much higher, reflecting the impact of the less concentrated distribution for pollution. The technique elasticity still dominates the scale elasticity, but the composition elasticity is now much larger. All remain significant at standard levels.

In column 3 we ask what transform of the dependent variable works best. Both the linear and the log specification are rejected in favor of the more flexible Box-Cox transform. The log specification does far better, as shown by a comparison of the log likelihoods. In addition, the elasticity estimates from column 3 square well with those found in the log specification. Therefore, for simplicity and ease of interpretation we remain with the log specification.

Overall these results indicate that our choice of transform and our choice of median sulfur dioxide figures were not critical in obtaining

---

41. For more information, our technical appendix is available at pacific.commerce.ubc.ca/download/appendix.pdf.

TABLE 7.8

Sensitivity Analysis for Dependent Variable, by Model Specification (estimation method: fixed effects)

Variable	Mean (1)	P90% (2)	P95% (3)	P99% (4)
Intercept	−4.297***	−3.216***	−2.662***	−2.394***
ξ = city economic intensity	0.102***	0.12***	0.1***	0.079**
$\xi^2/1,000$	−0.386	−0.462	−0.306	−0.226
Capital abundance (K/L)	0.71***	0.793***	0.769***	0.602***
$(K/L)^2$	−0.009	−0.019	−0.02	−0.002
Lagged per capita income	−0.182	−0.721	−0.995	−0.395
(Income)^2	0.633***	0.727***	0.744***	0.76***
$(K/L) \times (I)$	−0.441***	−0.429***	−0.39***	−0.444***
Trade intensity TI = $(X + M)/$GDP	−1.397*	−2.555**	−2.199**	−1.792*
TI × relative K/L	−3.144***	−3.217***	−3.143***	−3.027***
TI × (relative $K/L)^2$	0.213	0.447	0.521*	0.043
TI × relative income	1.203*	1.59**	1.309*	1.876**
TI × (relative income)^2	−0.385**	−0.418**	−0.323*	−0.647***
TI × (relative K/L) × (relative income)	1.102***	1.021***	0.864***	1.294***
Suburban dummy				
Rural dummy				
Communist country dummy				
Communist country dummy × income	7.428***	8.844***	10.198***	9.252***
Communist country dummy × (income)^2	−6.5***	−6.686**	−7.762***	−8.414***
Average temperature	−0.074***	−0.085***	−0.091***	−0.082***
Precipitation variation	9.094**	8.528*	9.206**	9.409**
Helsinki protocol	0.132	0.121	0.106	0.171*
Observations	2,555	2,555	2,555	2,555
Groups	290	290	290	290
R^2	0.1732	0.1829	0.1801	0.1657
Log likelihood	−1868	−2502	−2320	−2365
Hausman test/wald X^2 (df)	171.41	554.5	256.24	131.08
Scale elasticity	0.455***	0.536***	0.448***	0.353**
Composition elasticity	1.13***	1.043***	1.003***	1.005***
Technique elasticity	−1.42***	−1.697***	−1.715***	−1.419***
Trade Intensity elasticity	−1.022***	−1.264***	−1.247***	−0.865***

Note: The short descriptions refer to the following dependent variables: Mean = the log of the arithmetic mean of SO_2 concentrations; P90%, P95%, P99% = the log of the 90th, 95th, and 99th percentiles of SO_2 concentrations. All regressions use time-fixed effects. Empty cells were not estimated.

*$p < .05$.   **$p < .01$.   ***$p < .001$.

TABLE 7.9

Sensitivity Analysis for Dependent Variable Transformation, by Model
Specification (estimation method: fixed effects)

Variable	Log (1)	Linear (2)	Box-Cox (3)
Intercept	−4.299***	−0.475	2.854*
City economic intensity GDP/km²	0.089*	1.397**	0.156**
(City economic intensity)²/1,000	−0.34	−4.781	−0.577
Capital abundance (K/L)	0.437*	16.824***	1.233***
(K/L)²	0.008	−0.313	−0.006
Lagged per capita income	−0.228	−12.53	−0.622
(Income)²	0.578***	9.977***	1.052***
(K/L) × (I)	−0.386***	−6.568***	−0.728***
Trade intensity TI = (X + M)/GDP	−3.216**	10.254	−3.305*
TI × relative K/L	−2.121	−53.07***	−5.114**
TI × (relative K/L)²	−0.176	5.819	0.08
TI × relative income	2.614***	4.368	3.516**
TI × (relative income)²	−0.584**	−0.834	−0.817*
TI × (relative K/L) × (relative income)	0.924**	9.011*	1.574**
Communist country dummy × income	9.639**	−4.739	11.581*
Communist country dummy × (income)²	−8.806**	−3.75	−11.25**
Average temperature	−0.056*	−0.494	−0.088*
Precipitation variation	10.716*	−12.39	12.857
Helsinki protocol	0.016	2.745*	0.124
Observations	2,555	2,555	2,555
Groups	290	290	290
R²	0.1499	0.1459	0.1408
Log likelihood	−3905	−16520	−3421
Box-cox λ	0	1	0.2432
Scale elasticity	0.398**	0.601***	0.451**
Composition elasticity	0.975*	3.968***	1.857***
Technique elasticity	−1.266**	−2.822***	−1.714***
Trade intensity elasticity	−0.882***	−1.412***	−1.072***

Note: λ is the transformation parameter of the Box-Cox transformation.

our results. Even the simple linear specification gives similar results.
While the estimates naturally change somewhat, the economic interpretations we have stressed do not.

Alternative Theories: The Political Economy Motive

In our framework, governments use pollution policy to target pollution and not for other purposes. As a result, the pollution tax is set
equal to marginal damage, and changes in openness affect the pollu-

tion supply curve only through its impact on incomes and prices. More generally, pollution policy and openness may be linked through other channels if governments use pollution policy for other purposes. For example, if political economy motives are important, governments may adjust pollution taxes to try to undo the redistribution of income caused by increased openness.[42]

This potential link between openness and environmental policy adds a country-specific unmeasured factor to our simpler determinants of pollution. The factor is a country-type effect, and it is relevant to both a country's degree of openness and its pollution supply curve. In the political economy case, the unmeasured country type is described by its preferred and actual income distribution.

The impact this country-type effect has on our empirical results depends on whether it is time varying. If it is not time varying, then our fixed-effects implementation is appropriate even if country type is correlated with other right-hand-side regressors. For example, if country A has uniformly tighter policy because of political economy concerns, then this is reflected in country type. But country type variables are adequately dealt with in our fixed-effects implementation. If country type is uncorrelated with the variables on the right-hand side, then our random effects estimation is more efficient and still unbiased. On average, countries of different types would have different pollution levels, but they would respond similarly to changes in openness, scale, and so forth. Given that the panel is quite short for many countries, the assumption that country type is constant over time may be a reasonable way to deal with these additional policy linkages.

If the country-type effect is time varying, however, then it will be correlated with our measure of openness. Our results concerning the effects of further openness and income on pollution may be undermined. To investigate whether these motives could be responsible for our results, consider what is left out by our simpler specification. When openness increases, the political economy motive creates an unaccounted-for upward shift in pollution supply for a dirty good exporter. This leads to *less* pollution than our model would predict. Alternatively, the political economy motive produces an unaccounted-for outward shift in pollution supply for a dirty good importer. In this

---

42. In the model that formed the basis of the empirical work in this section, we allowed the marginal disutility of pollution to vary across consumers but assumed all individuals had the same income, and so the income redistributive motive did not arise.

case, the political economy motive leads to *more* pollution than our model would predict. In both cases, unaccounted-for shifts in supply work against the shift in pollution demand created by further openness. This tends to dampen the composition effect created by further openness.

Could unmeasured redistribution motives be responsible for the large technique effects we find? It is unclear since we do not have adequate data to investigate it formally. But this alternative theory leads to an unmeasured positive relationship between pollution and openness for some countries but an unmeasured negative relationship for others. Therefore, it is difficult to see how the omission of political economy determinants would necessarily manifest itself in a stronger measured negative relationship between income and pollution. The alternative theory does, however, suggest a smaller (than we would otherwise predict) change in the composition of output created by a fall in trade frictions. As such, another interpretation of our findings of a small trade-induced composition effect is that governments may be simultaneously dampening the impact of increased openness on pollution with compensating changes in pollution taxes.

To go further and disentangle the additional shifts in pollution supply suggested by the redistributive motive from the other effects in our data would require us to obtain information on the preferred and actual income distribution in many countries over time. This is perhaps best examined within a single country context where detailed examination of redistributive motives may be possible.[43]

7.7 Conclusion

This chapter argues that our theoretical model highlighting scale, technique, and composition effects is useful in thinking about the empirical relationship between openness to international markets and pollution. We adopted a reduced form specification linked to our theory and then estimated it paying special attention to the potentially confounding influences introduced by the panel structure of our data set. Our results consistently indicate that scale, technique, and composition effects are not just theoretical constructs with no empirical counterparts. Rather

---

43. We discuss here the extreme case where pollution policy is the only available instrument. There are many other instruments (such as income transfers) that can redistribute income. To the extent that these other instruments are available, then the dampening shift in pollution supply that we find below will be less relevant.

these theoretical constructs can be identified and their magnitude measured. Moreover, once measured, they can play a useful role in determining the likely environmental consequences of technological progress, capital accumulation, or increased trade. These estimates may also be useful in aggregate CGE modeling of the effects of various free trade agreements and other trade reforms (see, for example, Ferrantino and Linkins 1996).

This chapter has several findings. One is the surprising strength of factor endowment motives. If figures 7.7 and 7.8 are an accurate description of the trade-created composition effect, then relatively rich countries have a comparative advantage in dirty goods.[44] This implies that freer international trade will make poor developing countries cleaner with trade and not dirtier. It also implies that free trade is shifting dirty good production from lax regulation countries to tight regulation countries. On its own, this reallocation of production lowers world pollution levels, as we demonstrated in chapter 6. Moreover, if the policy response in relatively rich countries is quite income elastic, then it is possible that pollution will fall in both the developed and developing world with freer trade. Recall our discussion of this in chapter 4.

Another finding is the tentative answer we provide to the question in this chapter's title. As with any empirical exercise some questions remain unanswered, but overall our estimates indicate that increases in a country's exposure to international markets create small but measurable changes in pollution concentrations by altering the pollution intensity of national output. While our estimates indicate that greater trade intensity creates only relatively small changes in pollution via the composition effect, economic theory and numerous empirical studies demonstrate that trade also raises the value of national output and income. These associated increases in output and incomes will then affect pollution concentrations via our estimated scale and technique effects.

Our estimates of the scale and technique elasticities indicate that if openness to international markets raises both output and income by 1%, pollution concentrations fall by approximately 1%. Putting this cal-

---

44. Note that the positive relationship between trade intensity elasticities and relative income found in these figures is also found in every one of our sensitivity tests in tables 7.5 and 7.6 as well.

culation together with our earlier evidence on composition effects yields a surprising conclusion with regard to sulfur dioxide: freer trade is good for the environment.

A final result is our finding that the environmental consequences of growth depend on the source of growth. Growth in incomes created by neutral technological progress may be environmentally enhancing; income growth via freer trade appears benign; but income growth fueled by capital accumulation alone worsens the environment. Therefore, at first blush it appears there is no simple relationship between income per capita and pollution—the EKC is illusory. This interpretation is, however, too harsh and simplistic.

The EKC may still be alive, well, and consistent with our findings if there exists a stable relationship between the stage of economic development and the sources of economic growth: that is, if there exists something we can call a development path. If along this path capital accumulation becomes a less important source of growth as development proceeds, while technological progress becomes more important, then our results are consistent with pollution at first rising and then falling with income per capita. In a sense, we may have unpackaged the EKC, but we have not refuted its existence.

TABLE 7A.1
Country ISO-3166 Codes

ARG	Argentina	IND	India
AUS	Australia	IRL	Ireland
AUT	Austria	IRN	Iran
BEL	Belgium	IRQ	Iraq
BRA	Brazil	ISR	Israel
CAN	Canada	ITA	Italy
CHE	Switzerland	JPN	Japan
CHL	Chile	KEN	Kenya
CHN	China	KOR	South Korea
COL	Colombia	MYS	Malaysia
CSK	Czechoslovakia	NLD	Netherlands
DEU	Germany	NZL	New Zealand
DNK	Denmark	PAK	Pakistan
EGY	Egypt	PER	Peru
ESP	Spain	PHL	Philippines
FIN	Finland	POL	Poland
FRA	France	PRT	Portugal
GBR	United Kingdom	SWE	Sweden
GHA	Ghana	THA	Thailand
GRC	Greece	USA	United States
HKG	Hong Kong	VEN	Venezuela
IDN	Indonesia	YUG	Yugoslavia

8 Summary and Conclusions

The objective of this book has been to study the effect of international trade on the environment. We developed a unified theoretical framework to help the reader gain an understanding of the major forces at work, and we showed how this framework could serve as the basis for empirical investigation. In this chapter, we review the major insights of the book and present suggestions for future research.

8.1 Flexible Pollution Policy

A central message of this book is that allowing pollution policy to respond to the changes brought about by trade is essential to our understanding of how international trade affects the environment. While it is probably reasonable to assume that pollution policy is fixed in the short run, it is unwise to expect policy to remain unchanged in the long run. International trade can have a large impact on relative prices and incomes in small open economies. In these cases, we expect the scale and composition effects of international trade on pollution to be significant. Unless we allow for a possible policy response—and its resulting technique effect on pollution—it is unlikely that we will capture the full impact of international trade.

Our analysis in several chapters bears out the importance of allowing for flexible policy. The effects of economic growth on the environment depend critically on the strength of the policy response: the scale effect of growth tends to increase pollution; however, a strong policy response can reverse this. The environmental implications of trade liberalization are also heavily dependent on the policy response. This is particularly true for dirty good exporters: the scale and composition effects of trade tend to increase pollution; but trade may nevertheless be good for the environment if the policy-induced technique effect is strong enough. Policy responses also matter in a more subtle way because the composition effect of trade liberalization depends on a country's comparative advantage. Comparative advantage in turn relies on the interaction of factor endowments and income-generated differences in pollution policy.

Our empirical work supported the theoretical links we made between more stringent policy and real income gains. We consistently found a large and significant negative relationship between a country's real income per capita and its pollution concentrations, after controlling for other determinants. If we have controlled for the determinants of scale and composition effects adequately, then this result must reflect a tightening of pollution policy with income gains. Our finding that this link is very much weaker or even zero in Communist countries lends further credence to our interpretation. This suggests that our insistence on policy endogeneity is more than just a theorist's cry for logical completeness and internal consistency—policy responses are large, and they have important links to real income growth that we cannot ignore.

8.2 Growth Is Not Trade

Another major lesson from the book is that the environmental consequences of income growth depend on the source of this growth. This is because different sources of growth create different composition effects. We first demonstrated that composition effects matter by showing how changes in the "sources of growth" could generate an environmental Kuznets curve (EKC). We then demonstrated that trade liberalization brought similar real income gains to exporters and importers of dirty products but very different environmental consequences. Trade-inspired income gains were linked with lower pollution in clean good exporters and higher pollution in dirty good exporters. Our empirical work confirmed what theory had led us to suspect. We found a strong relationship between the composition of a nation's factor endowments and its pollution level. And our estimates show that the impact of international trade on the environment differs across countries depending on their comparative advantage.

These observations have several implications. One is simply that because the source of income growth is likely to differ both across time within any one country, and across countries at any point in time, it becomes far harder to rationalize the existing empirical EKC methodology that ignores the impact of composition effects. In fact we showed that it is quite difficult to render composition effects mute—even with our very simple model we require further restrictions on pollution supply and demand to generate the result that all sources of income growth have similar environmental effects. And our empirical estimates testify to the strength of composition effects. They imply that income growth fueled by capital accumulation has a very different environmental consequence than growth fueled by either technological progress or liberalized trade.

A second implication is that it is wrong to infer from the existing EKC literature that poor countries—those yet to reach the peak of a worsened environment—must choose between a worsened environment or income gains arising from liberalized trade. Since the income gains from trade are just one potential source of income growth, whether these gains lead to more or less pollution depends a great deal on a country's comparative advantage. If poor, less developed countries have a comparative advantage in relatively clean labor-intensive activities, then the composition effect created by trade tends to lower pollution and not raise it. Therefore income growth created by trade may help and not hurt the environments of very poor countries.

A final implication is that it is unlikely that international trade is either uniformly good or bad for the environment. As long as composition effects are not zero, the environmental consequences of trade liberalization will differ across countries. And if we are to isolate the impact of international trade on the environment, we must take careful account of how it creates composition effects. This necessitates a discussion of the factors determining comparative advantage and the inclusion of them in empirical estimation. While we have presented one method for capturing the composition effect created by trade, other—perhaps superior—methods may be available.

8.3 The Pollution Haven and Factor Endowments Hypotheses

A third major lesson of this book is that, while income-induced policy differences are critically important in understanding the effect of trade on the environment, the evidence does not support the notion that trade patterns are driven by pollution haven motives.

We spent a great deal of time incorporating income gains and income differences across countries into our analysis. We did this to separate the role of income differences from those created by differences in other national characteristics such as human and physical capital, and the fragility of environments. The importance of factors other than income was brought out early on in our discussion of the EKC and became a major theme in later chapters when we introduced the factor endowments hypothesis.

The factor endowments hypothesis turned out to be extremely important. Almost all of the dire predictions of the pollution haven hypothesis are reversed when factor abundance motives for trade are sufficiently strong. The factor endowments hypothesis also allows us to distinguish between situations where differences in regulation matter to trade in dirty goods—the pollution haven *effect*—from where they are the most crucial determinant of trade patterns—the pollution haven *hypothesis*. Without another motive for trade, these two results blur into one, and this has led to much confusion in the literature.

For example, our analysis indicates that it is quite consistent for differences in pollution regulation to affect trade flows at the margin (that is, there is a pollution haven effect), but at the same time for factor endowment differences to be a much stronger determinant of trade patterns than pollution regulation differences (that is, the strong form of the pollution haven hypothesis fails). Finding evidence that trade flows are primarily determined by factor endowments does not imply that pollution regulation differences are irrelevant; and finding evidence that trade flows are affected by differences in pollution policy, after controlling for all other determinants of trade, does not imply that countries with relatively strict environmental regulation will export dirty goods.

Since the pollution haven and factor endowments hypotheses offered such different predictions, we designed our empirical work to facilitate a weighing of their relative strength. Our results in this regard are surely provocative. Our empirical findings suggest that factor abundance motives for trade in dirty goods are more important than pollution haven motives. Since poor developing countries are capital-scarce, this implies that freer international trade will encourage dirty industry to migrate northward and not southward. This will make poor developing countries cleaner and not dirtier.

It also implies that free trade will shift dirty good production from lax-regulation countries to tight-regulation countries. And, as we demonstrated in chapter 6, this global composition effect tends to lower world pollution levels. Moreover, if the policy response in relatively rich countries is quite income elastic, then it is possible that freer trade will lower pollution levels in both the developed and developing world. Finally, the result that the costs of tighter regulation in rich developed economies are more than offset by other cost advantages undercuts arguments that freer trade necessarily creates regulatory chill in the North.

Again, the distinction between the pollution haven *effect* and the pollution haven *hypothesis* is important. Industry in the North always has an incentive to lobby against cost-increasing environmental regulation, given the existing trade regime. However, this does not imply that freer trade (a change in the trade regime) will exacerbate the effects of differences in environmental regulation. In fact the evidence is to the contrary—Northern countries are dirty good exporters, and so free trade should enhance opportunities for Northern dirty good producers.

While these results are provocative, they are not surprising if interpreted correctly. We have found that economic development, and not freer trade, may raise pollution levels. Our results are consistent with cities in developing countries getting dirtier as their share of dirty goods in national output rises; consistent with a falling reliance on Northern capital goods and industrial manufactures; and consistent with rising Southern exports of dirty goods. The counterfactual we consider is a situation where development proceeds in the South, but domestic production of dirty goods is protected from the North's competing imports. Under this interpretation, our result that free trade may be good for the environment is far less provocative than it appears.

Some will cry foul since economic development hinges on liberalized trade. Since many economists have linked freer trade with a host of related benefits, such as faster growth, technology transfer, reduced inefficiencies, hastened democracy, and improved political rights, how can we now argue for a narrow, theoretically based, view of trade's effect on the environment? We do so because it is the only sound argument we can make given the available empirical evidence. We leave it to future authors to provide the explicit links between these other potential impacts of openness and their consequences for the environment.

At present we can only note that when we considered the two most frequently mentioned induced impacts—faster capital accumulation and hastened technological progress—the results were ambiguous. Capital accumulation raises pollution, but neutral technological progress reduces pollution. Whether pollution rises or falls with trade liberalization will depend quite delicately on just what and how strong the induced effects are, and we have nothing to report on that score. Nevertheless, we are sympathetic to these criticisms. Our goal was to provide a theoretically grounded examination of how increased openness to trade may affect pollution levels. We fully recognize that our analysis is the first step in what should be a major empirical research program.

8.4 Directions for Future Research

One cost of developing a unified theoretical framework is that unity requires parsimony, and parsimony forces a researcher to make difficult choices. We chose to limit ourselves to a discussion of the impact of international trade on local pollution created by goods production. We also worked within a static, perfectly competitive general equilibrium framework where political economy elements appear only minimally and dynamic and strategic issues are entirely absent. These choices limited our methods and our results.

We made these choices for numerous reasons, some of which were spelled out in the introduction and elsewhere in the book. If we reconsider the main question facing this literature, "Is free trade good for the environment?" it is apparent that by our choice of local pollution, we have ignored a number of other potential channels through which trade can affect the environment. There is much scope for future work.

An extension of the methods developed here to consider global pollutants seems both useful and relatively easy. Our own previous work in this area (Copeland and Taylor 1995, 2000) adopted models that were, in effect, generalizations of the pollution haven models in chapter 5 to allow for global pollution. It now appears possible to incorporate a role for factor endowments into a tractable theoretical analysis of global pollution. Since the issues of global warming and shrinking biodiversity are unlikely to wane in future years, a more complete understanding of the linkages between global pollution and international markets is required. There is also great interest in linking international environmental agreements to international trade agreements, but thus far the literature on linkage has focused on the strategic impacts of such linkage within partial equilibrium settings. A generalization of our model of chapter 6 to include global pollution would allow for an examination of linkage issues in a more general setting.

Our exclusion of natural resource issues is potentially important. Many poor developing economies rely on natural resource rents for a significant fraction of their income, and the majority of domestic production is typically exported. For these countries the state of their natural resources may be a more important indicator of environmental quality than is the level of pollution in their urban centers. As a result, our analysis may have little direct relevance to their trade and environment issues. Our analysis does, however, raise one concern. In many cases natural resource deposits and low incomes per capita are found in the same location. When this is true, factor endowment motivations reinforce pollution haven motivations for trade. This suggests that the composition effect created by liberalized trade could be very significant for poor resource exporters. Working against this potential negative impact of trade is the potentially important positive role trade may play in fostering better resource management when it raises the value of natural resources. This impact is typically neglected in the theoretical literature linking natural resource use and international trade. Our finding of strong pollution policy responses to income gains suggests that taking the resource management regime as given is perhaps a mistake. A full consideration of this issue requires very different models and must be left for future research.

Another choice we made was to largely ignore the role of increasing returns to scale. We think there are two ways that increasing returns may be important in the local pollution context. First, it should be apparent that an extension of our methods to settings with monopolistic competition is easy to accomplish. This extension may be useful because such a model would predict that countries can gain from trade via enhanced product variety, without altering the allocation of their resources across sectors. Hence, gains from trade would occur despite a zero trade-induced composition effect. This was (virtually) impossible in our framework. Therefore, because our analysis ignores the gains arising from the division of labor and product variety, it may well underestimate the strength of technique effects.

We suspect that a similar result would be obtained by extending the increasing returns to abatement model of chapter 2 to a two-country trading setting. The analysis of trade between two otherwise identical countries would largely mimic that already in the literature on external increasing returns to scale and trade, but the results should indicate another benefit of trade that is absent in our analysis: the benefit of concentrating polluting industries in one location to exploit increasing returns in abatement. And hence, like the product variety example mentioned above, a consideration of increasing returns in abatement may suggest that we have underestimated the strength of technique effects.

Our focus on production-generated pollution meant that we neglected consumption-generated pollution, such as municipal waste, and exhaust from automobiles and home heating. An extension of our model to consider such pollution should be fruitful, both because it would allow the study of a different set of pollutants, and because there is less scope for composition effects to come into play when pollution is generated by consumption. With a pollutant such as automobile exhaust, it is the location of consumption, not production, that determines where pollution occurs, and hence while trade will affect the mix of products available, and therefore generate some changes in the composition of goods consumed, one would expect that scale and technique effects would be the major channels through which trade affects the environment.

On the empirical front several extensions are possible. One cost of our reduced form estimation is that structural parameters remain hidden. Reduced form estimation was essentially forced on us by the lack of data on regulations in many developing countries. If we adopt similar methods but restrict the sample to industrialized countries, we could then employ measures of pollution abatement costs as proxies for pollution regulations. Recall that our theory neatly links the pollution tax τ to the share of resources in the X industry used in abatement, θ. Exploiting this relationship would provide researchers with data on both the quantity and "price" for pollution, and this may allow for the identification of structural parameters. Extending our two-good model to many goods and exploiting the relationship between θ and τ may be one way to add much needed theory to the study of U.S. cross-sectional data on imports, factor shares, and pollution abatement costs.

In addition, we have largely ignored some of the complications introduced by policy linkages. Our focus on small countries meant that we ruled out strategic manipulation of trade policy and pollution policy in our analysis. As is well known in the international trade literature, a large country has an incentive to use trade barriers to improve its terms of trade. A number of papers, starting with Markusen 1976, have pointed out that if trade agreements preclude the use of trade barriers, then countries have an incentive to use pollution policy as a second-best instrument to improve the terms of trade. For example, a dirty good importer can provide an implicit subsidy to the dirty industry by weakening its pollution policy. This will increase world supply of the dirty good, lower its price, and thereby improve the country's terms of trade. While there has been much theoretical work on what we might call the "tariff-substitution motive" for manipulation of environmental policy, its empirical implications are not yet well understood.[1]

A shift to a narrower set of countries (say the OECD) with more detailed data may allow researchers to examine the strength of tariff-substitution effects as well as the political economy motives we discussed in chapter 7. To do so, researchers could exploit the more readily available data on voting patterns, membership in green movements, and factor shares over a narrower OECD panel to extend our very rudimentary accounting for country type. The EKC literature has also produced many papers where democracy, literacy, and other political economy variables are entered as additional regressors. Our simple Greens and Browns model could provide a framework for a more theoretically based examination of the linkages, since our reduced form provides a simple link between country type variables and pollution measures.

Our method for adding up scale, composition, and technique effects could also be enhanced by direct estimates of the income gains brought about by trade liberalization, and improved by explicit consideration of foreign direct investment and technology transfer. Work along the lines of Frankel and Romer (1999) linking openness to trade and income levels, or that of Coe and Helpman (1995) linking trade to total factor productivity, could provide us with additional methods for assessing trade's effect on the environment.

Finally, while we have chosen sulfur dioxide as our pollutant for study, researchers should extend and validate our methods using other pollutants. Given appropriate data, it should be straightforward to apply our techniques to other pollutants that are tightly linked with dirty manufactured goods production. It would be surprising if the

---

1. For example, suppose that once trade is liberalized, countries begin to use environmental policy to influence their terms of trade. A dirty good importer would loosen environmental policy, as noted above. This leads to an outward shift in the pollution supply curve that we have not accounted for in our empirical work. This works against the inward shift of the pollution supply curve caused by the composition effect of trade for a dirty good importer. Hence, as in our political economy example discussed in chapter 7, the tariff substitution motive may dampen the composition effect of trade.

strength of the technique effect were the same across all pollutants because our theory predicts that it should vary with marginal damage, which depends on a number of factors, such as toxicity and consumer awareness. Our method for disentangling scale and technique effects should be useful in this regard.

Extending our framework to examine pollutants less tied to production, such as automobile emissions, is surely possible but will require some model changes. Since the model we developed is quite similar to standard factor endowments models, researchers extending our work should be aware that they have at their fingertips a huge body of theoretical literature extending the original Heckscher-Ohlin framework to account for nontraded goods, factor mobility, distortions, and so on. Therefore, the basis for much of the work required in modifying or extending our framework is surely already present in the academic literature.

References

Aidt, T. S. 1998. "Political Internalization of Economic Externalities and Environmental Policy." *Journal of Public Economics* 69:1–16.

Anderson, K. 1992. "The Standard Welfare Economics of Policies Affecting Trade and the Environment." In *The Greening of World Trade Issues*, ed. K. Anderson and R. Blackhurst. London: Harvester Wheatsheaf.

Andreoni, J., and A. Levinson. 2001. "The Simple Analytics of the Environmental Kuznets Curve." *Journal of Public Economics* 80:269–86.

Antweiler, W., B. R. Copeland, and M. S. Taylor. 1998. "Is Free Trade Good for the Environment?" NBER Working Paper No. 6707.

———. 2001. "Is Free Trade Good for the Environment?" *American Economic Review* 91:877–908.

Asako, K. 1979. "Environmental Pollution in an Open Economy." *Economic Record* 55:359–67.

Barrett, S. 1994. "Strategic Environmental Policy and International Trade." *Journal of Public Economics* 54:325–38.

Barro, R., and J. Lee. 1993. "International Comparisons of Educational Attainment." NBER Working Paper No. 4349.

Baumol, W. J. 1971. *Environmental Protection, International Spillovers, and Trade.* Stockholm: Almqvist and Wiksell.

Baumol, W. J., and D. Bradford. 1972. "Detrimental Externalities and Non-convexity of the Production Set." *Economica* 39:160–76.

Becker, R., and J. V. Henderson. 2000. "Effects of Air Quality Regulations on Polluting Industries." *Journal of Political Economy* 108:379–421.

Bhagwati, J. N. 1968. "Distortions and Immiserizing Growth: A Generalization." *Review of Economic Studies* 35:481–85.

Bhagwati, J. N., A. Panagariya, and T. N. Srinivasan. 1998. *Lectures on International Trade.* 2d ed. Cambridge: MIT Press.

Bourguignon, F., and C. Morrison. 2001. "Inequality among World Citizens: 1820–1992." Discussion Paper No. 2001–18, DELTA, École Normale Supérieure, Paris.

Bovenberg, A. L., and R. A. de Mooij. 1995. "Environmental Levies and Distortionary Taxation." *American Economic Review* 86:985–1000.

Brander, J. A., and B. J. Spencer. 1985. "Export Subsidies and International Market Share Rivalry." *Journal of International Economics* 18:83–100.

Brander, J. A., and M. S. Taylor. 1997. "International Trade between Consumer and Conservationist Countries." *Resource and Energy Economics* 18:267–98.

Brecher, R. A., and C. F. Diaz Alejandro. 1977. "Tariffs, Foreign Capital, and Immiserizing Growth." *Journal of International Economics* 7:317–22.

Brown, D. K., A. V. Deardorff, and R. M. Stern. 1992. "A North American Free Trade Agreement: Analytical Issues and a Computational Assessment." *World Economy* 15:11–29.

Bruneau, J. 2000. "Essays in International Economics and the Environment." Ph.D. diss., University of British Columbia.

Cavlovic, T., K. Baker, R. Berrens, and K. Gawande. 2000. "A Meta-analysis of the Environmental Kuznets Curve Studies." *Agriculture and Resource Economics Review* 29:32–42.

Chay, K. Y., and M. Greenstone. 1999. "The Impact of Air Pollution on Infant Mortality: Evidence from Geographic Variation in Pollution Shocks Induced by a Recession." NBER Working Paper No. 7442.

Chichilnisky, G. 1994. "North-South Trade and the Global Environment." *American Economic Review* 84:851–74.

Coe, D. T., and E. Helpman. 1995. "International R&D Spillovers." *European Economic Review* 39:859–87.

Conrad, K. 1993. "Taxes and Subsidies for Pollution-Intensive Industries." *Journal of Environmental Economics and Management* 25:121–35.

Copeland, B. R. 1994. "International Trade and the Environment: Policy Reform in a Polluted Small Open Economy." *Journal of Environmental Economics and Management* 26:44–65.

Copeland, B. R., and M. S. Taylor. 1994. "North-South Trade and the Global Environment." *Quarterly Journal of Economics* 109:755–87.

———. 1995. "Trade and Transboundary Pollution." *American Economic Review* 85:716–37.

———. 1997. "A Simple Model of Trade, Capital Mobility, and the Environment." NBER Working Paper No. 5898.

———. 1999. "Trade, Spatial Separation, and the Environment." *Journal of International Economics* 47:137–68.

———. 2000. "Free Trade and Global Warming: A Trade Theory View of the Kyoto Protocol." NBER Working Paper No. 7657.

———. 2001. "Trade, Growth, and the Environment." Department of Economics, University of British Columbia. Photocopy.

Cox, D., and R. G. Harris. 1985. "Trade Liberalization and Industrial Organization: Some Estimates for Canada." *Journal of Political Economy* 93:115–45.

Daly, H. E. 1993. "Perils of Free Trade." *Scientific American* 269:50–57.

Dasgupta, S., B. Laplante, H. Wang, and D. Wheeler. 2002. "Confronting the Environmental Kuznets Curve." *Journal of Economic Perspectives* 16:147–68.

Dean, J. M. 1992. "Trade and Environment: A Survey of the Literature." In *International Trade and the Environment*, ed. P. Low. World Bank Discussion Papers, No. 159. Washington, D.C.: World Bank.

———. 2002. "Does Trade Liberalization Harm the Environment? A New Test," *Canadian Journal of Economics* 35:819–42.

Dixit, A. K. 1985. "Tax Policy in Open Economies." In *Handbook of Public Economics*, Vol. 1, ed. A. J. Auerbach and M. Feldstein. Amsterdam: North-Holland.

Dixit, A. K., and V. Norman. 1980. *Theory of International Trade*. Cambridge: Cambridge University Press.

Ederington, W. J., and J. Minier. 2003. "Is Environmental Policy a Secondary Trade Barrier? An Empirical Analysis." *Canadian Journal of Economics* 36, forthcoming.

Esty, Dan. 1994. *Greening the GATT*. Washington, D.C.: Institute for International Economics.

Ethier, W. 1982. "Decreasing Costs in International Trade and Frank Graham's Argument for Protection." *Econometrica* 50:1243–68.

Falvey, R. E. 1988. "Tariffs, Quotas, and Piecemeal Policy Reform." *Journal of International Economics* 25:177–83.

Feenstra, Robert C. 1996. "NBER Trade Database, Disk 1: U.S. Imports, 1972–1994: Data and Concordances." NBER Working Paper No. 5515.

———. 1997. "NBER Trade Database, Disk 3: U.S. Exports, 1972–1994, with State Exports and Other U.S. Data." NBER Working Paper No. 5990.

Ferrantino, M., and L. Linkins. 1996. "Global Trade Liberalization and Toxic Releases." U.S. International Trade Commission Discussion Paper.

Frankel, J. A., and D. Romer. 1999. "Does Trade Cause Growth?" *American Economic Review* 89:379–99.

Frankel, J. A., and A. K. Rose. 2002. "Is Trade Good or Bad for the Environment? Sorting Out the Causality." Harvard University. Photocopy.

Fredriksson, P. 1997. "The Political Economy of Pollution Taxes in a Small Open Economy." *Journal of Environmental Economics and Management* 33:44–58.

Fullerton, D., and G. Metcalf. 1998. "Environmental Taxes and the Double-Dividend Hypothesis: Did You Really Expect Something for Nothing?" *Chicago-Kent Law Review* 73:221–56.

Gale, L. R., and J. A. Mendez. 1998. "The Empirical Relationship between Trade, Growth, and the Environment." *International Review of Economics and Finance* 7:53–61.

Greenstone, M. 1998. "The Impacts of Environmental Regulations on Industrial Activity: Evidence from the 1970 and the 1977 Clean Air Act Amendments and the Census of Manufactures." Princeton Industrial Relations Section Working Paper.

Grossman G. M., and E. Helpman. 1994. "Protection for Sale." *American Economic Review* 84:833–50.

Grossman, G. M., and A. B. Krueger. 1993. "Environmental Impacts of a North American Free Trade Agreement." In *The Mexico-U.S. Free Trade Agreement*, ed. P. Garber. Cambridge: MIT Press.

———. 1995. "Economic Growth and the Environment." *Quarterly Journal of Economics* 2:353–77.

Harbaugh, W. T., A. Levinson, and D. M. Wilson. 2002. "Re-examining Empirical Evidence for an Environmental Kuznets Curve." *Review of Economics and Statistics* 84:541–51.

Harrigan, J. 1995. "Factor Endowments and the International Location of Production: Econometric Evidence for the OECD, 1970–1985." *Journal of International Economics* 39:123–41.

———. 1997. "Technology, Factor Supplies, and International Specialization: Estimating the Neoclassical Model." *American Economic Review* 87:475–94.

Hausman, J. A. 1978. "Specification Tests in Econometrics." *Econometrica* 46:1251–71.

Helpman, E., and P. R. Krugman. 1985. *Market Structure and Foreign Trade.* Cambridge: MIT Press.

Hilton, H., and A. Levinson. 1998. "Factoring the Environmental Kuznets Curve: Evidence from Automotive Lead Emissions." *Journal of Environmental Economics and Management* 35:126–41.

Jaffe, A. B., S. R. Peterson, P. R. Portney, and R. N. Stavins. 1995. "Environmental Regulations and the Competitiveness of U.S. Manufacturing: What Does the Evidence Tell Us?" *Journal of Economic Literature* 33:132–63.

John, A., and R. Pecchenino. 1994. "An Overlapping Generations Model of Growth and the Environment." *Economic Journal* 104:1393–1410.

Jones, L. E., and R. E. Manuelli. 1995. "A Positive Model of Growth and Pollution Controls." NBER Working Paper No. 5205.

Jones, R. 1965. "The Simple Analytics of General Equilibrium." *Journal of Political Economy* 73:557–72.

Kato, N., and H. Akimoto. 1992. "Anthropogenic Emissions of SO_2 and NOx in Asia: Emission Inventories." *Atmospheric Environment* 26A:2997–3017.

Kennedy, P. W. 1994. "Equilibrium Pollution Taxes in Open Economies with Imperfect Competition." *Journal of Environmental Economics and Management* 27:49–63.

Kraushaar, J. J., and R. A. Ristinen. 1988. *Energy and Problems of a Technical Society.* New York: John Wiley and Sons.

Krugman P. R., and M. Obstfeld. 2000. *International Economics.* 5th ed. Boston: Addison Wesley Longman.

Kuznets, S. 1995. "Economic Growth and Income Inequality." *American Economic Review* 45:1–28.

Levinson, A. 1996. "Environmental Regulations and Industry Location: International and Domestic Evidence." in *Fair Trade and Harmonization: Prerequisites for Free Trade*, ed. J. N. Bhagwati and R. E. Hudec. Cambridge: MIT Press.

———. 1999. "State Taxes and Interstate Hazardous Waste Shipments" *American Economic Review,* 89:666–77.

Levinson, A., and M. S. Taylor. 2001. "Trade and the Environment: Unmasking the Pollution Haven Effect." Georgetown University. Photocopy.

Lopez, R. 1994. "The Environment as a Factor of Production: The Effects of Economic Growth and Trade Liberalization." *Journal of Environmental Economics and Management* 27:163–84.

Low, P., and A. Yeats. 1992. "Do 'Dirty' Industries Migrate?" in *International Trade and the Environment*, ed. P. Low. World Bank Discussion Papers, No. 159. Washington, D.C.: World Bank.

Lucas, R. E. B., D. Wheeler, and H. Hettige. 1992. "Economic Development, Environmental Regulation, and the International Migration of Toxic Industrial Pollution: 1960–1988." In *International Trade and the Environment*, ed. P. Low. World Bank Discussion Papers, No. 159. Washington, D.C.: World Bank.

Mani, M., and D. Wheeler. 1997. "In Search of Pollution Havens? Dirty Industry Migration in the World Economy." World Bank Working Paper No. 16.

Markusen, J. R. 1976. "International Externalities and Optimal Tax Structures." *Journal of International Economics* 5:15–29.

———. 1989. "Trade in Producer Services and in Other Specialized Intermediate Inputs." *American Economic Review* 79:85–95.

Markusen, J. R., and J. R. Melvin. 1981. "Trade, Factor Prices, and the Gains from Trade with Increasing Returns to Scale." *Canadian Journal of Economics* 14:450–69.

Markusen, J. R., E. Morey, and N. Olewiler. 1995. "Competition in Regional Environmental Policies with Endogenous Plant Location Decisions." *Journal of Public Economics* 56:55–77.

McGuire, M. C. 1982. "Regulation, Factor Rewards, and International Trade." *Journal of Public Economics* 17:335–54.

Nordstrom, H., and S. Vaughan. 1999. *Trade and Environment*. Geneva: World Trade Organization.

Pargal, S., and D. Wheeler. 1996. "Informal Regulation of Industrial Pollution in Developing Countries: Evidence from Indonesia." *Journal of Political Economy* 104:1314–27.

Pethig, R. 1976. "Pollution, Welfare, and Environmental Policy in the Theory of Comparative Advantage." *Journal of Environmental Economics and Management* 2:160–69.

Rauscher, M. 1991. "National Environmental Policies and the Effects of Economic Integration." *European Journal of Political Economy* 7:313–29.

———. 1997. *International Trade, Factor Movements, and the Environment*. Oxford: Clarendon Press.

Richelle, Y. 1996. "Trade Incidence on Transboundary Pollution: Free Trade Can Benefit the Global Environmental Quality." University of Laval Discussion Paper No. 9616.

Sachs, J., and A. Warner. 1995. "Economic Reform and the Process of Global Integration." *Brookings Papers on Economic Activity* 1:1–119.

Samuelson, P. A. 1954. "The Transfer Problem and Transport Costs II: Analysis of the Effects of Trade Impediments." *Economic Journal* 64:264–89.

Selden, T. M., and D. Song. 1994. "Environmental Quality and Development: Is There a Kuznets Curve for Air Pollution Emissions?" *Journal of Environmental Economics and Management* 27:147–62.

Shafik, N. 1994. "Economic Development and Environmental Quality: An Econometric Analysis." *Oxford Economic Papers* 46:201–27.

Siebert, H. 1977. "Environmental Quality and the Gains from Trade." *Kyklos* 30:657–73.

Siebert, H., J. Eichberger, R. Gronych, and R. Pethig. 1980. *Trade and the Environment: A Theoretical Enquiry*. Amsterdam: Elsevier/North Holland Press.

Smulders, S. 2000. "Economic Growth and Environmental Quality." Tilburg University. Photocopy.

———. 2001. "Growth and Environment." Keynote lecture, Annual Conference of the European Association of Environmental and Resource Economists, Southampton.

Stokey, N. 1998. "Are There Limits to Growth?" *International Economic Review* 39:1–31.

Summers, R., and A. Heston. 1991. "The Penn World Tables (Mark 5): An Expanded Set of International Comparisons, 1950–1988." *Quarterly Journal of Economics* 106:327–68.

Tobey, J. A. 1990. "The Effects of Domestic Environmental Policies on Patterns of World Trade: An Empirical Test." *Kyklos* 43:191–209.

Ulph, A. M. 1996. "Environmental Policy and International trade When Government and Producers Act Strategically." *Journal of Environmental Economics and Management* 30:265–81.

———. 1997. "Environmental Policy and International Trade: A Survey of Recent Economic Analysis." In *International Handbook of Environmental and Resource Economics, 1997/98*, ed. H. Folmer and T. Tietenberg. Cheltenham: Edward Elgar.

United Nations Environment Programme. 1991. *Urban Air Pollution*. Nairobi: UNEP.

Walter, I. 1973. "The Pollution Content of American Trade." *Western Economic Journal* 11:61–70.

Weitzman, M. L. 1974. "Prices vs. Quantities." *Review of Economic Studies* 41:477–91.

Woodland, A .D. 1982. *International Trade and Resource Allocation*. Amsterdam: North-Holland Press.

World Bank. 1992. *World Development Report, 1992*. Oxford: Oxford University Press.

World Health Organization. 1984. *Urban Air Pollution: 1973–1980*. Geneva: Published under the joint sponsorship of United Nations Environment Programme and the World Health Organization.

World Resources Institute, the United Nations Environment Programme, the United Nations Development Programme, and the World Bank. 1998. *World Resources, 1998–99: A Guide to the Global Environment*. Oxford: Oxford University Press.

Xu, X. 1999. "Do Stringent Environmental Regulations Reduce the International Competitiveness of Environmentally Sensitive Goods? A Global Perspective." *World Development* 27:1215–26.

Index

abatement technology, 17–19; increasing returns to scale in, 97–103
abatement threshold model, 87–91
Aidt, T., 135n.32
Anderson, K., 107n
Andreoni, J., 70, 71, 97
Antweiler, W., 23n, 188n.4, 216n, 218n.5, 219n.7, 234n, 240n, 253
Asako, K., 107n
assimilative capacity of the environment, 170–71

Barrett, S., 18n.10, 159n.20
Barro, R., 241n.25, 243
Baumol, W., 16n.7, 107n
Becker, R., 220n
Bhagwati, J., 32n, 53n
Bourguignon, F., 144n.5
Bradford, D., 16n.7
Brander, J., 144n.6, 159n.20
Brown, D., 253, 256, 260
Bruneau, J., 21n

capital accumulation, 4; composition and scale effects of, 49–54; effects on pollution demand of, 59–60; empirical estimates of effects on pollution of, 259–60; and environmental Kuznets curve, 74–78, 218
capital mobility, 143n.3
Cavlovic, T., 68n.2
Chay, K., 247n
Chichilnisky, G., 70, 143n.4, 172n, 175
Coe, D., 283

comparative advantage, 113–14; due to differences in assimilative capacity of environment, 170–71; due to exogenous policy differences, 147–51, 155–56, 171–83, 192–95; due to factor endowment differences, 189–92, 196–213; due to income-induced policy differences, 159–64, 196–213; empirical evidence on, 253–57, 272; implications of theory for empirical work, 157–58, 195–96, 221, 239–41
composition effect, 2, 4, 45–47; of capital accumulation, 49–54; due to change in emission intensity, 54–56; empirical estimates of, 250–57; empirical identification of, 234–41; and environmental Kuznets curve, 78, 86, 91, 96; and trade liberalization, 112–17, 150; implications for world pollution, 164–70, 202–4, 212
Conrad, K., 159n.20
consumption-generated pollution, 282
Copeland, B., 7n.4, 9, 12, 13n.2, 16nn. 4 and 7, 18n.9, 19, 23n, 40n.25, 44n, 54n.33, 69n, 87n, 107n, 121n.13, 123n, 142n.2, 143n.3, 156n, 159, 164n, 166n, 187n.1, 188n.4, 216n, 218n.5, 219nn. 7 and 8, 234n, 240n, 253, 280
cost function: for clean good, 31; for net output, 22; for potential output, 21
cost minimization, 21–23
Cox, D., 259n

Daly, H., 67
Dasgupta, S., 68n.2